# Amphibious Anthropologies

CULTURE, PLACE, AND NATURE

*Studies in Anthropology and Environment*

K. Sivaramakrishnan, Series Editor

Centered in anthropology,
the Culture, Place, and Nature series
encompasses new interdisciplinary social
science research on environmental issues,
focusing on the intersection of culture, ecology,
and politics in global, national, and local contexts.
Contributors to the series view environmental
knowledge and issues from the multiple
and often conflicting perspectives
of various cultural systems.

# Amphibious Anthropologies

*Living in Wet Environments*

EDITED BY

Alejandro Camargo, Luisa Cortesi,
and Franz Krause

University of Washington
*Seattle*

*Amphibious Anthropologies* was made possible in part by a grant from the Samuel and Althea Stroum Endowed Book Fund.

Copyright © 2025 by Alejandro Camargo, Luisa Cortesi, and Franz Krause

Design by Mindy Basinger Hill

All rights reserved. No part of this publication may be reproduced or transmitted in any form or by any means, electronic or mechanical, including photocopy, recording, or any information storage or retrieval system, without permission in writing from the publisher.

UNIVERSITY OF WASHINGTON PRESS   *uwapress.uw.edu*

LIBRARY OF CONGRESS CATALOGING-IN-PUBLICATION DATA

Names: Camargo, Alejandro, editor. | Cortesi, Luisa 1980– editor. | Krause, Franz, editor.

Title: Amphibious anthropologies : living in wet environments / edited by Alejandro Camargo, Luisa Cortesi, and Franz Krause.

Description: Seattle : University of Washington Press, [2025] | Series: Culture, place, and nature | Includes bibliographical references and index.

Identifiers: LCCN 2024053087 | ISBN 9780295753881 (hardcover) | ISBN 9780295753898 (paperback) | ISBN 9780295753904 (ebook)

Subjects: LCSH: Bodies of water—Social aspects—Case studies. | Human ecology—Case studies. | Aquatic ecology—Case studies. | Human geography— Case studies.

Classification: LCC GF62 .A67 2025

LC record available at https://lccn.loc.gov/2024053087

♾ This paper meets the requirements of ANSI/NISO Z39.48-1992 (Permanence of Paper).

TO THE INHABITANTS OF WET ENVIRONMENTS

who have shared with us their time and knowledge

to help us understand life in amphibious worlds.

# Contents

Foreword by K. Sivaramakrishnan / *ix*

Acknowledgments / *xiii*

Introduction / FRANZ KRAUSE, LUISA CORTESI,
ALEJANDRO CAMARGO / *1*

### PART I. ON THE BRINK

1 / Postnatural Environmental Management
in an Amphibious Delta: Hybridity, Performativity,
and Indeterminacy at the Salton Sea / ALIDA CANTOR / *29*

2 / Between Hydro and Geo: Amphibious Spaces
of Social Exception / SIMONE POPPERL / *55*

3 / The Shape of Waterland: A Geomorphoanthropological
Commentary on Fluvial Infrastructures and Amphibious
Environmental Knowledge / LUISA CORTESI / *76*

### PART II. IN THE DAMP

4 / Keeping the Land Wet: "Wet Lands" and the Rise of
"Wetland Literacy" / PAOLO GRUPPUSO / *111*

5 / Situating Wetness in Soomaa, Estonia / FRANZ KRAUSE / *138*

6 / The Hyporheic Imaginary in Multispecies Watershed
Governance: How Beaver Collaborations Remix Patterns of Wet
and Dry in Northern California Streams / CLEO WOELFLE-HAZARD
AND DANIEL SARNA-WOJCICKI / *163*

PART III. THROUGH THE MUCK

7 / Restoring Wetlands in Alpine Ski Resorts:
The Biopolitics of Water, Land, and Snow / CÉLINE GRANJOU
AND STÉPHANIE GAUCHERAND / *195*

8 / Muddy Waters: Governing the Littoral in Andros Island,
The Bahamas / SARAH WISE / *219*

9 / The Contours of the Amphibious: Wetlands, Knowledge,
and Politics in Colombia / ALEJANDRO CAMARGO / *250*

Amphibious Epilogue / STUART MCLEAN / *276*

List of Contributors / *283*

Index / *287*

K. SIVARAMAKRISHNAN

# Foreword

Human history, through the ages, is replete with stories about the building of civilizations through various forms of domestication and containment of the natural world. Technological capability remained a powerful arbiter of the success and scope of such efforts. The twentieth century, not surprisingly, has seen some of the most ambitious efforts, as technological innovation and nation building combined to mount extraordinary projects for control and modification, by humans, of the nonhuman universe in which they lived. Burgeoning literature on the Anthropocene bears witness to the scale of these transformations and their devastating consequences.[1]

In contrast to this kind of world-historical work, environmental anthropologists and human geographers are responding to anthropogenic climate change with situated studies. They invite scholars and students to think themselves out of the ubiquitous modern tendencies to partition life and landscapes into governable units. This volume on amphibious anthropologies is a fine collection providing one compelling illustration of how various dichotomies may be questioned to propose alternative ways of imagining a just and sustainable future.

Studies on rivers, coastal zones, wetlands, marshes, floodplains, and low-lying islands have shown that vast engineering ingenuity and enormous investment was lavished on reclaiming land from water, or protecting land from water, particularly in the last two hundred years. As Dilip da Cunha (2019, 1) has noted, human habitation of the planet was so often predicated on separating land from water. This was done in service of irrigation and agrarian empires but also urbanization, industrial development, and state building. Displacement, aggravated floods, and the pollution of water bodies followed. Ambitious projects changed the course of rivers, drained marshes and fens, and blocked seawater ingress along coasts. The unfortunate results of much of this activity, exacerbated by climate change, have provoked a fundamental reevaluation of the very basic distinctions between land and water that shaped human history so profoundly in recent centuries.

The essays brought together in this collection deliberate on amphibiousness and wetness as essential conditions of human and nonhuman existence. They find often-forgotten or discarded understandings of water and its place in and around land. All this to offer new approaches to studying, in a more-than-human approach, what the environment and sustainable life within it looks like when water is indivisible from other natural phenomena and when human striving respects and works with the way water finds its place. They do this first and foremost through a very capable survey of available writing across disciplines that helps them elicit their guiding principles and overarching framework of amphibiousness. This work is done in a clear, well-written introduction to the volume by three scholars who have felicitously brought their experience together. Krause, Cortesi, and Camargo map out the reach and value of their organizing concepts with admirable lucidity.

An important contribution of the volume is to move beyond an imagination of amphibious zones as refugia, places that bred resistance and outlawry or presented difficult frontiers for human settlement. Such writing, often portraying marshes, river islands, and deltaic regions as eluding conquest by empires or control by states, remains human-centric even as it seizes upon the challenges posed by recalcitrant ecological conditions. This also, frequently, has led to a romanticization of people who dwelled in these amphibious areas, failing to note their struggles, dissensions, and ultimately persistent accommodation of both internal hardships and external threat. In *Amphibious Anthropologies*, the authors present human coexistence with watery or wet environments as a more subtle process of adaptation and respectful adjustment. Neither the human nor the nonhuman prevails here—considerable wisdom and resilience can be found, amid struggle and uncertainty.

The individual chapters cover a range of situations and issues from the

Americas, Europe, the Middle East, and South Asia, and they offer a dismantling of the classificatory regimes of devastating consequence that marked modernity. They also analyze the ways in which people lived in wet environments. Several themes unite the chapters organically. These include considerations of knowledge from within amphibious communities and that which directs interventions to alter them or even, increasingly, preserve these damp or wet places. In different ways, the chapters bring out the reckoning with the limitations of modern visions of engineered land- and waterscapes that occurs in these amphibious regions and amphibious societies.

All this—rich and mostly ethnographic empirical material—is used to argue that finding ways to advance a more-than-human shared existence is a vital necessity if planetary environmental crises are to be understood historically, with due respect to place-based experiences and outcomes, and then to be resolved justly. As happens in the best of edited collections, individual chapters are brought into a vibrant conversation with each other, and they work well together to highlight in distinct ways the larger arguments laid out elegantly in the opening chapter.

Three segments organize the chapters. They show that containment and collaboration remain contrasting imperatives in the way people deal with water in its environment. The compulsions of production—of livelihood, wealth, and power—and the urge to conserve favored forms of water in the landscape may express divergent human tendencies, but they manifest, often, in strikingly similar ways. These kinds of insights abound in this volume, and they reveal not only the limitations of prevailing ideas but also the challenges of starting afresh in times of evident ecological and social distress around the world. Amphibiousness emerges as not confounding to human endeavor to live sustainable lives but in fact an inspiration to imagine sustainability in new ways.

NOTE

1. Three works that provide broad assessments, from different vantage points, are McNeill and Engelke 2016; Angus 2016; and Yusoff 2018.

## REFERENCES

Angus, Ian. 2016. *Facing the Anthropocene: Fossil Capitalism and the Crisis of the Earth System*. New York: Monthly Review Press.

da Cunha, Dilip. 2019. *The Invention of Rivers: Alexander's Eye and Ganga's Descent*. Philadelphia: University of Pennsylvania Press.

McNeill, John, and Peter Engelke. 2016. *The Great Acceleration: An Environmental History of the Anthropocene since 1945*. Cambridge: Harvard University Press.

Yusoff, Kathryn. 2018. *A Billion Black Anthropocenes or None*. Minneapolis: University of Minnesota Press.

# Acknowledgments

We are grateful to the contributors of this volume for their patience and persistence. It was a long road, but we are profoundly pleased to have completed this collective project with you. Thanks to the University of Washington Press editorial team (Emily Feng, Justine Sargent, Lorri Hagman, Caitlin Tyler-Richards, Larin McLaughlin, and all those who make the publishing wheels turn, whose names we never knew) for their unwavering support. Warm thanks to K. Sivaramakrishnan, the series editor, for opening its possibilities for the reader, as well as to Stuart McLean for closing the circle, and to the two anonymous reviewers for their helpful suggestions and generous reading. We are grateful to Sugeeta Roy Choudhury, who worked meticulously to prepare the manuscript, and Ben Pease, who prepared the maps for chapter 3. Our gratitude is also due to the DFG project number 276392588 for covering some of the costs of putting the manuscript into shape.

Alejandro Camargo thanks the people of the rivers, marshes, and streams of Colombia for sharing their knowledge about the world that exists between land and water.

Luisa Cortesi is grateful to James Scott, Michael Dove, K. Sivaramakrishnan, Paul Kockelman, Jim Saiers, and K. Hebert for early discussions on amphibiousness. She thanks her colleagues and many friends and interlocutors in Bihar, India, in particular the late Naniji Urmila Devi, the late Pawan K. Bind, and the late Prem K. Sharma, but also Rajenderji, Chandrashekarji, Rameshji, Vinayji, and Eklavji, for teaching her about amphibious living. She is indebted to the SSRC, the Wenner Gren Foundation, the De Karman Foundation, the Agrarian Studies Program, the MacMillan Center at Yale, and the Fulbright-IIE.

xiv *Acknowledgments*

Franz Krause acknowledges support by the Estonian Research Foundation ETAG and the German Research Foundation DFG for his research and thinking about amphibious anthropologies. He is grateful to his many teachers, peers, and research participants who shaped his understanding of vibrant life in wet environments, many of whom contributed to this collection in one way or another.

# Amphibious Anthropologies

# Amphibious Anthropologies

FRANZ KRAUSE / LUISA CORTESI / ALEJANDRO CAMARGO

# Introduction

From the Mesopotamian marshes of southern Iraq and the intertidal wetlands of the Yellow Sea in China to Lake Chad in West-Central Africa and the rivers in North Bihar, India, stories about the radical transformations of wet environments dramatically connect the lives of people, plants, and animals across the globe. Floods are inundating otherwise arid environments, while areas generally considered too wet are now scorched by droughts. Unpredictable water regimes haunt scenarios of sea level rise with melting ice caps, and people are displaced by landscapes that are too dry or too wet to be bearable.

This book is about the experiences and meanings of living in environments of ever shifting wetness. With climate change, many places are becoming wetter, forcing people to learn how to manage inconsistent and threatening waters, exactly at the same time when others, who have long made a living in wet environments, struggle to maintain wetness in the face of its disappearance. The wet and the dry are out of control. This has probably always been the case—in fact one wonders who ever thought they could be controlled. But recent events make blatantly evident how misplaced any idea about predicting and controlling water has been, especially in times in which unpredictability has become the only predictable aspect of the hydrological cycle. While the trends and extremes of climate change have raised a general awareness of wet environments as shifting, vulnerable, but potentially also disastrous ecologies, this book examines existing forms of amphibious life that may provide lessons for living with climate change in places where water and land have been opposed in thinking and practice, often with devastating consequences.

Wet environments have increasingly become places for reckoning the planetary uncertainties and disturbances of our current epoch. Take the cases of Bangladesh, Indonesia, and Tuvalu, where the ocean is already pushing people to relocate and change their livelihoods. Or the cases of the islands in Japan, Hawaii, and Russia that have sunk over the last few years. Although those islands were uninhabited, scientists argue that what has happened to them is a warning of what populated places in the middle of or near the ocean are likely to face (Chow 2019; Storlazzi et al. 2018). The recent past is a clear sign of what is to come: a report coauthored by the UN Office for Disaster Risk Reduction (UNDRR and CRED 2020) identifies floods as the single most disastrous hazard in terms of occurrences and people affected. More than three thousand flood disasters were reported across the world between 2000 and 2019, affecting 1.65 billion people. Yet floods do not happen only in floods-prone areas. Places that have been facing severe water scarcity are suddenly realizing the difficulties created by its abundance. The Warragamba Dam, for example, provides most of Sydney's drinking water. Drawn to less than half of its water-storage capacity in 2019 due to prolonged drought and growing water consumption, in 2020 the dam was suddenly threatened with flooding. From "too empty," the reservoir became "too full" in a matter of a few months (Wheeler 2022). Yet, many places struggle to maintain the wetness that characterized them. Scientists have recently warned that 54–57 percent of the world's wetlands have been lost (Davidson 2014), and that these ecosystems are disappearing three times faster than forests (Ramsar Convention on Wetlands 2018). Lake Poopó, Bolivia's second-largest water body, stands out as a dramatic instance, as it dried up in 2015 due to climatic, mining, urban, and agricultural pressures, unsettling regional ecology and forcing people to migrate (Perreault 2020).

While stories of transformation and loss in wet environments offer a gloomy global picture, the experience of wetness is not solely a dystopian reality. A paradigm shift from flood control to living with floods is resonating in different contexts. Decades of flood control through polders, dams, and embankments have proven counterproductive, as separating land from water eventually increases flood risk (Cortesi 2021). Inspired by the communities whose everyday life unfolds in the midst of dynamic floods, some suggest letting cities and formerly enclosed lands be flooded

(Warner, van Staveren, and van Tatenhove 2018; Liao, Le, and Van Nguyen 2016). Others report that people periodically open gaps in embankments to let water and sediment in. While not a simple process, letting water and land merge again has revitalized fractured landscapes in structural ways: waterlogging has eased, rivers have grown deeper, increased sediments have raised the land inside the previously subsiding polders, and with improved water circulation the endangered Ganges River dolphin has returned in Bangladesh (Warren 2018). An even more localized approach to biophysical feedback mechanisms reveals that, in some cases, coastal wetlands may persist, prosper, and coexist with humans in spite of sea level rise (Schuerch et al. 2018). People live in, and experiment with, wetness as it mutates, moves, fades away, and returns.

Wetness is perhaps a third space beyond the opposition of land and water. Different from the sociological use of the term, the concept of a third space has been used in anthropology, geography, and related fields to characterize various phenomena that lie beyond established categories and are not adequately described as mixtures of them. Postcolonial theorist Homi Bhabha has famously conceptualized the ubiquitous field of cultural contact as a third space, characterized by contradictions, tensions, and ambivalence. His rendering of the third space emphasizes that culture is not a clear and fixed artifact but perpetually remade through interpretation from different perspectives (Bhabha 1994). Urbanist Edward Soja, in turn, developed the idea of thirdspace (in one word) to designate an understanding of inhabited, enacted, and lived space that encompasses the physical and imagined aspects of space, which he called first and second space, respectively (Soja 1996). Also here, the *third* refers to a dimension beyond an apparent opposition, in this case between physicality and imagination. More recently, anthropologist Michael Fischer used the term *third space* to refer to the moment between nostalgia and apocalypse, between the Holocene and the Anthropocene, between the disruptive times of the present and the possibilities of emerging futures. In Fischer's sense, the third space is a temporal phenomenon, the meantime between what was and what might be in the long run (Fischer 2018). This use of the term, too, renders a perspective of being in the midst of things, not looking back or projecting forward, and thereby opens up a dimension beyond apparent opposition.

Aligned to these discursive, spatial, and temporal renderings of third spaces, our understanding of wetness pivots on its circumvention of the opposition between land and water. Wetness is less a state between water and land than an attention to the materialities, processes, and experiences that constitute the lived spaces where water in myriad forms plays a pivotal role, in an emerging present that recognizes the multiple positionalities from which it is perceived and engaged (Krause 2024). For example, when people in Bangladesh open the gaps in the embankments to let water, sediment, and aquatic species in, they allow wetness to reach a land that had been classified otherwise through long, inequality-inflected histories of colonial land distribution and myopic landscape engineering (Dewan 2021).

In this space of wetness, to flourish is to lead an amphibious life in which plants, humans, other animals, water, and land "intra-act" (Barad 2007), thereby creating new expectations for the future. Flourishing, here, is not to be confused with the pursuit of benefit-maximizing strategies of a neoliberal subject in the context of adverse uncertainty (Krause and Eriksen 2023). Instead, it refers to the situated making ends meet in a shifting, unbounded, and emerging universe. Amphibious anthropologies, therefore, narrate the everyday tensions and possibilities of a disturbing world from the third space of wetness. Living in wet environments is an everyday foray into the interstices of land and water, where creativity resonates with uncertainty amid stories of disaster, modernization, colonialism, and capital accumulation.

## FROM SEPARATED ELEMENTS TO WET WORLDS

Focusing on amphibious lifeworlds centers the conversation around living with wetness. Social scientists and humanities scholars are well positioned to undertake this work, because disciplines such as anthropology, geography, and history have long examined how wet environments, ideas about them, and practices come together. Consider geographer Bernard Nietschmann's classic monograph *Between Land and Water: The Subsistence Ecology of the Miskito Indians, Eastern Nicaragua* (1973). As a pioneer work in cultural ecology, this study narrates the life of the Miskito people between the ocean and a forest-bordered lagoon as they integrate into capitalist exchange relations. Wetness is interwoven with people's activities as they fish in the sea, rivers, swamps, and creeks; cultivate cassava; and hunt turtles, peccary, and deer in the forest and shoal areas. Changes in wind and water patterns transform this "land-water zone," as Nietschmann calls it, especially when rivers inundate the coastal lowlands.

Wetness, however, is not solely a material condition in which water, land, humans, and other animals meet. It also permeates subjectivities, trajectories, and worldviews. Ethnographies of the Bar Nor, or "Mangrove man," of the mangrove swamps of Papua New Guinea (Lipset 1997); the Waí Mahá, or "Fish People," of the Amazonian rivers of Colombia (Jackson 1983); and the Uru-Qotzuñi, or the "Water People," of the Poopó lake in Andean Bolivia (Munter, Trujillo, and Rocha-Grimoldi 2019) expose how wetness transcends human-nature frontiers in intimate ways.

A fundamental contribution of this literature to the way in which we understand wetness today has to do with the approach to water as a multiscalar and political phenomenon (Strang 2004) and a "theory machine" (Helmreich 2011) to facilitate new ways of thinking (Chen, MacLeod, and Neimanis 2013) or formulate "wet ontologies" (Steinberg and Peters 2015). Under the banner of hydrosociality, for instance, geographers and anthropologists have examined how water flows are deeply embedded in the dynamics of capitalism, power, and authority (Swyngedouw 2005; Bakker 2012; Harris 2022) and how water is implicated in struggles over justice and equality (Mehta, Veldwisch, and Franco 2013; Boelens, Perreault, and Vos 2018).

This perspective has helped us reframe questions regarding places such as irrigation landscapes, where water and agricultural land are closely connected. Irrigation has long been a terrain of ethnographic enquiry, with anthropologist Clifford Geertz's work in the "wet villages" of Bali (1972) as an important landmark in this tradition. Power relations are intrinsic to the organization and management of irrigation landscapes (e.g., Lansing 2009) but also to the everyday politics of those who routinely divert, block, release, or channel water to connect rivers with arable land (Oorthuizen 2003; Barnes 2014). When power imbalances prevent water from infiltrating land through irrigation, resistance to water dispossession becomes a part of farmers' everyday life (Birkenholtz 2016). Dwellers of mangrove forests face similar situations as they fight the privatization of their territories due to the expansion of tourism and conservation (Hiraldo 2018). Research in urban areas has also exposed the politics of wetness, as the transformation of water into land via land reclamation projects result in the racialization and displacement of people (Collins 2017). Conversely, when water takes over land through floods, stories of informal settlements and the unevenness of real estate development come to the surface (Ranganathan 2015; Ley 2021). Wetness, this literature about water warns us, configures contested environments and unequal power relations.

Since the late 1990s, social science scholarship about water has expanded both geographically and theoretically in order to counteract a land bias in cultural theory. This scholarship has called attention to the manifold epistemologies and ontologies involved in the production of waterworlds (Barnes and Alatout 2012; Hastrup and Hastrup 2015) and has identified useful descriptive idioms such as "aquatic space" (Oslender 2016) and "waterland" (Cortesi 2022). It has focused on material properties of wet worlds such as fluidity, depth, liquidity, and volume, thus moving away from "hydrotopias," or stereotypical understanding of water as wet, moving/flowing, tasteless, odorless, colorless or green-bluish, as opposed to land as dry, stable, solid, red-brownish (Cortesi 2022).

Here we understand the amphibious as constituted by neither land-based nor water-centered relations but as bringing forth its own assemblages. These may borrow elements from water- or land-related spheres but are not reducible to a combination or mixture of the two.

## GENEALOGIES OF THE AMPHIBIOUS

The focus on water has gone some way toward decentering the implicit bias toward terra firma in analyzing social and cultural life. However, there is a tendency for this decentering to obliquely reinscribe water and land as separate and opposed elements. Focusing, instead, squarely on the amphibious can help us avoid this pitfall. Sociologist Orlando Fals Borda (1979) was perhaps the first to explicitly use the term *amphibious* to refer to the specific material-semiotic assemblages of ecologies, technologies, practices, and beliefs that characterize life in the Mompos Depression, a low-lying area at the confluence of the Magdalena River with other major rivers in northern Colombia. He opens his multivolume work on this area's inhabitants with a delineation of the *fundamentos de la cultura anfibia* (foundations of amphibious culture). Fals Borda defines it, in good culturalist-cum-Marxist fashion of the time, as "a complex of behaviors, beliefs and practices related to the handling of the natural environment, technology (productive forces) and the norms of agricultural production, fishing and hunting that prevail in the communities" (Fals Borda 1979, 21B).[1] However, this innovation, along with other pioneering work of Fals Borda (see Oslender 2016), has remained largely invisible in the English-speaking world (with the exception of the recent book by Rappaport 2020).

In Colombia itself, the theme of the amphibious has had more resonance, as the recent two-volume publication titled *Colombia Anfibia: Un país de humedales* suggests (Amphibious Colombia: A country of wetlands, Jaramillo Villa et al. 2015, 2016). Published by the biodiversity research center Instituto Humboldt and directed at a broad, nonspecialist readership with ample images, simple language, and copious graphic design, these books foreground ecological dimensions and human-induced threats of various water bodies in the country, raising awareness of the importance of water in the Colombian landscape. A short section on "amphibious cultures" (Jaramillo Villa et al. 2015, 42–43) explicitly draws on Fals Borda's work. The Amphibious Colombia books, however, do not focus on documenting unorthodox ways of life and underappreciated wetland ecologies as much as they are part of a larger scientific project of inscribing water management, adaptation to climate change, and conservation into Colombian subjectivities, transposing knowledge about biodiversity into political claims, as Camargo discusses in his chapter.

For this book's endeavor to develop a more explicit approach to am-

8 *Krause, Cortesi, Camargo*

phibious lifeworlds, we also rely on sociologist Therezinha J. P. Fraxe's *Homens anfíbios: Etnografia de um campesinato das águas* (Amphibious men: Ethnography of a water peasantry), where she develops the idea of an amphibious landscape to describe the wetlands and rural livelihoods of the Amazon (Fraxe 2000). In the last decade, research in anthropology, geography, and related fields has begun to use the term more widely and collect a growing repertoire of studies and reflections. Among these, anthropologists Karine Gagné and Mattias Borg Rasmussen's "An Amphibious Anthropology: The Production of Place at the Confluence of Land and Water" (2016) is useful for focusing on the making and transformation of place in order to find a common frame of reference for water and land. Their collection represents an important step from focusing on water in opposition to land toward considering their entanglements as socially and culturally relevant.

The work of anthropologists Atsuro Morita (e.g., 2016; 2017) and Casper Bruun Jensen (2017; see also Morita and Jensen 2017) makes further inroads into an amphibious analytic, by approaching technologies, infrastructures, land uses, and worldviews as amphibious phenomena, not reducible to terrestrial and aquatic dimensions. We read these works as establishing the amphibious as a frame of reference for the dynamics of wet environments that are not only constituted by "land + water" but develop in other configurations, for example "waterland" (Cortesi 2022). Amphibious landscapes and socialities, in these accounts, preexist those of water and land, the latter extracted, for example, in the drive toward a "terrestrialization" of towns in the Danube Delta (Richardson 2018) and the Chao Phraya Delta (Morita and Jensen 2017), or the colonial production of land as physical and fiscal realities in India and Bangladesh (D'Souza 2006; Dewan 2021). These studies show that amphibious relations often precede the separation and subsequent recombination of land and water, an argument that the contributions to this volume elaborate in detail.

Our understanding of amphibious lives is guided, furthermore, by a keen attention to their temporality. Wetness is often seasonal—think of the monsoon (da Cunha 2019; Bremner 2020)—and can be capricious and difficult to predict, as floods and droughts have amply demonstrated. What does this imply for more-than-human amphibious relations? Anthropologist Mark Harris (1998; 2000), writing about the inhabitants of a riverbank village on the middle Amazon, has analyzed the rhythmicity of social and ecological life, where the village's wetness is always transforming as the river swells and recedes. Life on the Amazon, according to Harris, is not so much determined by this shifting wetness as it comes into being in response to and anticipation of ever-transforming wet opportunities and limitations. Developing this insight, anthropologist Franz Krause (2022) has illustrated how amphibious assemblages continually arise through situated practices and rhythmic social and material dynamics.

Indeed, amphibious materialities and the infrastructures designed to manipulate them play central roles in an approach to the amphibious that takes more-than-human relations to heart. For example, in *Liquid Landscape*, Michele Navakas (2018) portrays historical accounts of Florida's materiality that did not fit the dominant narrative of US colonization, which was based on terrestrial metaphors and practices of enclosure and taking root. Instead, she discovers metaphors and practices from an amphibious realm that supplied alternative narratives of settler attachments in North America, including the figure of the water lettuce as discovered in Florida: growing in large, floating communities, it is resilient to storms and floods and easily finds a new home after disruptions. This metaphor also mirrors the traditions and narratives surrounding Florida's Everglades, where unorthodox forms of wetness long facilitated the flourishing of unorthodox forms of social life (Ogden 2011). Historian David Biggs (2010), in turn, illustrates how the Mekong Delta has long been a "quagmire" for colonial governments and US American armies trying in vain to control a recalcitrant population in an equally recalcitrant terrain. Governing the Mekong Delta has therefore meant governing its waters and sediments through developing and maintaining complex infrastructural arrangements (Biggs et al. 2009). Anthropologist Luisa Cortesi shows how, in North Bihar, India, infrastructures that are designed for flood control, irrigation, and drainage not only physically separate water and land but conceptually and cognitively separate the two even in places where people consider them as two sides of the same coin (Cortesi 2021; see also Morita and Jensen 2017; Dewan 2021). Together, these works enable us, in conversation with the contributions to this volume, to formulate a thorough approach to the amphibious that considers human engagements with shifting aspects of wetness as social, temporal, and material.

## A NEW UNDERSTANDING OF THE AMPHIBIOUS

Building on these considerations, the present collection develops an approach that we call amphibious anthropologies. This plural term reflects not only the multiple locations—from the United States to India, and from Estonia to the Bahamas—and disciplinary groundings of the contributions, from anthropology to geography and science-and-technology studies. It also hints at the gamut of ways in which amphibious relations and practices matter in the lives of differently situated humans and the landscapes they inhabit. *Anthropologies* therefore does not so much refer to the discipline of anthropology as to the variety of experiences, socialities, and struggles in and around wet environments. What makes these anthropologies amphibious is their empirical location in contexts where shifting configurations of wetness matter to those involved through work or residence, as well as their more general tendency to blur taken-for-granted distinctions. In the contributions to this collection, attention to the details of living in wet environments brings to the fore that oppositions like conservation and use, insider and outsider, rational and affective, or natural and artificial often do not hold.

In short, this book considers the amphibious as a framework that allows the multiple, defiant ethnographic insights and multidisciplinary discussions in this volume to speak to each other and to make a wider argument. This argument proceeds in three interrelated ways, each corresponding to one part in the book. In the first part, On the Brink, we discuss different ways in which the amphibious elides modernist classifications and can serve as a provocation to reassess both these classifications and the people and places marginalized by them. In the second part, In the Damp, we elaborate how wetness is a multiple phenomenon, which manifests differently for differently situated people and is represented in potentially contradictory ways. In the final part, Through the Muck, we probe the implications of imagining and performing places and processes as amphibious for resource management, conservation, and governance and argue that this approach is necessarily temporal, more-than-human, and affective.

Together, these discussions suggest an analytical lens that articulates the predicaments of life in wet places in terms that are not reducible to the languages of land and water. They propose a range of methods for investigating how these places—including their inhabitants and the discourses about them—come into being. And they provide a vocabulary that melts the Western distinction between land and water, and the associated registers of modernity, colonialism, and control.

## ON THE BRINK

Amphibious lives have long been on the brink. By *brink*, we do not primarily mean the margins between water and land, but rather the physical in-betweenness of amphibious landscapes, their social and cultural ambiguity (see Gruppuso and Krause 2025). *Amphibious*, recites the *Oxford English Dictionary*, does not only mean inhabiting—or being suited for—both land and water, but it also means more generally "having two lives; occupying two positions; connected with or combining two classes, ranks, offices, qualities." Similarly, amphibians are not only creatures that live in both land and water but also those who have "two modes of existence; fig. of doubtful nature" "or a double character."[2] The amphibious is what blurs categorical distinctions, is an in-between, adaptable to different modalities, exploiting liminal spaces and polysemic possibilities. By proposing the amphibious as a model for thriving despite uncertainties, we aim to turn what was to be eradicated, separated, controlled (Giblett 1996) into a model for a sustainable future. Inhabiting the brink, dichotomies must be released in order to make it through.

Alida Cantor, in chapter 1, narrates the Salton Sea in California as an assemblage of lively matter and influential processes, amphibiously upsetting dichotomies of natural/artificial, wet/dry, alive/dead, resource/waste, beneficial/nuisance, fixed/fluid, and restored/wasted, setting up a practice of ontological disruption that not only reveals the existential crisis of environmental categories but also has implications for how nature is understood, imagined, and therefore decided upon and managed (Yates, Wilson, and Harris 2017; Cortesi 2013). In Cantor's analysis, the Salton Sea performs an interference with the logic of identity descriptors and definitions. It challenges the heteronormativity of the environmental resource: Is this thing, made of out-of-control, dirty water, a lake? What does it mean to call it a lake? Is this an environmental thing, is this nature, or its distortion? And therefore, what is "environmental" after all? The Salton Sea successfully provokes all these questions, and thus pushes to legitimize deviation from purportedly stable categories.

When we think about wetness as slippery, slimy terrain, our attention remains above the surface, with a certain solidity on which we can stand (Ingold 2010). What if we pull such a premise from under our feet? A sinkhole in the borderlands of Israel, Jordan, and Palestine, the topos of chapter 2, is precisely the receding of such assumptions: water and land are all the more entangled underground; the amphibious is "voluminous" (Billé 2020) rather than territorial. Simone Popperl examines sinkholes frozen midcollapse and asks us to take the risk of thinking through them, through the distinctions they blur, the influence they negatively exert. Sinkholes render visible the sociopolitical forms of adaptation necessary for Ibrahim, for example, who has become the caretaker of a settlement-owned tourist beach where sinkholes have punctured the ground enough for the facilities to be closed down. Ibrahim's identity and labor seem to hang on those fractures, as he has regained, if temporarily, some of the freedom his Bedouin family had in this landscape, decades and waves of colonization ago. Sinkholes destabilize the deeply and painfully contested lands of Israel and Palestine, depriving power from two components it depends on, land and control, and perhaps the conventions and discourses that hold them up.

In the floodplains of North Bihar, Luisa Cortesi reflects on the shapes and forms of dealings with water and the types of knowledge and politics such shapes support, further suggesting a possible way forward. In chapter 3, she contrasts what Ingold (2007) calls "lines of occupation" and "lines of habitation" by focusing on the shapes that the enactment of different ontologies of water and land instill in the world: the linear, parallel, and perpendicular shapes of colonial and state-sponsored infrastructure of water management such as embankments and dams in opposition to the concave and convex shapes of the floodplain dwellers' ways of managing water in an amphibious landscape. While the former, making water and land into separate entities, rests on what she calls an "ecology of absences," the latter acknowledges the intrinsic relations between land and water in a radically wet landscape, where life with wetness is not governed by oppositional lines but understood and negotiated in curved movements and shapes. Recognizing these shapes and their associated imaginations and practices in a potential field that Cortesi calls "geomorphoanthropology" takes an amphibious epistemology, one that leverages the possibility of humble shifting between knowledges and is conscious of its political value.

## IN THE DAMP

Amphibious lives emerge in the damp. But what this damp is, and how different people and their administrations relate to it, is hard to pin down. As Anuradha Mathur and Dilip da Cunha (2020) argue, "wetness" is everywhere before it becomes "water" somewhere, in rivers or the sea. "In India," claims da Cunha, "wetness does not flow as rivers do; instead, it is held for varying extents of time . . . in soils, aquifers, glaciers, snowfields, tanks, building materials, agricultural fields, air, and even plants and animals that come alive and thrive for the period of the monsoon" (2019, 10–11). Practically and theoretically engaging with such wetness may inspire what Jason Cons calls a "damp ontology" (2020), a reality characterized by wetness and seepage rather than clear-cut objects.

Separating wetness, conceptually and physically, into water bodies distinct from terra firma not only is unfeasible but also introduces a hierarchy in which land is superior and water is placed at its service, thus turned into an attribute. Stuart McLean (2011, 609) diagnosed "an unmistakable partiality for terra firma and a concomitant desire to reduce liquidity and wetness to predicates of the solid substance of dry land." This relates to the difficulty in grasping, conceptually and technically, the volatility inherent in the damp, which makes wetness an ever-elusive phenomenon, illustrated for example in the unsolved challenges of representing wetlands on modern maps and in narratives (Huijbens and Pálsson 2009). Remaining attentive to wet sociomateriality might require an approach akin to what Arjun Appadurai and Carol Breckenridge (2009) have called "wet theory," which enables thinking outside of hard categorical boundaries. Whereas the previous part elaborates the implication of this in-betweenness, the three chapters in this part focus on the frictions between inhabiting and maintaining wet environments, on the one hand, and processes that sideline wetness and its more-than-human inhabitants, on the other.

Chapter 4 starts from the conundrum that the prosperous economy of fishing, hunting, farming, and buffalo breeding in the Agro Pontino in Lazio, Italy, survived the drainage of the marshes by the Fascist Regime in the first half of the last century but did not survive the more recent categorization of the area as "protected wetland" and the consequent conservation policies. Paolo Gruppuso explains that such classification does not recognize the complex more-than-human ecologies of the wetlands. Buffalo, for example, theoretically destructive for water bodies, are instead hydrophilic animals whose presence facilitates the maintenance of canals by preventing aquatic plants' overgrowing and obstructing water flow. Gruppuso sees the origin of the problematic effects of conservation in the very category of wetland, which denotes an area between the wet and the dry. He juxtaposes it with the local understanding of Agro Pontino as wet land. What to an external eye may look like a certain category of place, a wetland, is better understood, says Gruppuso, as the multispecies taskscape of a wet land.

Chapter 5 shows that wetness is richer and more diverse than its relative water content: it is a property of amphibious life, emerging out of people's social and material practices and aspirations, caught up in their activities, projects, ideals, and embodied experiences. Franz Krause argues for appreciating the situatedness of wetness in the context of changing social and cultural practices in an Estonian wetland. He traces the particular perceptions of different wetland inhabitants. While some feel left behind in a wet heterotopia, others specifically seek out wet places for realizing projects that would be impossible on dry ground. The rhythmic spatial and temporal dimensions of wetness matter: where does wetness occur, and for how long or during what moments? And so does the otherness implied in wet land, which can be a stigma as well as a commodity in different contexts. Amphibious anthropologies, argues Krause, must not take wetness as a physical background, to which social life responds, but approach amphibious predicaments themselves as situated in concrete lifeworlds.

Chapter 6 analyzes a project of beaver reintroduction in Northern California. It unpacks a story of ingenuity, where observations of the ecological value of beavers reveal the positive economic effects of their protection and thus find their way into governance, as well as a narrative of transformation, grounded in values of collaboration, identity, connection, and a recovery of knowledge within a history severed by settler colonialism. Cleo Woelfle-Hazard and Daniel Sarna-Wojcicki propose a "hyporheic imaginary" that counters the modernist drive for speed and effectiveness, and its implications in boom and bust economies, by slowing things down, meandering and seeping rather than flowing in a single, straight, powerful line. Drawing attention to the hyporheic zone, which is the wet space under and around open water bodies, the authors oppose rigid demarcation of water/land, dead/alive, or enemy/collaborator, thus destabilizing the ground on which the colonial narrative of human domination has historically formed.

## THROUGH THE MUCK

An amphibious understanding of wet environments benefits from long-term observation, an inclination to poetry, and the practice of manual labor (Cortesi 2013). For all the attention to conceptual challenges, the broader institutional concerns cannot be left unattended. The challenge here is to find ways of aligning the static expectations and aspirations of planners, scientists, policymakers, and engineers with the shape-shifting movements of wet landscapes and their inhabitants, without missing the socioeconomics in which they are embedded, conscious of the specific socioecological values any managing model enacts. In short, a lot to ask. But any engagement with these issues must go through the muck. An amphibious approach to understanding and managing landscapes can warn against reproducing the colonial impetus of separation, stability, and control (da Cunha 2019; Lahiri-Dutt and Samanta 2013) and against reducing wet landscapes to "heterodystopias" (Cons 2018) by projecting on them terra firma ideas of crisis and coping. It can also support the building of unlikely alliances, avoid futile rigid categorization, and recognize ambiguities rather than trying to obliterate them.

In chapter 7, situated in a sky resort in the French Alps, Céline Granjou and Stéphanie Gaucherand explore how the practice of wetland management and the manufacturing of wetness becomes entrenched in the managers' subjectivities through discourses and practices of care and affect. Ecological and affective benefits, even those that include nonhuman phenomena, are both a goal and a strategy for wetland restoration: wetlands are sponges, the authors say, and you can love your sponge for what it does. Framed by a reflection on the rigid land-water divide in ecology—the disciplinary background of one of the coauthors—Granjou and Gaucherand focus on the ideas and effects of what they call amphibious functionality, which describes the more-than-human assemblages required for thriving wetlands. These include not only ideas, techniques, and materials but also their generative relations to ethics: by maintaining infrastructures and conversations, ski lift operators come to care for wetlands. Framing wetlands as "functional," as opposed to "natural," the authors illustrate how the maintenance of amphibious relations is not necessarily a question of restoration but a forward-looking endeavor that works through connectivity, unlike the often individuated rhetoric involved in species conservation.

The model of amphibious governance elaborated by Sarah Wise in chapter 8 focuses on the waxing and waning of activities, histories, and ecologies on which families, personal relationships, and knowledge(s) of tidal areas in The Bahamas are based. There, the idea of the amphibious serves to oppose the supposition that governing quickly and radically changing spaces necessarily leads to enclosure and de facto privatization. This provides a new critique of the tragedy of the commons parable—debunking the belief that harvests regulated neither by state nor by the market imply suboptimal outcomes. Wise proposes unorthodox, temporally and socially sensitive forms of littoral governance: the amphibious, says Wise, is simply a condition sine qua non for management in the tidal context, where the fixity of land is swept away more often than not.

In chapter 9, Alejandro Camargo presents the amphibious as a space of knowledge production and political deliberation among scientists, communities, and government agents. In the aftermath of catastrophic floods in 2010, the Colombian government funded a scientific study intended to determine the boundaries of wetlands across the country. Concerns regarding climate change and wetland loss justified the need to understand the geographical extent of wetlands accurately in order to support conservation and sustainable management. Yet making the boundaries of wetlands visible is not merely a geographical endeavor but also a political project. Boundaries also set limits to extractivism, urbanization, and agricultural expansion, thereby placing scientific work within a network of power relations. Scientists have drawn upon Orlando Fals Borda's idea of the amphibious as a strategy to move scientific knowledge toward the sphere of public opinion and thus foster consciousness regarding the ecological importance of wetlands among Colombians. The amphibious becomes both a way to understand a national territory and a conceptual device to mobilize different actors around conservation and sustainability.

## LEARNING FROM THE AMPHIBIOUS

As a collection, and alongside the many more detailed elaborations and inspirations from individual contributions and the existing literature on which we build, this book offers three take-home lessons. First, the amphibious is processual and relational rather than categorical. Indeed, shifting conditions of wetness and their imbrication in social, cultural, and economic lives defy and confuse, time and again, the categories imposed on them through science and governance. A key characteristic of amphibious life lies in its uncertain transformations, its nonlinearity, and the havoc this wreaks not only on the agencies charged with governing it but also on the people unable to adequately—that is, flexibly—deal with shifting wetness due to governmental restrictions.

Second, the amphibious is an inhabited place rather than a physical given. The fact that a geographical location is experiencing shifting water content does not make it an amphibious place. For this to happen, we need living beings to frequent, inhabit, use, struggle, and think about the place and its dynamic affordances. Amphibious anthropologies describe the more-than-human encounters and predicaments in wet landscapes, where people struggle to make ends meet in the face of uncertain hydrologies, often disastrous colonial histories, and the constant friction with mainstream, land-based ideas and policies.

Finally, amphibious landscapes are conflictual spaces, where the kinds of wetness, the kinds of relations, and the benefits arising from them are contested and unstable. No single solution, no lasting accord can govern amphibious lives, as neither their social nor their material aspects are ever fixed and are often transforming in much more salient ways than on terra firma. Instead, they require constant renegotiations of evolving human interests, dynamic regimes of wetness, and inhabitants' livelihoods and prospects.

Amphibious anthropologies, as we have called these studies of wet environments that center on their inhabitants' predicaments, creativities, and imaginations, benefit from conversations between a range of disciplinary approaches, from anthropology and ecology to geography, history, sociology, and science-and-technology studies. The contributions to this volume and the literature we draw on provide some examples, and there are certainly more: geographer Camargo explores the political implications of mapping wetlands in Colombia; geographer Cantor probes three conceptual approaches—hybridity, performativity, and indeterminacy—for what they can tell us about the Salton Sea; anthropologist and STS (science-and-technology studies) scholar Cortesi links infrastructural shapes with contrasting ways of inhabiting and therefore knowing a floodplain; multidisciplinary sociologist Granjou and ecologist Gaucherand combine hydrology, STS, and affect theory to understand Alpine wetland restoration; anthropologist Gruppuso explores the political agency of the wetlands concept; anthropologist Krause's ethnographic study with wetland inhabitants reveals the situatedness of wetness; anthropologist and communicator Popperl tells a story of sinkholes and borders based on multilingual ethnographic fieldwork; anthropologist and environmental scientist Wise suggests a governance model suited to hydrosocial peculiarities; and STS scholar Woelfle-Hazard and environmental scientist Sarna-Wojcicki engage feminist science studies, Indigenous studies, and political ecology to explore the multispecies politics of flood and drought management.

In these transdisciplinary explorations, the amphibious is simultaneously an environmental context (a landscape of shifting wetness), a methodological approach (using mixed and flexible methods, less in conversation with each other than as an open exploration), and a theoretical concept (addressing the spaces, practices, and knowledges of the in-between, unconstrained by the binaries of "land" and "water" or "this" and "that"). The amphibious, therefore, refers as much to a material and epistemological reality, shaping and being shaped by the lived experience and practices of humans and other beings across the Earth, as it denotes a world to think with. Through the understandings of the amphibious elaborated in this volume, we complicate the very ideas of water and land as well as the ways we respond to the rapid and profound environmental transformations of our time. The amphibious is a world to think with because it forces us to see reality as entanglements, as temporal configuration of relations and materialities that sometimes manifest themselves as continuums and sometimes as ruptures, but never as isolated parts. With the amphibious, we reimagine the ways we do research and theorize life in uncertain times.

## NOTES

1   "Aquí los viajeros nos referimos a un complejo de conductas, creencias y prácticas relacionadas con el manejo del ambiente natural, la tecnología (fuerzas productivas) y las normas de producción agropecuaria, de la pesca y de la caza que prevalecen en las comunidades de reproducción de la depresión momposina" (translation by the authors).

2   *Oxford English Dictionary* (2020) "amphibious, adj." and "amphibian, adj. and n."

## REFERENCES

Appadurai, A., and C. A. Breckenridge. 2009. Foreword. In *Soak: Mumbai in an Estuary*, edited by A. Mathur and D. da Cunha, 1–3. New Delhi: Rupa & Co.

Bakker, K. 2012. "Water: Political, Biopolitical, Material." *Social Studies of Science* 42 (4): 616–23.

Barad, K. 2007. *Meeting the Universe Halfway: Quantum Physics and the Entanglement of Matter and Meaning*. Durham, NC: Duke University Press.

Barnes, J. 2014. *Cultivating the Nile: The Everyday Politics of Water in Egypt*. Durham, NC: Duke University Press.

Barnes, J., and S. Alatout. 2012. "Water Worlds: Introduction to the Special Issue of Social Studies of Science." *Social Studies of Science* 42 (4): 483–88.

Bhabha, H. 1994. *The Location of Culture*. London: Routledge.

Biggs, D. 2010. *Quagmire: Nation-Building and Nature in the Mekong Delta*. Seattle: University of Washington Press.

Biggs, D., F. Miller, C. T. Hoanh, and F. Molle. 2009. "The Delta Machine: Water Management in the Vietnamese Mekong Delta in Historical and Contemporary Perspectives." In *Contested Waterscapes in the Mekong Region: Hydropower, Livelihoods and Governance*, edited by F. Molle, T. Foran, and M. Käkönen, 203–25. London: Earthscan.

Billé, F., ed. 2020. *Voluminous States: Sovereignty, Materiality, and the Territorial Imagination*. Durham, NC: Duke University Press.

Birkenholtz, T. 2016. "Dispossessing Irrigators: Water Grabbing, Supply-Side Growth and Farmer Resistance in India." *Geoforum*, no. 69, 94–105.

Boelens, R., T. Perreault, and J. Vos, eds. 2018. *Water Justice*. Cambridge: Cambridge University Press.

Bremner, L. 2020. "Sedimentary Logics and the Rohingya Refugee Camps in Bangladesh." *Political Geography*, no. 77, 102109.

Chen, C., J. MacLeod, and A. Neimanis, eds. 2013. *Thinking with Water*. Montreal: McGill-Queen's University Press.

Chow, D. 2019. "Three Islands Disappeared in the Past Year. Is Climate Change to Blame?" NBC News. June 9, 2019. https://www.nbcnews.com/mach/science /three-islands-disappeared-past-year-climate-change-blame-ncna1015316.

Collins, E. 2017. "Reclamation, Displacement and Resiliency in Phnom Penh." In *Other Geographies: The Influences of Michael Watts*, edited by S. Chari, S. Freidberg, V. Gidwani, J. Ribot, and W. Wolford, 199–213. London: Wiley-Blackwell.

Cons, J. 2018. "Staging Climate Security: Resilience and Heterodystopia in the Bangladesh Borderlands." *Cultural Anthropology* 33 (2): 266–94.

———. 2020. "Seepage: That Which Oozes." In *Voluminous States: Sovereignty, Materiality, and the Territorial Imagination*, edited by F. Billé, 204–16. Durham, NC: Duke University Press.

Cortesi, L. 2013. "Nature Is Hard to Know: Conflicts over Floods as Struggles of Knowledge." In *Agony of Floods: Flood-Induced Water Conflicts in India*, edited by E. Prasad. K. J. Joy, S. Paranjape, and S. Vispute. Delhi: Routledge.

———. 2021. "The Ontology of Water and Land and Flood Control Infrastructure in North Bihar, India." *Journal of the Royal Anthropological Institute* 27 (4): 870–89.

———. 2022. "Hydrotopias and Waterland." *Geoforum*, no. 131, 215–22.

da Cunha, D. 2019. *The Invention of Rivers: Alexander's Eye and Ganga's Descent*. Philadelphia: University of Pennsylvania Press.

Davidson, N. 2014. "How Much Wetland Has the World Lost? Long-Term and Recent Trends in Global Wetland Area." *Marine and Freshwater Research* 60 (10): 934–41.

Dewan, C. 2021. *Misreading the Bengal Delta: Climate Change, Development, and Livelihoods in Coastal Bangladesh*. Seattle: University of Washington Press.

D'Souza, R. 2006. *Drowned and Dammed: Colonial Capitalism and Flood Control in Eastern India*. New Delhi: Oxford University Press.

Fals Borda, O. 1979. *Historia doble de La Costa*. Vol. 1, *Mompox y Loba*. Bogotá: Carlos Valencia Editores.

Fischer, M. M. 2018. *Anthropology in the Meantime*. Durham, NC: Duke University Press.

Fraxe, T. J. 2000. *Homens anfíbios: Etnografia de um campesinato das águas*. São Paulo: Annablume.

Gagné, K., and M. Borg Rasmussen, eds. 2016. "An Amphibious Anthropology: The Production of Place at the Confluence of Land and Water." Themed section, *Anthropologica* 58 (2): 135–249.

Geertz, C. 1972. "The Wet and the Dry: Traditional Irrigation in Bali and Morocco." *Human Ecology* 1 (1): 23–39.

Giblett, R. 1996. *Postmodern Wetlands: Culture, History, Ecology*. Edinburgh: Edinburgh University Press.

Gruppuso, P., and F. Krause. 2025. "Displacing the In-Between: Wetlands, Urbanity and the Colonial Logic of Separation." In *Beyond Perception: Correspondence with Tim Ingold's Work*, edited by C. Gatt and J. P. L. Loovers. London: Routledge.

Harris, L. M. 2022. "Learning from Aotearoa: Water Governance Challenges and Debates." *New Zealand Geographer* 78 (1): 104–8.

Harris, M. 1998. "The Rhythm of Life on the Amazon Floodplain: Seasonality and

Sociality in a Riverine Village." *Journal of the Royal Anthropological Institute* 4 (1): 65–82.

———. 2000. *Life on the Amazon: The Anthropology of a Brazilian Peasant Village.* Oxford: Oxford University Press.

Hastrup, K., and F. Hastrup, eds. 2015. *Waterworlds: Anthropology in Fluid Environments.* Oxford: Berghahn Books.

Helmreich, S. 2011. "Nature/Culture/Seawater." *American Anthropologist* 113 (1): 132–44.

Hiraldo, R. 2018. "Experiencing Primitive Accumulation as Alienation: Mangrove Forest Privatization, Enclosures and the Everyday Adaptation of Bodies to Capital in Rural Senegal." *Journal of Agrarian Change* 18 (3): 517–35.

Huijbens, E. H., and G. Pálsson. 2009. "The Bog in Our Brain and Bowels: Social Attitudes to the Cartography of Icelandic Wetlands." *Environment and Planning D: Society and Space* 27 (2): 296–316.

Ingold, T. 2007. *Lines: A Brief History.* London: Routledge.

———. 2010. "Footprints through the Weather-World: Walking, Breathing, Knowing." *Journal of the Royal Anthropological Institute*, no. 16 (May): S121–39.

Jackson, J. E. 1983. *The Fish People: Linguistic Exogamy and Tukanoan Identity in Northwest Amazonia.* Cambridge: Cambridge University Press.

Jaramillo Villa, Ú., J. Cortés Duque, and C. Flórez Ayala, eds. 2015. *Colombia Anfibia: Un país de humedales.* Vol. 1. Bogotá: Instituto de Investigación de Recursos Biológicos Alexander von Humboldt.

———. 2016. *Colombia Anfibia: Un país de humedales.* Vol. 2. Bogotá: Instituto de Investigación de Recursos Biológicos Alexander von Humboldt.

Jensen, C. B. 2017. "Amphibious Worlds: Environments, Infrastructures, Ontologies." *Engaging Science, Technology, and Society*, no. 3, 224–34.

Krause, F. 2022. "Rhythms of Wet and Dry: Temporalising the Land-Water Nexus." *Geoforum*, no. 131, 252–59.

———. 2024. "Afterword: Wet Ethnographies." *Ethnos* 89 (3): 500–509.

Krause, F., and T. Hylland Eriksen. 2023. "Inhabiting Volatile Worlds." *Social Anthropology/Anthropologie Sociale* 32 (4): 1–13.

Lahiri-Dutt, K., and G. Samanta. 2013. *Dancing with the River: People and Life on the Chars of South Asia.* New Haven: Yale University Press.

Lansing, J. S. 2009. *Priests and Programmers: Technologies of Power in the Engineered Landscape of Bali.* Princeton: Princeton University Press.

Ley, L. 2021. *Building on Borrowed Time: Rising Seas and Failing Infrastructure in Semarang.* Minneapolis: University of Minnesota Press.

Liao, K. H., T. A. Le, and K. Van Nguyen. 2016. "Urban Design Principles for Flood Resilience: Learning from the Ecological Wisdom of Living with Floods in the Vietnamese Mekong Delta." *Landscape and Urban Planning*, no. 155, 69–78.

Lipset, D. 1997. *Mangrove Man: Dialogics of Culture in the Sepik Estuary*. Cambridge: Cambridge University Press.

Mathur, A., and D. da Cunha. 2020. "Wetness Is Everywhere: Why Do We See Water Somewhere?" *Journal of Architectural Education* 74 (1): 139–40.

Mehta, L., G. J. Veldwisch, and J. Franco. 2013. "Water Grabbing? Focus on the (Re)appropriation of Finite Water Resources." *Water Alternatives* 5 (2): 193–207.

McLean, S. 2011. "Black Goo: Forceful Encounters with Matter in Europe's Muddy Margins." *Cultural Anthropology* 26 (4): 589–619.

Morita, A. 2016. "Infrastructuring Amphibious Space: The Interplay of Aquatic and Terrestrial Infrastructures in the Chao Phraya Delta in Thailand." *Science as Culture* 25 (1): 117–40.

———. 2017. "From Gravitational Machine to Universal Habitat: The Drainage Basin and Amphibious Futures in the Chao Phraya Delta, Thailand." *Engaging Science, Technology, and Society*, no. 3, 259–75.

Morita, A., and C. B. Jensen. 2017. "Delta Ontologies: Infrastructural Transformations in the Chao Phraya Delta, Thailand." *Social Analysis* 61 (2): 118–33.

Munter, K. D., F. Trujillo, and R. C. Rocha-Grimoldi. 2019. "Atencionalidad y líneas de vida en la malla Poopó-uru-qotzuñi ('gente del agua')." *Antípoda: Revista de antropología y arqueología*, no. 34, 19–40.

Navakas, M. C. 2018. *Liquid Landscape: Geography and Settlement at the Edge of Early America*. Philadelphia: University of Pennsylvania Press.

Nietschmann, B. 1973. *Between Land and Water: the Subsistence Ecology of the Miskito Indians, Eastern Nicaragua*. New York: Seminar Press.

Ogden, L. A. 2011. *Swamplife: People, Gators, and Mangroves Entangled in the Everglades*. Minneapolis: University of Minnesota Press.

Oorthuizen, J. 2003. *Water, Works and Wages: The Everyday Politics of Irrigation Management Reform in the Philippines*. New Delhi: Orient Longman.

Oslender, U. 2016. *The Geographies of Social Movements: Afro-Colombian Mobilization and the Aquatic Space*. Durham, NC: Duke University Press.

Perreault, T. 2020. "Climate Change and Climate Politics." *Journal of Latin American Geography* 19 (3): 26–46.

Ramsar Convention on Wetlands. 2018. *Global Wetland Outlook: State of the World's Wetlands and their Services to People*. Gland, Switzerland: Ramsar Convention Secretariat.

Ranganathan, M. 2015. "Storm Drains as Assemblages: The Political Ecology of Flood Risk in Post-colonial Bangalore." *Antipode* 47 (5): 1300–1320.

Rappaport, J. 2020. *Cowards Don't Make History: Orlando Fals Borda and the Origins of Participatory Action Research*. Durham, NC: Duke University Press.

Richardson, T. 2018. "The Terrestrialization of Amphibious Life in a Danube Delta 'Town on Water.'" *Suomen antropologi: Journal of the Finnish Anthropological Society* 43 (2): 3–29.

Schuerch, M., T. Spencer, S. Temmerman, M. L. Kirwan, C. Wolff, D. Lincke, and S. Brown. 2018. "Future Response of Global Coastal Wetlands to Sea-Level Rise." *Nature*, no. 561, 231–34.

Soja, Edward W. 1996. *Thirdspace: Journeys to Los Angeles and Other Real-and-Imagined Places*. Cambridge, MA: Blackwell.

Steinberg, P., and K. Peters. 2015. "Wet Ontologies, Fluid Spaces: Giving Depth to Volume through Oceanic Thinking." *Environment and Planning D: Society and Space* 33 (2): 247–64.

Storlazzi, C. D., S. B. Gingerich, A. van Dongeren, O. M. Cheriton, P. W. Swarzenski, E. Quataert, C. Voss, D. Field, H. Annamalai, G. Piniak, and R. McCall. 2018. "Most Atolls Will Be Uninhabitable by the Mid-21st Century Because of Sea-Level Rise Exacerbating Wave-Driven Flooding." *Science Advances* 4 (4): eaap9741.

Strang, V. 2004. *The Meaning of Water*. Oxford: Berg.

Swyngedouw, E. 2005. "Dispossessing H2O: The Contested Terrain of Water Privatization." *Capitalism Nature Socialism* 16 (1): 81–98.

UNDRR (UN Office for Disaster Risk Reduction) and CRED (Centre for Research on the Epidemiology of Disasters). 2020. *Human Cost of Disasters: An Overview of the Last 20 Years (2000–2019)*. https://www.undrr.org/publication/human-cost-disasters-overview-last-20-years-2000-2019.

Warner, J. F., M. F. van Staveren, and J. van Tatenhove. 2018. "Cutting Dikes, Cutting Ties? Reintroducing Flood Dynamics in Coastal Polders in Bangladesh and The Netherlands." *International Journal of Disaster Risk Reduction*, no. 32, 106–12.

Warren, C. 2018. "As Sea Levels Rise, Bangladeshi Islanders Must Decide Between Keeping the Water Out—or Letting It In." *Science Magazine*. March 1, 2018. https://www.sciencemag.org/.

Wheeler, T. 2022. "Raising Warragamba Dam Probably Can't Stop Floods. There's a Simpler Solution Closer to Home." *Guardian*. October 30, 2022. https://www.theguardian.com/australia-news/commentisfree/2022/oct/31/raising

-warragamba-dam-probably-cant-stop-floods-theres-a-simpler-solution
-closer-to-home.

Yates, J., N. Wilson, and L. Harris. 2017. "Multiple Ontologies of Water: Politics, Conflict and Implications for Governance." *Environment and Planning D: Society and Space* 35 (5): 797–815.

## PART I

## On the Brink

ALIDA CANTOR

# 1. Postnatural Environmental Management in an Amphibious Delta
## *Hybridity, Performativity, and Indeterminacy at the Salton Sea*

Standing at the shores of the Salton Sea, California's largest lake, one can see sparkling water stretching out as far as the eye can see. An odor of sulfur permeates the air as a beach made of the bones of dead fish and birds crunches below one's feet. The lake, rich with bird life, is drying up at an alarming rate, leaving behind a playa of fine toxic dust that threatens local air quality and human health. Yet it has received relatively little attention from environmentalists and others beyond the immediate region. Meanwhile, politicians and water managers debate potential management options at a pace that may be too slow for the lake and its future.

Why is the Salton Sea drying up, and why does it matter? The vast lake, approximately nine hundred square kilometers in size and located in Southern California's arid Imperial Valley, relies primarily upon agricultural wastewater as a source of inflow. Across the flat, hot desert landscape, a network of canals bring Colorado River water to vast agricultural fields, standing starkly green against the desert's softer sage and brown. Silty muddied canals then flow from the agricultural fields, delivering runoff water to the thirsty Salton Sea. But in recent years, the lake's inflow has been reduced because of rural-to-urban water transfers (negotiated as part of the 2003 Quantification Settlement Agreement, an agreement between Imperial Irrigation District, San Diego County Water Authority, and other local, state, and federal entities with the goal of reducing California's overall use of Colorado River water). The water transfer agreements included provisions for Salton Sea restoration, but debates have ensued over who should foot the bill and what exactly restoration should entail (Cantor and Knuth 2019).

The lake's future is currently far from certain. What is certain is that without mitigation or restoration of some sort, the water transfer will accelerate the lake's increasing salinity and receding shorelines, with potentially catastrophic effects on wildlife habitat for migrating birds, as well as air quality in a region already suffering from high childhood asthma rates and other environmental justice issues (Cohen 2014; Cohen and Hyun 2006; DeBuys 2001; Buck 2020). The lake has arguably been rendered a "sacrifice zone" (Voyles 2017; Cantor 2017; Cantor and Knuth 2019; Voyles 2021). Political economic disparities and environmental justice issues are on clear display as urban Southern California benefits from access to water (Cantor 2021) while Imperial Valley residents suffer the deadly consequences of severely impaired air quality (Jones and Fleck 2020; Johnston et al. 2019).

The debates over the Salton Sea's future are about more than environmental management decisions: they tap into an existential crisis regarding the lake's identity. Although the lake is currently the largest in the state of California, it has been a dried-up lake bed at times throughout history. The low-lying area has historically filled up and dried over centuries as part of the shifting Colorado River Delta system, but its most recent formation as a large lake originated from a flood typically attributed to an accidentally breached Colorado River irrigation canal in 1905 (DeBuys 2001; Voyles 2016; Ross 2020). For the past hundred years, under settler colonial water management practices (Voyles 2021), the Colorado River has remained fixed in its course in the interest of supporting capitalist agriculture (e.g., Claire and Surprise 2022), cutting off the fluctuations that once periodically filled the low Salton Sink. Meanwhile the lake itself has persisted because of runoff water from surrounding irrigated agriculture. This unconventional origin story makes it difficult to position the Salton Sea within conventional environmental binaries. Because it is not an obviously natural—or naturally wet—place, the Salton Sea has struggled to gain environmentalist attention and support for restoration, which is itself an ambiguous concept in an "unnatural" environment (Voyles 2016; Cantor 2016; Cantor and Knuth 2019).

It is in this context that I apply the lens of amphibious anthropologies to examine the case of the Salton Sea.[1] The perspective of amphibious anthropologies examines the complicated and vulnerable nature of environments that lie somewhere in between land and water: tidelands, wetlands, floodplains, and so on (Krause 2017; Gagné and Rasmussen 2016; see also introduction to and other chapters within this volume). In various contexts, amphibious places, which defy binaries of wet and dry, have been considered wastelands, dangerous disease vectors, areas for drainage and exploitation, and valuable habitat, to name a few. An anthropological perspective examines how different amphibious environments shape social meanings, interpretations, practices, and identities. An amphibious perspective contributes to a better understanding of how humans interact with, categorize, and manage these ambiguous sites that are neither wet nor dry. The lens of amphibious anthropologies provides a useful tool for thinking about the Salton Sea, as its position at the edge of wet/dry boundaries complicates its management.

This discussion engages with theories of relational materiality, inspired by science-and-technology studies (STS) and actor-network theory (Alaimo and Hekman 2008; Coole and Frost 2010; Whatmore 2006; Latour 2005; Law 1992; Deleuze and Guattari 1987). This perspective emphasizes non-human agency, proposing the idea of "vibrant matter" (Bennett 2009), which is lively and undetermined (Hird 2012; Gregson and Crang 2010), and challenging binaries including separation of social and natural realms (Haraway 1991). Importantly, Indigenous STS scholar Kim TallBear (2017) notes that the approach, sometimes called "new materialism," is not necessarily "new" at all. The divide between nature and culture is a largely European construct that Indigenous thinkers have long rejected; attempts to claim this approach as new risk ignoring long-held Indigenous traditions. As such, I avoid the term *new materialism* and instead use *relational materiality* to refer to the collection of theoretical perspectives that take seriously the agency of nonhumans while critically examining nature/society binaries.

Discursive debates over the Salton Sea have consequences for the lake's management, and critical theoretical perspectives may provide openings for reframing and reconsidering the Salton Sea. Over time, different understandings and interpretations of the Salton Sea's identity—as wet or dry, natural or artificial, dead or alive—have played into the difficult management challenges that the lake faces. I consider how theories of hybridity, performativity, and indeterminacy may inform environmental management in an amphibious and ambiguous landscape.

## HYBRIDITY: MOVING BEYOND BINARY CONSTRUCTIONS

Salton Sea historian William DeBuys notes that "deltas are the most inconstant of landforms" (2001, 58). Deltas fluctuate and change, and they are neither consistently wet nor dry; as such they present a unique set of hydrosocial relations that is uniquely amphibious (Krause 2017).

As part of the Colorado River Delta system, the low-lying Salton Sink has historically periodically filled to form the ancient Lake Cahuilla and then dried up again. The Salton Sea's lake bed had been dry for several centuries, from around 1600 (Singer 2001) until 1905, when a project constructing irrigation channels to divert Colorado River water into the dry area to support capitalist and colonial agricultural expansion went awry. The entire Colorado River changed course, rushing through the irrigation channel cuts to fill the Salton Sink in a flood that lasted for over a year. After this flood, the new lake was expected to dry up eventually due to the lack of natural inflow. However, due to continued inflows of Colorado River water running off from irrigated agricultural fields surrounding the Salton Sink, the Salton Sea still exists. Instead of drying up, the Salton Sea is now the largest lake in California. In 1924 and 1928, the Salton Sea was legally designated by President Calvin Coolidge as an "agricultural sump," a permanent drainage reservoir for the storage of agricultural wastewater. Today, the Salton Sea is fed through a system of agricultural drainage canals filled with slow-moving, brown, brackish water.

Feminist scholars in STS have for decades worked to break down binaries such as human/natural and have linked binary constructions to relationships of domination (Plumwood 1993; Haraway 1991). Queer theory and "queer ecologies" (Mortimer-Sandilands and Erickson 2010) further challenge questions of constructions of the "natural" and the "deviant." Considering the Salton Sea through this lens, the lake is difficult to categorize along numerous binaries, including wet/dry and artificial/natural. Over time, the Salton Sink has been both wet and dry. The lake's current form is not clearly attributable to "natural" inflows of water nor to deliberate human action. Questions of whether the Salton Sea ought to be wet or dry and, relatedly, whether it is a "natural" versus an "artificial" or "man-made" place are not just epistemological debates; these questions have had serious material consequences when taken up as assumptions by managers (Voyles 2016; Cantor 2017).

Ecofeminist scholar Val Plumwood describes dualism as "the logic of colonization" (Plumwood 1993, 41). She argues that a range of dualist constructions, including culture/nature, mind/body, and male/female, overlap with one another and should be considered as part of an interrelated system of domination, rather than being considered as independent of one another. In this case, constructions of the Salton Sea as wet/dry—the focus of this chapter, as part of a collection of works on amphibious places—are entangled with other binary categories, including natural/man-made, natural/artificial, fixed/fluctuating, and alive/dead. Perceptions of the public and environmental managers regarding whether the lake ought to exist or not—whether it should be wet or dry—are inextricably tied to whether it is a "natural" and "living" place as opposed to an "unnatural" and "dying" place (the issue of the Salton Sea as "dying" is elaborated by Voyles [2017] in her description of the Salton Sea as an "invalid"). These questions, framed around binary constructions, have mattered in terms of the ability of advocates to gain legal protection, political support, and funding for environmental restoration for the lake (Cantor 2016).

The ambiguity of a water body that is part of a shifting delta system, has periodically shifted from wet to dry and back again over time, yet is currently fixed in its existence as a lake raises legal issues that cause difficulties when it comes to environmental management and protection. Cantor (2016) describes these issues in depth in a discussion of why the Salton

Sea is ineligible for certain legal protections. Although the Salton Sea has been California's largest inland body of water for the last hundred years, it was dry—not a lake—in 1850, when California was granted statehood. At this point in time, the state took legal title to the land underneath all navigable bodies of water. Because the Salton Sink was, at that point, dry, the land underneath what is now the lake is not owned by California; instead, the lake bed represents a patchwork of ownership and is primarily held by the Imperial Irrigation District, the US Bureau of Reclamation, and the Torres Martinez Desert Cahuilla Indians. The consequence is that the Salton Sea is ineligible for certain conservation measures afforded to other bodies of water (Cantor 2016). Temporality clearly matters here: the lake has changed over time, and the specific forms it has taken at different particular points in time make a difference in its legal status. In this way, the Salton Sea's amphibious identity as a fluctuating, nonequilibrium delta ecosystem compounds difficulties in securing environmental protection and presents legal-political challenges when it comes to management.

The discursive debates over whether the Salton Sea is an "accident" or a "natural" place have broader ramifications for environmental management beyond the legal, as well. On the one hand, the Salton Sea is frequently referred to in media and public discourse as a human-created "accident" (see, for example, Frankel 2015). The "accident" discourse is not unfounded: the current form of the Salton Sea dates back to the aforementioned 1905 flooding, and the lake's levels have been maintained as a result of continued industrial agricultural irrigation. On the other hand, contrary to the argument that the lake is an "accident" caused by humans, the lake's existence can also be attributed to a number of "natural" nonhuman factors, including the Salton Sink's low-lying topography and the Colorado River Delta's historically unpredictable, shifting course. Recent scholarship analyzing historic geological and hydrological data pushes back on the "accident" narrative, making the case that the 1905 flood was a result of regional climate and floodplain dynamics (Ross 2020). This lack of agreement around the Salton Sea's identity as a natural versus an artificial place impacts the discourses around the Salton Sea's potential futures. For example, early in my research, I interviewed a water policy expert with deep knowledge of the Salton Sea, who said, "One of the challenges is that people see this as an artificial system, which is more of a political and perceptual problem. And . . . that gets people saying it should just dry up, it's not natural, it should just dry up, we should let it go."

As this policy expert explained, the "perceptual problem" of seeing the Salton Sea as artificial leads to a particular management approach of "letting it go." Yet, despite the common designation of the Salton Sea an artificial lake, it is clear that the amphibious Salton Sea has existed in different forms throughout history. Before its most recent filling in the early 1900s, the Salton Sea had been dry since around 1600 (Singer 2001; Laflin 1995). Prior to that dry period, geological and archaeological evidence suggests that the ancient Lake Cahuilla existed in the current Salton Sea's lake bed, multiple times and much larger than the current Salton Sea (Singer 2001). It is estimated that the lake filled up and dried again approximately every four hundred to five hundred years. This longer historical perspective is well recognized by the area's contemporary Native American inhabitants. The Imperial Valley area is the homeland of numerous bands of Cahuilla Native American tribes, who inhabited the desert and mountain areas and used Lake Cahuilla as a resource when it was full (Voyles 2021). The area was colonized first by the Spanish and then in the mid-1800s by the United States. The Imperial Valley's population remained low until the turn of the twentieth century, when land developers began to cultivate commercial irrigated agriculture based on water diversions from the Colorado River (DeBuys 2001). Today the area is home to the Torres Martinez Desert Cahuilla Indians, who hold land on the northwestern shores of the Salton Sea. In an interview that took place on Torres Martinez tribal lands on the edge of the Salton Sea, a member of the Torres Martinez tribe noted the historic importance of Lake Cahuilla's ever-shifting shoreline for tribal members in the area:

> Back in our ancestors' times we had a lot of fish tribes, there was fishing, and the Salton Sea wasn't a dead sea, right, it was a flowing, living sea at that time. The sea is one part of our history and tradition. It's still there. It hasn't changed just because of, you know,

different physical aspects, it's still there. And I know the elders see it and still remember it being active and alive, so that's how they see it and how they tell the younger ones. We used to do this, we used to fish and we used to swim. And that was a big part of their life back then.

Today, high-water marks can be seen about 230 feet higher than the lake's current elevation (Laflin 1995), and fish traps built by Cahuilla people can be found in the mountains far above the lake. On a field tour of the area with a local water district manager, he gestured to the mountains surrounding the lake. He explained:

You know, the Salton Sea, one of my pet peeves is that the Salton Sea is not a mistake. It is a remnant of an old lake system that used to occur and dry up on a cyclical basis throughout time. And when they stopped the flow to the Salton Sea in 1906, they intervened in a natural system, and that was when mankind intervened in a natural process. Otherwise it would've filled up all the way and covered everything. I mean, Lake Cahuilla was a big lake. It would take twenty-eight years to fill and sixty-five years to dry, and it would just do it over time. When we did work over on the east side, we found the fish traps, which are these stone rings built in a series. As ancient Lake Cahuilla's shoreline diminished, they would be at different elevations.

The water manager's description of the fish traps, along with the comment about the lake's continued existence from the Torres Martinez tribal member, highlights that the Salton Sea was previously a system that fluctuates over time. Historically, local Native American tribes would use the changing Salton Sea — the "flowing, living sea" — to their advantage as a way to trap fish. The Salton Sea's changes were perceived as a part of what made the Salton Sea "active and alive." The concept of the Salton Sea as a flowing, living system that actively changes over time contrasts starkly with the idea of the Salton Sea as an artificial, human-created accident. In this way, overlapping binaries—fluctuating/fixed and alive/dead—take on relevance in the context of the Salton Sea.

The difference between a "flowing, living sea" and a fixed, dead body of water is more than just a matter of opinion. It is, as Yates, Harris, and Wilson (2017) describe, an ontological disjuncture that carries political implications. Importantly, these overlapping dualisms—wet/dry, natural/unnatural, alive/dead, fluctuating/fixed—influence potential visions and versions of the lake's future. These dualisms are leveraged by environmental managers to support various goals. For example, some managers argue that since the lake is an accidental, man-made feature in a naturally dry place, it should be allowed to dry up unimpeded. However, this view certainly has negative consequences for the communities of people, migrating birds, and fish that reside in and around the lake. Others have put forth proposals that seek to maintain the current boundaries of the wet lake's shore through massive engineering efforts that stretch the definition of "restoration"—with their own set of problematic consequences for people and ecosystems (Cantor and Knuth 2019).

It is in this context that rethinking the Salton Sea as a hybrid, as proposed by Rudy (2005), may be a step toward moving past binaries. In her excellent and thorough book focusing on the impacts of settler colonialism at the Salton Sea, Voyles (2021) describes such binary thinking as a hallmark of colonialism that contrasts with more relational ways of thinking. These insights from critical scholars encourage us to consider specific ways in which the lake's plight matters for different human and nonhuman actors and to think about who might benefit or lose in what ways from different solutions proposed for the lake's future.

## PERFORMATIVITY: DESIRABILITY AND DEVIANCE

Framings of the Salton Sea as "dead" or "a mistake," due to its supposedly accidental origins, may support certain management goals ("let it dry up") but are not necessarily conducive to addressing the management issues at hand, including how to support existing bird life and how to manage dust issues caused by the shrinking shoreline. Turning the attention to performativity may change the focus of the conversation: examining the performative roles of the Salton Sea as a lively ecosystem can deemphasize the question of what the Salton Sea *is* and switch the focus to what it *does*.

The Salton Sea plays many roles: to name a few, it is a vibrant ecosystem, home, habitat, and suppressor of toxic dust. Barad (2003), drawing from Butler's conceptualizations of gender performativity (e.g., Butler 1990), proposes the concept of "posthumanist performativity" in her discussion of "how matter comes to matter." Barad calls for a "robust account of the materialization of *all* bodies—'human' and 'nonhuman'—and the material-discursive practices by which their differential constitutions are marked" (810). She challenges us to think about "phenomena," temporarily stabilized iterations of particular intra-acting practices and relationships, rather than "things." Applying this idea to the Salton Sea, we can view the lake as a dynamic set of relationships that is performatively enacted in particular ways. This perspective takes the weight off the problematic questions of the lake's identity—what the lake is (wet/dry, dead/alive). Instead, we can consider the Salton Sea as an intra-acting set of relationships and practices. This reduces the emphasis on the troublesome and ultimately unanswerable questions of whether the Salton Sea is or ought to be wet or dry and whether the water body is an accident or "natural" and instead emphasizes the importance of ensuring that important roles of ecosystem, home, and habitat continue in a meaningful way.

California water managers are well aware of the importance of the roles played by the Salton Sea. For example, in an interview that took place at a conference in a shiny hotel in Los Angeles, an LA city water manager noted that regardless of how the Salton Sea was created, an ecosystem, community, and economy has since formed around the lake: "So, you look at the Salton Sea, well, the Salton Sea is interesting. There was kind of a remnant sea there, and the Salton Sea was mostly created by accident because of farming problems. You know, where the Colorado River breached itself. And then you have fish established, and the whole community and the economy established, and so, you know, so all of a sudden it's the norm. So if you undo it, now you are undoing everything."

The LA water manager recognizes that ecological and human communities have formed around the existence of the Salton Sea in its current formation as a lake. He recognizes that despite LA's interest in securing the water that feeds into the Salton Sea to support urban water supplies, the lake's disappearance would have severe consequences for this established network, which includes the humans and nonhumans who rely upon the lake as well as the lake itself.

The Salton Sea performs a particularly significant role in terms of habitat. The lake is a key hub for migrating fish-eating birds traveling the Pacific Flyway (Redlands Institute 2002; DeBuys 2001; Bradley and Yanega 2018). Over four hundred species of birds, including several endangered species, use the lake for habitat. As a report by international bird conservation group Audubon (Wilsey et al. 2017) emphasizes, migratory birds rely heavily upon the linked system of saline lakes of the Intermountain West; each node, including the Salton Sea, is key in maintaining habitat connectivity along the Pacific Flyway.

Migrating birds rely particularly heavily on the lake since 90 percent of California's wetland habitat has disappeared over the past century (Wilson 2010). This means that birds rely upon the few remaining regional wetlands and lakes for survival. On a visit to the Sonny Bono National Wildlife Refuge, known for having the highest diversity of bird species of any Western US wildlife refuge, a staff member explained that the Salton Sea, with its shallow shoreline and abundant fish, performs an important role in standing in for this missing habitat:

> In California, we've lost more than 90 percent of our wetlands in the last hundred years. And the Salton Sea has really provided a lot of that wetland area for birds, and has become one of the primary stopping points for migrating birds. . . . Also, a lot of people want to say the Salton Sea is a mistake or an accident. Migratory birds have been using it for thousands and thousands of years. And so, I argue that now it is not a mistake. It's maintained in a different way, by agricultural drainage water right now, and not by natural flooding cycles of the Colorado River, which historically it was maintained, and it was historically a much bigger wetland than currently is

maintained. So yeah, I just argue that no, it's been here for a very long time, and there's evidence that there's been Native American campsites excavated a couple of places, up here in this part of the Salton Sea—and at those campsites they've found, I think it was well over a hundred species of different bird bones, mimicking bird life exactly what we see today.

The wildlife refuge staff member notes that the current formation of the Salton Sea is performing a similar function as historical flooding cycles of the Colorado River and that this role is particularly important, given the decimation of California's wetlands. A restoration ecologist I interviewed agreed that whether or not the Salton Sea is artificial, it presents very real habitat for birds: "The Salton Sea was an accident in the historical time. It's well understood that over geologic time the river has wandered around, and the Salton Sea had water in it, and then it didn't have water in it. Now it has water in it. It was a human caused accident rather than a change of the natural flowing of the river, but there it is. The habitat issue is very real, regardless of whether it's an artificial lake or whether it's a natural lake." From the restoration ecologist's perspective, the lake's habitat value—what it *does*—outweighed the question whether or not the lake is artificial or not—what it *is*.

When I spoke with a staff member at a bird conservation nonprofit organization, I heard a perspective that also emphasized the lake's habitat performance. She explained, "I don't really care that it's an accident, because water is such a scarce resource in California, way more so than it used to be. So, the Salton Sea is now being used by a lot of birds, and they need it whether it's accidental or not. The Central Valley used to be full of water, but it's not anymore. The Colorado River, these places are all gone for the most part, but at least we still have the Salton Sea. It's an accident, but it's helping to replace everything else that's gone." The bird conservationist differed slightly from the National Wildlife Refuge manager previously described, in that she does, in fact, see the Salton Sea as an "accident." However, even so, she also emphasizes the importance of the Salton Sea in terms of ecological functionality despite the lake's "accidental" origins. Her perspective emphasizes the importance of the Salton Sea given that the Colorado River no longer reaches its terminus because of overallocation of the river system.

Considered together, the above three interviewees differ in their assessment of whether the lake is an accident or not, but they all agree that the lake is now performing an important role, especially when it comes to providing bird habitat. The bird conservationist went on to discuss the Salton Sea's positioning within a broader context, which includes the Colorado River Delta: "The Salton Sea is accidental, it's not a naturally occurring lake, but it's basically become a surrogate for the Colorado River Delta, which is basically gone. . . . So it might be accidental, but it has happened at a good time when the Colorado River is being drained." In this perspective, the Salton Sea is not just providing habitat but providing replacement habitat for other, even more degraded, ecosystems, including the Colorado River. Recent efforts have actually attempted such a restoration of the Colorado River Delta. In 2014, a historic binational agreement between the United States and Mexico, Minute 319, brought a temporary "pulse flow" of water all the way down the usually dry delta of the Colorado River for several weeks. The goal was to engineer a spring flood in an ecosystem where such floods have been cut off for decades. Ecologically, the experiment was successful: willows and other vegetation flourished in the wake of the engineered flood. In 2017, Minute 323 extended the original pulse flow agreement; however, timing and sizes of additional pulse flow releases remain uncertain (Benson 2017). If the Colorado River pulse flows are successful in restoring bird habitat, it is unclear how this will factor into the arguments for restoration of the Salton Sea: will this potential alternative habitat undermine efforts at the Salton Sea or strengthen the case for habitat connectivity along the entire Pacific Flyway? The answer remains to be seen.

The engineering of temporary pulse flows to create habitat in the Colorado River Delta raises parallels with other anthropogenic wetland landscapes: for example, further north on the Pacific Flyway, the engineered floodplain of the Yolo Bypass provides a habitat stand-in for California's Sacramento–San Joaquin Delta (Milligan and Kraus-Polk 2017). These engineered amphibious landscapes play an important role in ensuring habitat connectivity in the face of widespread wetland drainage and destruction. Such human-generated yet ecologically important landscapes feature large in contemporary scholarship and activism attempting to conceptualize what successful forms of conservation might look like in the new epoch of the Anthropocene (Kareiva, Lalasz, and Marvier 2011; Collard, Dempsey, and Sundberg 2015).

At the same time, the Salton Sea performs in ways less desirable from a human perspective as well. In its current form, sustained by agricultural runoff water, the Salton Sea is an unstable ecosystem characterized by eutrophication and high salinity, with algae and fish populations experiencing periodic spikes and crashes driven by runoff-related nutrient surges. The lake was once a highly prolific fishery; sport fish (in particular orangemouth corvina) were introduced in the 1950s, and during the 1950s and 1960s, the lake became a popular destination for fishing. However, in the 1980s and 1990s, eutrophic lake conditions caused large-scale fish and bird die-offs that blemished the lake's reputation and led to its reputation as a polluted and undesirable body of water. Today, tilapia are the only fish that live in the sea (along with very small populations of endangered native desert pupfish).

After the large bird and fish die-offs in the 1990s, the lake's shoreline is ringed with tiny bones that look like crunchy sand, dotted with larger skeletons of dead birds. The lake is known not only for its macabre beaches but also for its offensive odors. In 2012, an event known as "the Big Stink" occurred when hydrogen sulfide gases bubbled to the surface of the Salton Sea, creating terrible smells that spread for hundreds of miles. The *New York Times* described the incident as an "olfactory insult: a sulfurous smell, like rotten eggs, wafting across hundreds of miles" (Lovett 2012). A local author I interviewed, who has lived in and written extensively about the desert region, discussed the causes of the smelly event: "The reason behind the Big Stink was not the dead fish; it was actually hydrogen sulfide. It was after a really bad wind event—the Salton Sea is famous for getting really bad winds . . . and after that, it stirred the sea up, and all the hydrogen sulfide at lower levels of the water is allowed to escape and get blown across the sea and into the residential areas." She went on to explain that while on the one hand, the smells confirmed general perceptions of the Salton Sea as a "gross" place, on the other hand, the Big Stink at least temporarily secured attention for the pressing need to do something at the Salton Sea. The author continued, "In a sense, that event alone has definitely helped with policy in the last few months. The important thing about the Big Stink, even though people saw the problems, it means that others were quick to see that something does need to be done, which I think is important. They noticed for the first time that people who were saying that something needs to be done about the Salton Sea, because it affects everybody, they finally got to see that that is actually true."

As the Big Stink illustrates, the Salton Sea performs in ways that many people (particularly local residents) find undesirable—by stinking and killing wildlife—as well as in ways that are seen as more desirable, such as providing valuable habitat that makes up for the loss of similar habitat elsewhere. The Salton Sea is an assemblage of lively material processes akin to Bennett's "vibrant matter" (Bennett 2009): algae and bacteria flourish; birds and fish thrive, die, and stink. Not only do these material processes matter for the birds and fish and bacteria themselves, on their own terms, but they also matter in the ways that they affect the humans who react to the sights and smells with visceral repulsion. These visceral reactions are translated into the stuff of policy: it becomes difficult to argue for recognition of what is traditionally thought of as "environmental" value at a place that kills fish and birds and smells awful (Cantor 2021). However, as the local author observes, when it comes to getting political attention for the lake, these undesirable performances can be just as influential as the lake's more desirable functions.

Using a "queer ecologies" framework (Mortimer-Sandilands and Erickson 2010), the Salton Sea can be considered a "deviant" body of water in its refusal to behave in ways that are deemed appropriate. In challenging heteronormativity, queer studies has problematized the concept of "natural" and advanced a politics of deviation. The Salton Sea's fecundity has rendered it toxic, as high nutrient levels drive algae blooms, causing eutrophic conditions linked to the fish and bird deaths and the noxious smells described above (Cohen, Morrison, and Glenn 1999). These undesirable performances render the Salton Sea outside the realm of the properly environmental, complicating efforts to advance a conservation agenda on any conventional terms.

Focusing on the Salton Sea's performativity — what the lake does, the relationships supported by the lake — as opposed to its identity as either a wet or dry, or natural or artificial, place has the potential to reframe debates around the lake's management. Despite the lake's unconventional origins, my interviews revealed that many environmental managers do recognize that the Salton Sea performs vibrant and important ecological roles in its current form. Community members such as the author quoted above also pointed to the political power of undesirable performances like the Big Stink that drew broader attention to the need to manage the lake better. Amphibious places like the Salton Sea are lively, active systems. And queer theory makes room to envision a politics where such amphibious systems need not be rejected on the basis of their deviance. The driving question, discussed in the following section and in the conclusion, becomes how to actually manage this place in a way that recognizes the diverse and fluctuating life that has taken up residence there.

## INDETERMINACY: THE TROUBLES OF RESTORATION IN AN UNKNOWABLE ENVIRONMENT

The Salton Sea has been, for the last century, uncontrollable and uncertain — yet another aspect that complicates efforts to manage the lake. The Salton Sea's most recent formation stems from water out of control: when engineers and canal builders in 1905 miscalculated the strength of the Colorado River, they did not expect that the ensuing flood would take several years to control and would result in a lake that would persist for over a century. Fifty years later, when real estate developers plotted housing around the lakeshore, they did not foresee the lake's unstable levels and ecological crashes that would contribute to the decline of real estate prices and the ultimate collapse of the Salton Sea as a tourist destination. As a result, there are "ghost communities" around the lake: areas with roads, telephone poles, and street signs all laid out in anticipation for houses that were never built and neighbors that never arrived. Today, the lake's managers face a new suite of unknowns, including potential ecological tipping points as well as changing water policies that might impact the amount of water available as inflow to the Salton Sea.

STS perspectives on water, including within this volume on amphibious environments (and see, for example, Bear and Bull 2012; Gibbs 2013; Bull 2011; Lavau 2013), emphasize the lively properties of water as a nonhuman actor with agency of its own (Bear and Bull 2012). As such, water evades control and is characterized by indeterminacy. The ambiguity and indeterminacy of flows of wastewater clash with efforts to control and manage these flows (Hird 2012). As Hird (2012) describes, fixes are temporary and "management of waste ultimately fails. Fails to be contained, fails to be predictable, fails to be calculable, fails to be a technological problem (that can be eliminated), fails to be determinate" (465). The Salton Sea, as an ecosystem that is dependent upon wastewater, exemplifies this failure to be calculable, predictable, and contained.

Salton Sea managers and scientists readily admit that the lake encompasses a wide range of unknowns. Even those with intimate knowledge of the science and context of the lake note that there are many factors of uncertainty that make the lake difficult to manage. For example, an irrigation district employee, who has become a Salton Sea expert out of necessity, emphasized the uncertainties around the ecological future of the Salton Sea: "The model suggests that the Salton Sea will reach sixty parts per thousand salinity in about . . . three to five years, and the [tilapia] fishery will collapse. Nobody knows that, quite frankly; it's just what the models show. It could be fifty-nine parts. It could be sixty-two or sixty-five. Or it could be that we get a real cold spell at fifty-nine and that knocks the fishery over. We just don't know."

Even those most well-versed in the lake's science freely admit that it is impossible to completely contain, comprehend, or manage the material and ecological processes at the Salton Sea. In Sacramento, far from the Salton Sea in a tall building at the California capital, a state agency employee involved in Salton Sea policy and management points out that this makes it difficult to manage the lake: "If they could figure out how to stabilize it, so people know what to expect of it. . . . Right now it's so hard because no one can plan anything around it because they don't know what it's going to be." Moreover, even the idea of "restoring" the Salton Sea is surrounded by ambiguity. A county government agency official who is invested in economic development efforts explained in an interview, "*Restoration* is that nebulous word, what are we restoring it to? The 1900s? To 1905? So I avoid that term and the ambiguities and fights that come with it. I use the term *revitalization*. Revitalization, OK, basically means anything better than what we have now. And no one seems to object to that."

However, this uncertainty does not mean that the lake should not be managed at all. While a perspective of indeterminacy recognizes that humans are clearly not in control of everything, this does not let people off the hook for taking responsibility. A framing of indeterminacy may encourage a more open and deliberate consideration of what types of futures could be envisioned, what might be most desirable and just for human and nonhuman species, and how we might get there, while simultaneously recognizing that humans may not be able to control all factors and processes. This is particularly the case given that the Salton Sea is an ecosystem in which humans are already inextricably involved. Even though complex systems may not be fully legible or controllable, human actions have already influenced the Salton Sea and will continue to do so. Ecosystem collapse, in this case, is human-created, a result of political and power inequalities, which necessitates deliberate (and potentially expensive) human mitigation (Buck 2020). Indeed, as Cohen (2014) describes, the choice of "no action" should itself be viewed as a management choice that comes with a cost and a set of consequences. Even in its unpredictability and complexity, it is undisputable that human actions and human-driven systems are interconnected with the Salton Sea, and managers must make choices despite the potential for failure.

As an indeterminate system that cannot be fully known, yet nevertheless requires human management of some sort to avoid ecological and public health disaster, the Salton Sea can be seen as an ecosystem of the Anthropocene (Cantor and Knuth 2019). Recently, scholars critically examining the Anthropocene have renewed calls for "postnatural conservation," arguing for the need to break down nature-society binaries and recognize the ways in which humans are entangled with the nonhuman world (Collard, Dempsey, and Sundberg 2015; Lorimer 2015).

A Salton Sea expert who works at an environmental nonprofit organization described the concept of postnatural conservation in a phone interview, emphasizing the context of California water management more broadly: "We've so altered the landscape that those species that have managed to figure out a way to persist in the altered landscape, they've now become dependent on that altered landscape. . . . So they are clinging to this altered habitat for their survival, and then when you start to make changes to it, that obviously has an impact. In California, [National Wildlife Refuges] are extremely managed. They can't persist untouched. They have to be managed in order to be usable. . . . You have to manage the altered stuff as well." It is notable that such ideas of "postnatural conservation" are being taken up within the environmental community by people such as this environmental NGO employee. She recognizes that places like the Salton Sea require environmental management regardless of whether they fit conventional definitions of natural or environmental places. This involves recognition that environmental management does not hinge on a place being natural, wild, or even attractive in a conventional sense, but instead emphasizes the multispecies relationships supported by the place.

In recent years, ecologists have begun embracing a practical approach of "reconciliation ecology," which emphasizes the responsibility of humans to intervene in ecosystem management (Moyle 2014; Rosenzweig 2003). Reconciliation ecology may provide a useful framework for guiding managers' efforts to seek solutions for the lake that support existing human and nonhuman life. As ideas and practices of postnatural conservation flourish, critical scholars encourage us to carefully consider the political questions of how different visions of social natures are produced and negotiated, whose visions are implemented, and who benefits in what ways (Mansfield et al. 2015). The Salton Sea requires management in spite of its indeterminacy, but at the same time, given the nebulousness of the idea of restoration at the lake, many different competing agendas and visions are at play, with potentially uneven payoffs for different actors (Cantor and Knuth 2019). As managers and politicians negotiate and implement their visions of socionatures toward their various goals, it is important to remember this is not a neutral process and deserves careful critical consideration.

## CONCLUSION

The Salton Sea, like many amphibious environments discussed in this volume, is a lively place that does not fit neatly into conventional categories. The lake is a valuable bird habitat supporting a wide variety of life, yet it also threatens to kill with its deadly toxic air emissions. Its past and present forms have all been very much shaped by human management decisions, yet it is a seemingly uncontrollable place that people are now struggling to manage. The ebbs and flows of the lake's waters over time have resulted in not only a complex patchwork of property rights but also conflicting ideas of nature, both of which impact contemporary discussions about the lake's management. Different people have different visions of what restoration should look like, based on different fundamental assumptions of what the lake *is* in essence.

In many ways the Salton Sea is not unique. There are many uncertain, ambiguous, and complex environmental places and problems that require human intervention and care in the Anthropocene (e.g., Marris 2013; Lorimer 2015; Errington and Gewertz 2018). Amphibious ecosystems such as wetlands, swamps, and river delta systems defy categorization and present persistent management challenges. Careful consideration of this case can shed light on the particular challenges of managing such places.

First, the Salton Sea illustrates the difficulties of decision-making in a context of uncertainty. It is difficult to predict exactly what the future of the Salton Sea might look like. The lake faces many threats and uncertainties, including the potential for inflows to be further reduced as regional water managers renegotiate allocations of the Colorado River in the context of drought, and the uncertainties associated with state and private restoration funding. In addition to these political and institutional uncertainties, ecological uncertainties underlie the insecure future of the Salton Sea. Biologists have noted that the lake may have unknown ecosystem tipping points, and the specific impacts of climate change are also uncertain. These multiple, overlapping dimensions of uncertainty and indeterminacy make the lake, and those who live near it and rely upon it, particularly vulnerable.

Second, the Salton Sea, like other amphibious ecosystems, is constantly fluctuating. As a delta, the ecosystem has changed over time and taken on different forms, making it difficult to identify a clean baseline for "restoration." The Salton Sea illustrates the challenges that arise when managers attempt to "fix" fluctuating amphibious places by pinning them down and controlling them. These challenges can have ripple effects that go on for generations. In the case of the Salton Sea, management actions taken by settler colonists in the early 1900s have instigated a cascade of consequences (Voyles 2021). Irrigating the desert landscape, as well as fixing the dynamic ecosystem of the Colorado River in place through modern water management, have altered river flow patterns fundamentally. At the same time, at this point, simply restoring the natural variability in flow patterns by letting the Salton Sea dry up would cause irreparable harm to existing avian and human communities. Finding ways to rethink restoration in fluctuating, nonequilibrium ecosystems is a key project for socioecological thinkers in the Anthropocene (Cantor 2017).

Third, the Salton Sea resists categorization. When managers and policy actors do try to categorize it, it is sometimes with labels that render it disposable. Though *amphibious* often evokes the sense of abundant water, the Salton Sea is in an arid landscape, an ephemeral lake that is a remnant of a river delta system. As such, the Salton Sea does not behave in a way that fits neatly into categories set by modern water management practices: the lake is neither "naturally" wet nor totally dry, it provides important habitat even though it is "unnatural," it occasionally produces uncontrollable offensive odors, and it will require proactive management to avoid socioenvironmental disaster. There is much at stake, including the livelihoods of workers entangled with Imperial Valley's irrigated capitalist agriculture, the migration paths of birds traveling along the Pacific Flyway, the region's potential future as it is now being reimagined as a lithium production hotspot, and the health and quality of life for those who breathe the air around the region. While wealthier urban cities benefit in material ways from the water transfers, the poorer, heavily Latino communities around the lake suffer from the degraded air quality. The area around the Salton Sea has been treated as a sacrifice zone, bringing environmental justice concerns into clear focus (Voyles 2017; Cantor 2017; Cantor and Knuth 2019).

The Salton Sea, as an amphibious landscape, encompasses webs of relationships between humans, nonhumans, irrigation and infrastructure, dust, politics, money, and water. This complex place, like many amphibious landscapes in the Anthropocene, cannot be completely controlled—yet in order to avoid an ecological and environmental justice disaster, still requires deliberate human involvement and management. By adopting an amphibious approach, managers may be able to shift their efforts toward multispecies stewardship, responsibility for caring for existing life and relationships, and ongoing adaptation given the many persistent uncertainties.

## NOTE

1    This chapter is based primarily on fieldwork that took place from 2013 to 2016. I conducted over fifty in-depth, semistructured interviews with research interlocutors involved in management and planning processes around the Salton Sea and other saline California lakes at multiple levels, including community members, environmental and environmental justice advocates, local and state government officials, government agency employees at the local and state levels, and water lawyers. I spent time at and around the Salton Sea and toured related sites, including restoration projects, farms, government offices, wildlife refuge areas, nearby communities, and local and regional water infrastructure. I also conducted participant observation at community meetings, board meetings, and events and have, since the period of interview data collection, continued to review relevant archival documents including newspaper articles, legal and policy documents, and technical and historical documents.

## REFERENCES

Alaimo, S., and S. J. Hekman. 2008. *Material Feminisms*. Indiana University Press.

Barad, K. 2003. "Posthumanist Performativity: Toward an Understanding of How Matter Comes to Matter." *Signs* 28 (3): 801–31.

Bear, C., and J. Bull. 2012. "Water Matters: Agency, Flows, and Frictions." *Environment and Planning A* 43 (10): 2261–66.

Bennett, J. 2009. *Vibrant Matter: A Political Ecology of Things*. Durham, NC: Duke University Press.

Benson, E. 2017. "Why a Colorado River Reunion with the Sea Isn't a Guarantee." *High Country News*. October 6, 2017.

Bradley, T. J., and G. M. Yanega. 2018. "Salton Sea: Ecosystem in Transition." *Science* 359 (6377): 754–54.

Buck, H. J. 2020. "Understanding Inaction in Confronting Ecosystem Collapse: Community Perspectives from California's Salton Sea." *Ecology and Society* 25 (1): 27.

Bull, J. 2011. "Encountering Fish, Flows, and Waterscapes through Angling." *Environment and Planning A* 43 (10): 2267.

Butler, J. 1990. *Gender Trouble: Feminism and the Subversion of Identity*. Routledge.

Cantor, A. 2016. "The Public Trust Doctrine and Critical Legal Geographies of Water in California." *Geoforum*, no. 72, 49–57.

———. 2017. "Material, Political, and Biopolitical Dimensions of 'Waste' in California Water Law." *Antipode* 49 (5): 1204–22.

———. 2021. "Hydrosocial Hinterlands: An Urban Political Ecology of Southern California's Hydrosocial Territory." *Environment and Planning E* 4 (2): 451–74.

Cantor, A., and S. Knuth. 2019. "Speculations on the Postnatural: Ecomodernist Restoration in California's Desert Renewable Energy Boom." *Environment and Planning A* 51 (2): 527–44.

Claire, T., and K. Surprise. 2022. "Moving the Rain: Settler Colonialism, the Capitalist State, and the Hydrologic Rift in California's Central Valley." *Antipode* 54 (1): 153–73.

Cohen, M. 2014. *Hazard's Toll: The Costs of Inaction at the Salton Sea*. Oakland, CA: Pacific Institute.

Cohen, M. J., and K. H. Hyun. 2006. *Hazard: The Future of the Salton Sea with No Restoration Project*. Oakland, CA: Pacific Institute.

Cohen, M. J., J. I. Morrison, and E. P. Glenn. 1999. *Haven or Hazard: The Ecology and Future of the Salton Sea*. Pacific Institute for Studies in Development, Environment and Security.

Collard, R.-C., J. Dempsey, and J. Sundberg. 2015. "A Manifesto for Abundant Futures." *Annals of the Association of American Geographers* 105 (2): 322–30.

Coole, D., and S. Frost. 2010. *New Materialisms: Ontology, Agency and Politics.* Duke University Press.

DeBuys, W. E. 2001. *Salt Dreams: Land and Water in Low-Down California.* Minneapolis: University of Minnesota Press.

Deleuze, G., and F. Guattari. 1987. *A Thousand Plateaus.* Minneapolis: University of Minnesota Press.

Errington, F., and D. Gewertz. 2018. "Managing an Endangered Species: Palliative Care for the Pallid Sturgeon." *American Ethnologist* 45 (2): 186–200.

Frankel, T. C. 2015. "California's Largest Lake Is Slipping Away amid an Epic Drought." *Washington Post.* May 28, 2015.

Gagné, K., and M. B. Rasmussen. 2016. "Introduction — An Amphibious Anthropology: The Production of Place at the Confluence of Land and Water." *Anthropologica* 58 (2): 135–49.

Gibbs, L. M. 2013. "Bottles, Bores, and Boats: Agency of Water Assemblages in Post-colonial Inland Australia." *Environment and Planning A* 45 (2): 467–84.

Gregson, N., and M. Crang. 2010. "Materiality and Waste: Inorganic Vitality in a Networked World." *Environment and Planning A* 42 (5): 1026–32.

Haraway, D. 1991. "A Cyborg Manifesto: Science, Technology, and Socialist-Feminism in the Late Twentieth Century." In *Simians, Cyborgs and Women: The Reinvention of Nature.* New York: Routledge.

Hird, M. J. 2012. "Knowing Waste: Towards an Inhuman Epistemology." *Social Epistemology* 26 (3–4): 453–69.

Johnston, J., M. Razafy, H. Lugo, L. Olmedo, and S. Farzan. 2019. "The Disappearing Salton Sea: A Critical Reflection on the Emerging Environmental Threat of Disappearing Saline Lakes and Potential Impacts on Children's Health." *Science of the Total Environment*, no. 663, 804–17.

Jones, B., and J. Fleck. 2020. "Shrinking Lakes, Air Pollution, and Human Health: Evidence from California's Salton Sea." *Science of the Total Environment*, no. 712, 136490.

Kareiva, P., R. Lalasz, and M. Marvier. 2011. "Conservation in the Anthropocene." *Breakthrough Journal*, no. 2, 26–36.

Krause, F. 2017. "Towards an Amphibious Anthropology of Delta Life." *Human Ecology* 45 (3): 403–8.

Laflin, P. 1995. "The Salton Sea: California's Overlooked Treasure." *Periscope, Coachella Valley Historical Society.*

Latour, B. 2005. *Reassembling the Social: An Introduction to Actor-Network-Theory*. Oxford University Press.

Lavau, S. 2013. "Going with the Flow: Sustainable Water Management as Ontological Cleaving." *Environment and Planning D*, no. 31, 416–33.

Law, J. 1992. "Notes on the Theory of the Actor-Network: Ordering, Strategy, and Heterogeneity." *Systems Practice* 5 (4): 379–93.

Lorimer, J. 2015. *Wildlife in the Anthropocene: Conservation after Nature*. Minneapolis: University of Minnesota Press.

Lovett, I. 2012. "Lake Is Blamed for Stench Blown across Southern California." *New York Times*. September 11, 2012.

Mansfield, B., C. Biermann, K. McSweeney, J. Law, C. Gallemore, L. Horner, and D. K. Munroe. 2015. "Environmental Politics after Nature: Conflicting Socioecological Futures." *Annals of the Association of American Geographers* 105 (2): 284–93.

Marris, F. 2013. *Rambunctious Garden: Saving Nature in a Post-wild World*. Bloomsbury.

Milligan, B., and A. Kraus-Polk. 2017. "Inhabiting the Delta: A Landscape Approach to Transformative Socio-ecological Restoration." *San Francisco Estuary and Watershed Science* 15 (3).

Mortimer-Sandilands, C., and B. Erickson. 2010. *Queer Ecologies: Sex, Nature, Politics, Desire*. Indiana University Press.

Moyle, P. B. 2014. "Novel Aquatic Ecosystems: The New Reality for Streams in California and Other Mediterranean Climate Regions." *River Research and Applications* 30 (10): 1335–44.

Plumwood, V. 1993. *Feminism and the Mastery of Nature*. Routledge.

Redlands Institute. 2002. *Salton Sea Atlas*. Redlands, CA: ESRI Press.

Rosenzweig, M. L. 2003. "Reconciliation Ecology and the Future of Species Diversity." *Oryx* 37 (2): 194–205.

Ross, J. E. 2020. "Formation of California's Salton Sea in 1905–07 Was Not 'Accidental.'" *2020 Desert Symposium*. April 17–20, 2020, California.

Rudy, A. P. 2005. "Imperial Contradictions: Is the Valley a Watershed, Region, or Cyborg?" *Journal of Rural Studies*, no. 21, 19–38.

Singer, E. 2001. *Geology of the Imperial Valley, California*. San Diego, CA: San Diego State University Center for Inland Waters.

TallBear, K. 2017. "Beyond the Life/Not-Life Binary: A Feminist-Indigenous Reading of Cryopreservation, Interspecies Thinking, and the New Materialisms." In *Cryopolitics: Frozen Life in a Melting World*, edited by J. Radin and E. Kowal, 179–202. MIT Press.

Voyles, T. 2016. "Environmentalism in the Interstices: California's Salton Sea and the Borderlands of Nature and Culture." *Resilience: A Journal of the Environmental Humanities*, no. 3, 211–41.

———. 2017. "The Invalid Sea: Disability Studies and Environmental Justice History." In *Disability Studies and the Environmental Humanities: Toward an Ecocrip Theory*, edited by S. Ray and J. Sibara. University of Nebraska Press.

———. 2021. *The Settler Sea: California's Salton Sea and the Consequences of Colonialism*. University of Nebraska Press.

Whatmore, S. 2006. "Materialist Returns: Practicing Cultural Geography in and for a More-Than-Human World." *Cultural Geographies* 13 (4): 600–609.

Wilsey, C. B., L. Taylor, N. Michel, and K. Stockdale. 2017. *Water and Birds in the Arid West: Habitats in Decline*. New York: National Audubon Society.

Wilson, R. M. 2010. *Seeking Refuge: Birds and Landscapes of the Pacific Flyway*. University of Washington Press.

Yates, J. S., L. M. Harris, and N. J. Wilson. 2017. "Multiple Ontologies of Water: Politics, Conflict and Implications for Governance." *Environment and Planning D: Society and Space* 35 (5): 797–815.

SIMONE POPPERL

# 2. Between Hydro and Geo
## *Amphibious Spaces of Social Exception*

As the Dead Sea's salty waters recede, by more than a meter per year at this point, they leave eerie traces of former shorelines in the desiccated desert landscape (Niemi, Ben-Avraham, and Gat 1997). Old docks dangle uselessly over the dry ground meters from the water's edge. Beachgoers are left to pick their way daintily across more and more burning sand and sharp stones with each passing day as they seek the cool relief of saline buoyancy in the blue-green inland lake. The receding water has left its mark under this shoreline too, in the form of a frightening geologic phenomenon: sinkholes.

Sinkholes as large as a city block opened regularly around the Dead Sea during my fieldwork period, dotting the gray-brown shoreline with deep, dark circles.[1] Their location in border regions between Palestinian, Jordanian, and Israeli territory makes them difficult to quantify because security regimes restrict researchers' and residents' movement. Interlocutors estimated that four thousand to five thousand of them dotted the landscape of the lowest place on Earth in 2016. By 2023, that number has nearly doubled to eight thousand. As the soft earth along the Dead Sea's shores caves in, the sinkholes take in concrete, asphalt, electrical wires, metal pipes, donkeys, cars, bulldozers, and occasionally people. Even as they collapse, Dead Sea sinkholes create new economic and social possibilities for some people and foreclose possibilities for others.

The Dead Sea sinkhole problem reveals that colonial violence is enacted not just against people but also against landscapes—and sometimes underground. Analyzing it requires engaging a settler colonial interpretive frame, which has seen a resurgence in recent social scientific work about

## 56 Popperl

Palestine forty-four years after the publication of Ibrahim Abu-Lughod and Baha Abu Laban's *Settler Regimes in Africa and the Arab World: The Illusion of Endurance* (1974). I engage that theoretical frame here to think through human-nonhuman relations and the social worlds brought into being by hydrogeologies in the occupied Palestinian territories (oPt), Israel, and Jordan. Around the world, other subterranean geopolitical phenomena are upending settler colonial projects.[2] The Dakota Access Pipeline deep under Sioux treaty lands has been repeatedly threatened by Indigenous activism. Peruvian corporate mining campaigns have created a mountain politics of pollution and containment (Li 2015). In the oPt, sinkholes are disrupting global commodity chains, settler colonial infrastructures, agricultural practices, and security regimes. I focus here on what these sinkholes create and generate. I document the social relations brought into being by these hydrogeologic phenomena formed by the interaction of waters (hypersaline and fresh) and land. Rather than simply foreclosing the possibilities for human social life, Dead Sea sinkholes have allowed people to break social, religious, and political conventions and to advocate for more government attention to rural concerns. This generative potential of Dead Sea sinkholes—which have emerged in part because of the contemporary project of settler colonization—can disrupt the ongoing settler colonial project in the Jordan Valley by altering power relations among settlers, nation-states, and Indigenous communities. As water and land act on each other, the amphibious realities they impose on humans are processual and relational—sinkholes are always midcollapse, and they alter the way humans relate to each other and the landscape of the Dead Sea.

### MIDCOLLAPSE

As my friend and interlocutor Ibrahim unlocked the chain-link gate at the entrance to a recently closed Israeli settlement–run Dead Sea beach in the Palestinian West Bank, he said pointedly, "I have something to show you." His raised eyebrows marked the drama of what I saw.

Where just two days before had been a large circle of gravel marking

FIG. 2.1. The destruction of the new sinkhole, 2015. Photo by Simone Popperl.

the outline of an older sinkhole filled in with sand and gravel, a new sinkhole now gaped in the parking lot. It was over seven meters deep and ten meters wide. The asphalt parking lot around the gravel circle had cracked in a ripple pattern. It appeared to me that the earth was in the process of falling away but had frozen midcollapse. The reasons for these Dead Sea sinkholes are well understood by scientists: they form due to interactions among the geological composition of the Dead Sea's shoreline, groundwater, and the hypersaline and mineral-rich waters of the sea. Other aspects of these sinkholes are less clear. These hydrogeologic phenomena, and the amphibious subsurface material relations they index, enact new social, economic, and political entanglements in Dead Sea borderlands.

Across the mineral-rich water on Jordan's Dead Sea coastline, muddy sinkholes that swallowed a Jordanian tile factory in 2008 sprouted long stalks of electric-green bamboo that swayed in the wind by the time I first visited them in 2015. Around these sinkholes, the ground was littered with cigarette butts, crushed soda cans, and the occasional empty bottle of arak (anise-flavored liquor), evidence that the site served as an escape from the pressures of small-town life for some local Jordanian residents. Residents spoke of these places not as "wet" or "dry" but as "sinking" or "stable." The interaction of water and land is nevertheless what makes these places stand out. These amphibious formations bring opportunities for leisure and become verdant spaces of ecological and social exception in the desert landscape. My analysis here will be confined to the sinkhole problem in the West Bank and Israel; the geopolitics of the Dead Sea's western shores are complex enough. Sinkholes, however, are not confined to one side of the sea. Indeed, similar economic, political, and scientific quagmires exist in Jordan as well.

Attention to the social, economic, and political effects of the material interaction between land and water (expressed in the *hydrogeo* of *hydrogeologic*) gives rise to novel questions for anthropological research. Taking seriously not only the amphibiousness of social worlds but also the generative and destructive potential of how land and water act on each other in material ways will be critical in ethnographic analyses of all

FIG. 2.2. Large sinkhole in Jordan's Lisan Peninsula, 2015. Nearby arak bottles not pictured. Photo by Simone Popperl.

manner of things against the backdrop of accelerating climate change. The amphibious materiality of this landscape disrupts social worlds but also renders them unstable. Recent anthropological work on water and waterworlds (Anand 2011; Anand 2012; Anand 2017; Barnes 2014, Barnes and Alatout 2012; Espland 1998; Hastrup 2013; Helmreich 2009; Limbert 2001; Shallot 2010), mining (Ballard and Banks 2003; Smith 2011), and earthquakes (Tironi 2015), as well as recent debates about the Anthropocene as a geologic epoch (e.g., Zalasiewicz et al. 2010; Olson and Messeri 2015), all represent considered efforts to untangle either the hydro or the geo through ethnographic research. Missing from these discussions so far is an effort to analyze points at which water and earth interact, comingle, act on each other, and, in so doing, make the hydro and the geo impossible to separate. This chapter brings these interactions into the center of the frame through the ethnographic object of Dead Sea sinkholes. Indeed, the interaction between water and earth has animated the sinkhole problem at the Dead Sea and contemporary history of settlement in the area as well.

Dead Sea sinkholes all form the same way and originate from the same problem. Rapid recession of highly saline Dead Sea water exposes seventy-thousand-year-old subterranean salt pockets to fresh groundwater running into the inland lake from the highlands of Amman and Jerusalem (Closson and Karaki 2009; Yechieli et al. 2003). The fresh water dissolves these buried pockets of salt, leaving underground vacuums of unknowable size. So how has the sea's water come to be so shockingly depleted? The answer lies at the intersection of the hydro and the geo.

Sinkholes, swamps, bogs, and eroding shorelines are not always treated as places to be wiped away by the humans who interact with them but sometimes as places of social, political, and even economic possibility. Anthropological work on bogs, wetlands, and swamps has begun to explore the value and sociality of amphibious places (Catellino 2015; Kelman 2007; McLean 2008; McLean 2011; Ogden 2011; Scaramelli 2018). Turning ethnographic attention to sovereignty in amphibious places can elucidate the processes through which communities stake claims over those places, even as they erode, sink, or shift, taking wires, pipes, roads, and valuable arable land with them (McLean 2011). While Anand's notion of "hydraulic citizenship" points to a form of sociality created by urban water infrastructures (Anand 2011), my work calls attention to what I call "amphibious entanglements" brought to bear by phenomena in which the hydro and the geo are inexorably intertwined. In the Dead Sea area and other settler colonial contexts, we cannot take for granted the *terra* of *terra nullius*.[3] Likewise, we cannot take for granted the extraordinary amount of work that goes into fixing what counts as "territory."[4] While much attention has been paid to how territory is rhetorically rendered empty (*nullius*), amphibious landscapes call for greater focus on terra. Terra in this example is hydrogeologically constituted, inexplicable without an understanding of both hydro and geo material properties, as well as how the two interact. In this chapter, I bring into focus hydrogeologic social worlds circulating around phenomena in which the hydro and the geo are coconstitutive.

## END OF THIS PLACE

My interlocutors repeatedly identified the first appearance of sinkholes around the Dead Sea in the 1980s as a "surprise." They agreed that these amphibious apparitions had a distinctly human cause: the extreme depletion of the Dead Sea as a result of the overuse of both the sea itself by Israeli and Jordanian factories and of Jordan River water by Israel, Syria, and Jordan. When showing me the new sinkhole, my friend Ibrahim explained, "On the first day of Ramadan, on the eighteenth of June, a big new sinkhole opened up. This is the end of this company. This place is closed forever." The new sinkhole opened beneath the parking lot and two shipping container buildings that used to serve as rooms for pricey mineral spa treatments. The displaced buildings now stuck out of the hole at odd angles, along with several discombobulated palm trees. Ibrahim invited me to take photos of the damage, repeating, "This is the end of this place. That's it; it's over." He goes on: "All of this is from God. The sinkholes come because the water is going away, and the water is going away because of the factories in the South." Ibrahim was convinced that this new sinkhole means the beach would never reopen. Ibrahim had remained hopeful that it might reopen in the months since it had been closed to visitors. But now, he was sure, its fate was sealed.

The history of the Dead Sea concession is a hydrogeologic history. I will now recap a few key pieces of this history to demonstrate how hydro and geo are inseparable in the history of the Dead Sea concession and, thus, Dead Sea sinkholes. Public interest first turned to the industrial potential of the Dead Sea and its minerals at the turn of the twentieth century, though people have extracted chemicals from the Dead Sea since at least the time of the Pharaohs, who transported crucial compounds used in mummification from the Dead Sea to the Nile Valley (Nissenbaum and Buckley 2013). The Ottomans commissioned expeditions to the Dead Sea to test the viability of extracting salts (Norris 2011). Sultan Mehmed V issued an imperial charter in 1911 for the extraction of bromine from the sea to three Ottoman subjects: Djindjöz Bey, Zuad Bey, and Djenab Chehabeddin Bey. The imperial order required Djindjöz Bey, Zuad Bey, and

## 62 Popperl

Djenab Chehabeddin Bey to begin extracting bromine within two years after Mehmed V issued it. By 1915, no extraction had been initiated. The Ottoman Porte nullified the concession with an imperial decree, but interest in the Dead Sea's mineral wealth was already emerging from another source: a Russian Jewish industrialist fleeing the Bolshevik Revolution named Moshe Novomeysky.

Novomeysky's interest in the Dead Sea had been piqued by a geologic report passed on to him in 1906 by German botanist and fellow Zionist professor Otto Warburg (Novomeysky 1958; Novomeysky 1956; Norris 2013). The report was the work of another German scientist, a geologist named Max Blanckenhorn, who wrote about the Dead Sea after undertaking a study of the area sponsored by European Zionists with Ottoman permission in 1904. Blanckenhorn's research suggested to Novomeysky that "the salts contained in those waters very closely resembled that of the salts in Siberian lakes from which I had already commercially extracted chemicals necessary as raw materials for industry" (Novomeysky 1958, 11). He applied to the Ottoman Empire for an extraction enterprise at the Dead Sea in 1907 before his arrival in Palestine, but his application was denied. He visited the area anyway in 1911, and he returned in 1920 as an immigrant, ready to lobby the young British Mandate government for unprecedented mineral rights.

In the absence of the geological data needed to help make the importance of the concession clear to potential allies in the British administration, Novomeysky undertook a range of tests and expeditions to the Dead Sea himself. This was an essentially hydrogeologic research mission, and the data he collected was everything Novomeysky had hoped it would be— scientific proof of the validity and value of a mineral industry on the Dead Sea's shores. After a lengthy and convoluted campaign for a concession of the Dead Sea's minerals from the young British Mandate governments of Palestine and Transjordan, Novomeysky secured for himself and his company the unrestricted rights to the wealth of bromine, magnesium, phosphate, phosphorus, and salt of the Dead Sea in 1930. He set up a company, Palestine Potash Limited, based in England and Palestine, and began his extractive work in a small factory on the northern end of the Dead Sea, where the Jordan River flows into the hypersaline lake.

Novomeysky was a meticulous documentarian, in part because he needed historical and scientific evidence to secure and defend the Dead Sea concession. He was a bombastic and passionate writer, publishing two book-length memoirs: *My Siberian Life* (1956), about his adventures and exploits before his arrival in British Mandate Palestine, and *Given to Salt* (1958), a detailed accounting of how Novomeysky secured the Dead Sea concession (Novomeysky 1958; 1956). Novomeysky was an unreliable, self-interested, colonial narrator, obscuring and misrepresenting crucial pieces of the story surrounding Palestinian co-investors and Arab workers in his plants (see Norris 2011). Novomeysky's story obscures the efforts, experiences, and contributions of nonwhite people; he left an extremely detailed and yet extremely flawed history of the Dead Sea concession. Yet, the legal frameworks he helped put in place still govern the Dead Sea's shores. These frameworks allow for unchecked industrial evaporation on a scale so large that the Dead Sea is disappearing, and sinkholes are taking the shoreline with it.

In the manner of other Ottoman concessions, the Dead Sea Concession gave Novomeysky the exclusive rights to extract, sell, and export minerals from the Dead Sea (see Norris 2014; Shahvar 2002; Tezçakar 2010; among many others on Ottoman Concessions). The crucial piece in this story is once again at the hydro-geo nexus: in granting Novomeysky the rights to Dead Sea minerals in situ, the British effectively gave his company the right to exploit whatever he could using the water and the unique geological properties of the area. Novomeysky's operation employed the following procedures, as detailed in his memoir *Given to Salt*: "We used the water of the River Jordan, which constantly pours nearly 2,000 million gallons daily into the Dead Sea, as the instrument for the decomposition of the carnality—i.e., the separation of the two salts, potassium and magnesium chloride, based on the differences in their solubility" (Novomeysky 1958, 80). As the fresh water from the Jordan River acted on the geological substrates at the edge of the Dead Sea, mineral commodities began their

FIG. 2.3. What remains of workers' quarters at the Southern Works, 2015. Photo by Simone Popperl.

journey from extraction to markets elsewhere in the region and around the world. This method remained in effect until Jewish paramilitary groups evacuated the northern factory during the Nakba in 1948. Mineral extraction at the Dead Sea was from then on confined to Novomeysky's second factory, with its vast evaporation ponds at the southern tip of the Dead Sea. It was the economic possibilities afforded by the interaction of water and minerals that catalyzed contemporary Jewish settlements near the Dead Sea, since workers were needed in the factories. The modern kibbutzim Ein Gedi, Mitzpe Shalem, and Qalia all owe their founding to the hydrogeologic economic miracle Novomeysky initiated.

By the mid-2010s, the Jordan River trickled a meek thirteen million gallons of fresh water per day into the Dead Sea near the former site of Novomeysky's northern factory as a result of the river's diversion for irrigation upstream. The legacy of Novomeysky's unchecked rights to exploit the Dead Sea's mineral wealth exists in the corporate structures of Dead Sea

Works, whose parent company Israel Chemicals Limited was bought after it was denationalized by Israeli billionaire investors the Ofer brothers in 1999. Along with Israel Chemicals Limited's manufacturing infrastructures and financial holdings, the Ofer brothers effectively also bought the Dead Sea concession in 1999, now guaranteed by the State of Israel. With it, they gained special rights to expand Dead Sea Works' factories and pump Dead Sea water into their evaporation pools in whatever quantities they chose, thereby rapidly decreasing the water levels of the Dead Sea and creating the hydrogeologic shoreline conditions in which sinkholes began forming in the 1980s. Thanks to Novomeysky's 1927 concession from the British Mandate governments of Palestine and Transjordan, Dead Sea Works' monopoly over chemical and pharmaceutical products produced from Dead Sea minerals was nearly complete—only the emergence of sinkholes in their evaporation ponds are holding them back. An interlocutor expressed the paradox this way: the rapid recession of Dead Sea water makes Dead Sea Works' operations run faster, as the mineral concentration in the brine increases. But as sinkholes regularly open in the ponds, valuable industrial machinery disappears. In the absence of outside checks on extractive industries at the Dead Sea, the interaction between the hydro and the geo limit its production capacity.

## SINKING ECONOMIES AND NEW MOBILITIES

Let me return to the ethnographic present and the sinkhole Ibrahim has shown me. Sinkholes do not foreclose economic possibilities everywhere as they have at Dead Sea Works. At the settlement-owned tourist beach where Ibrahim works, sinkholes have made his employment as a caretaker possible. When small sinkholes began emerging in the parking lot and among the plastic deck chairs that once held tourists from all over the world as they napped in the heat, the managers of the beach saw no alternative but to close it to tourists temporarily. To protect their buildings from theft, they hired Ibrahim to live in the building that used to house the manager's office and keep people out of the closed area until the permanent fate of the beach was decided.

FIG. 2.4. Tourists at the beach before its closure, 2013. Photo by Simone Popperl.

FIG. 2.5. The same beach, abandoned after its closure because of sinkhole activity, 2015. Photo by Simone Popperl.

When I got to know Ibrahim a few months after the beach's initial closure, he and the beach's managers thought the beach would soon reopen. They thought they could stabilize the shoreline by filling all the sinkholes with sand and gravel. Any geologist would scoff at a plan like this: since sinkholes form as a result of interconnected underground caverns that are impossible to map, it is impossible to restabilize sinkholes with more material. Eventually, the new sand and gravel will collapse into the caverns as well, and this is exactly what happened when the new sinkhole opened in the parking lot on June 18. At that point, Ibrahim's role as caretaker began to seem redundant. He and the beach's management seemed to realize that the beach would remain closed forever.

Ibrahim's employment with the settlement was made possible because of the sinkholes, but they now threatened to make his position obsolete. To explain why requires a quick detour into the bureaucratic mechanisms of Israeli occupation in the West Bank. The West Bank, occupied by Israel since the end of the 1967 Six-Day War, was fragmented into three jurisdictional zones when the Palestinian Liberation Organization and the Israeli government signed the US-brokered Oslo Accords in the 1990s: (1) Area A, where the Palestinian Authority was to have full military and civil authority; (2) Area B, where the Palestinian Authority was to have civil authority and the Israeli army was to have military authority; and (3) Area C, where the Israeli government maintains civil and military authority. These three zones are noncontiguous, and territory can be reclassified by the Israeli Civil Administration, headquartered in a large settlement outside Ramallah called Beit El. Land around the Dead Sea and in the Jordan Valley is Area C. During the Oslo negotiations, the Israeli government cited security concerns as the reason it needed to maintain military and civil control over the West Bank's borders at the expense of the territorial sovereignty of a future Palestinian state. The Jordan River Valley represents that border from Lake Tiberius down to the Red Sea.

The West Bank tourist beach where Ibrahim worked is Area C but is just over four kilometers south of the military checkpoint the IDF operates to keep Palestinians without formal permission from entering Israel. Palestinians without permission to enter Israeli territory in the form of Israeli

68  *Popperl*

citizenship or working papers were thus barred from accessing these beach facilities even before sinkholes closed them. Ibrahim's extended Bedouin family lives near Bethlehem but comes from land where Kibbutz Ein Gedi now stands, on the Israeli coast of the Dead Sea. For many years, Ibrahim bounced between hospitality jobs in Dead Sea settlements that cater to Hebrew-speaking Jewish Israelis and English-speaking tourists in Area C, north of the checkpoint. At these Israeli-run hotels and resorts in the occupied Palestinian territories, Ibrahim said that the long hours and his somewhat limited foreign-language skills hampered his progress and kept his salary relatively low. When the beach closed, one of his former managers referred him for the job of caretaker, and he acquired the working papers that legally allowed him to cross the checkpoint into Israel for the first time. The hydrogeologic phenomenon of the sinkholes opened a new role for him in the Dead Sea tourism industry in spite of his marginal social position (Yiftachel 2006), and they provided an opportunity for him to circumvent the bureaucratic restrictions of his political status (Tawil-Souri 2011).

Ibrahim gained what he described as an extraordinary opportunity with the closing of the beach: the chance to live on the very edge of his beloved Dead Sea twenty-four hours a day, to be provided room and board in addition to a salary just to keep tourists away, and to legally obtain permission to move around what is today Israel. He was to safeguard the settlement's remaining structural investments while the fate of the beach was decided in corporate boardrooms and government meetings seventy-five kilometers away in Jerusalem. Once large sinkholes began to emerge at the site, as they did on June 18, Ibrahim rightly realized that his sinkhole-created job would likely soon be obsolete. By the end of the summer, Ibrahim had received a phone call from his manager informing him that his caretaker services were no longer needed since the beach would be permanently closed. He began trying to negotiate employment in a Dead Sea spa-products factory a short distance away so he could stay close enough to the shoreline he loves. His experience illustrates the way the amphibious interactions that create sinkholes also produce complex economic, political, and social entanglements and possibilities.

The damage that results from sinkholes threatens the livelihoods of factory workers, industrialists, farmers, animal herders, tour guides, and others, even as it opens new possibilities, like for the provisional reclamation of Ibrahim's political and labor rights. Sinkholes force organizations seeking to profit from the Dead Sea to adapt their methods and technologies of extraction and to develop their own informal warning systems. Likewise, they force the Israeli and Jordanian governments to come face-to-face with the needs of local residents who lack political capital, such as when farmers demand that access roads be rebuilt and electrical grids be replaced. As such, sinkholes can be forces for innovation and collective action as well as destruction. It is thus the interaction between hydrologic and geologic forces that produces a coconstituted amphibious world where power relations are upended to the advantage of people who have been marginalized by them, even as the infrastructures these forces destroy render the landscape increasingly uninhabitable to humans.

## SINKHOLES AND SMALL-TOWN POLITICS

In the early 1980s, when the Israeli government was investing heavily in tourist development in the town of Neve Zohar, on the southern tip of the Dead Sea near industrial evaporation ponds owned by Dead Sea Works, sinkholes began appearing near the construction of a new beach facility. Unsure of the scope of the problem, the Tamar Regional Council opted to continue construction apace. Soon, the situation became untenable as new roads collapsed and construction equipment was swallowed by the holes. The Neve Zohar development project was all but abandoned. Today, only a small number of sun-faded, hand-painted signs advertising vacation rooms to let in English and Russian stand among the small concrete residences as reminders that the Israeli government once envisioned a thriving tourist economy there.

Not long after sinkholes began appearing in Neve Zohar, the problem spread north to Kibbutz Ein Gedi, a settlement founded in 1948 near the speculated site of an ancient biblical outpost of the same name, just a few kilometers south of the Green Line dividing Israeli and Palestinian territory. Since the late 1980s, sinkholes have destabilized the kibbutz's original corrugated metal barracks and swallowed 80 percent of the kibbutz's date trees. In January 2015, sinkholes opened along a small section of the main road that connects Ein Gedi to its neighboring communities and closed the Ein Gedi public beach, including campsites, the gas station, and the snack shop.

The contemporary history of Ein Gedi is important here. Before the 1948 war and the Nakba, two kibbutzim on the Dead Sea supplied Novomeysky's Palestine Potash Limited with workers: Ein Gedi and Beit HaArava. Jewish settlers founded Ein Gedi just before the 1948 war, on the site of a town by the same name mentioned in the Bible. According to the Bible, Ein Gedi's dates were celebrated for their quality and taste. Damage to the contemporary Ein Gedi's date plantation was a source of sorrow and pain for informants who live at the kibbutz.

Like many other kibbutzim founded around the same time, Ein Gedi and Beit HaArava served as garrison towns during the 1948 war. Shortly after violence began, David Ben-Gurion (who commanded the militias that became the Israeli army at independence) ordered Kibbutz Beit HaArava evacuated and closed. He determined that Ein Gedi would serve as a border town until the West Bank, occupied by Jordan at the end of the war, could be conquered for Israel. As a result, the first twenty years of Kibbutz Ein Gedi's existence was fraught for my interlocutors who lived there during that time. They often told me stories of the Jordanian snipers that occasionally aimed at them from the cliffs nearby. Coincidentally, Ibrahim's Bedouin tribe originates from the same place, but they were displaced when settlers arrived to found Ein Gedi as a Jewish outpost. The family was eventually forcibly settled in a cluster of dwellings near Bethlehem. Ibrahim's employment at the closed tourist beach a few kilometers north held an additional resonance for him because of his family's origins.

One dark night with stars sparkling in the warm breeze in 2015, I sat in an air-conditioned conference room at the Ein Gedi Hotel with the kibbutz community while one of their number, a geologist, endeavored to convey to the group the severity of the sinkhole problem on the kibbutz's land. After a lengthy discussion of the geologic origins of the Dead Sea and its place in Jewish theology, a kibbutz member in his midfifties interrupted the geologist: "So, are you finally getting to the sinkholes at the end of all this?" The geologist quickly shot back, "We're all getting to the sinkholes in the end," and the room erupted with laughter. All kidding aside, the geologist proceeded to explain the hydrogeologic origins of the sinkholes and the methods he had helped develop for predicting this type of sinkhole. He told the room, "All around the world, sinkholes are caused by different things, but these we understand have a human cause"—the depletion of Dead Sea water, which, thanks to the Dead Sea concession, cannot legally be limited by the Israeli government. In the geologist's expert opinion, the Israeli government needed to find another way to reverse the rapid water loss in the Dead Sea. The transportation authority should divert Route 90 away from the sinkhole area, he opined, cutting directly through the kibbutz's remaining date plantations and an archaeological site from which Ein Gedi gets entrance fees. The room groaned. For this community, sinkholes were destroying a way of life dating back to biblical times.

Discussion about what the Israeli government would do about the damage wrought by sinkholes on Kibbutz Ein Gedi continued for six months. I attended regular kibbutz community meetings, usually led by the geologist, which played out the classic trope of small-town politics in which the people's interests were opposed by a corrupt governing body—in this case, the Tamar Regional Council. Ein Gedi residents, I came to understand, thought of Jerusalem and Tel Aviv as the center and themselves as the settler colonial periphery, devoting their lives to maintaining the Jewish state's frontiers as they made the desert bloom. These dynamics were made clear as residents debated what to do about Route 90—the road that connects Ein Gedi and its tourist hotels, spring water factory, and date plantations to Jerusalem. After one especially frustrating meeting that devolved into ad hominem attacks against members of the local council (one of whom is currently being prosecuted by the Israeli government for eliciting bribes), a middle-aged woman in rugged khaki pants and a pink work shirt cried out, "But why should the government listen to *us*? We're only a small group of people far from the capital. Why would they do anything to help us?"

Ultimately, thanks to the fervent lobbying of the community, the geologist's plan prevailed over other more elaborate and less feasible schemes.

72 *Popperl*

Each time I arrived at Ein Gedi, a little more of the date plantation had been uprooted and a few more segments of new asphalt had been laid down. A small army of traffic guards had been hired by the Israeli government to help cars, buses, and large delivery trucks navigate the one-lane route through the construction zone. During the day, the guards took turns stopping cars under the baking sun while their colleagues sat beleaguered in the paltry shade of a sun umbrella; at night, a single guard would be left to stand under a blinding construction lamp. It was grueling work, but it was work in service of the Zionist ideal of maintaining Jewish roots in the now eroding soil of the biblical land of Israel.

It was work needed to maintain the terra of this terra nullius, in the face of the amphibious interactions that upended it. In spite of the preexisting power imbalance Ein Gedi residents perceived between themselves and the state, the hydrogeologic threat to settler control over the Dead Sea landscape gave them the upper hand. In this case, amphibiousness rendered the periphery more powerful than the center, even as the periphery itself was midcollapse.

### CONCLUSION

Interactions between water and minerals have long defined the economic potential of the Dead Sea, inspired its contemporary settlement, begun to limit seemingly illimitable industrial mining rights dating back to the Ottoman Empire, and allowed individuals like Ibrahim and the residents of Kibbutz Ein Gedi to maneuver within the power of the Israeli state. These hydrogeologic worlds underground define the conditions of possibility of future human life in the region. When "stable" and "unstable" are more salient categories than "wet" and "dry" on the shoreline of a massive inland lake, it becomes incumbent on us to rethink the way we understand the territoriality of these places.

Human social worlds are directed not simply by water and land but rather by different waters (salty, fresh, potable, toxic, mineral-rich) and lands (arable, barren, sandy, rocky, stable, sinking), as well as the hydrogeologic forces through which these interact. The social relations brought into being by sinkholes as hydrogeologic phenomena—formed by the very interaction of water (hypersaline and fresh) and land—reveal that around the Dead Sea, the *terra* of *terra nullius* must be understood in hydrogeologic terms.

## NOTES

1   I conducted fourteen months of ethnographic fieldwork for this project between 2012 and 2015 in the Occupied West Bank, Israel, and Jordan. This included participant observation in communities struggling with new sinkholes; site visits to closed sinkhole areas; interviews with scientists, entrepreneurs, tourists, residents, and others interacting with sinkholes; and archival research.

2   By "subterranean geopolitical phenomena" I mean social and political movements engendered by the materialities of what is underground, including fossil fuels and rare earth minerals and efforts to extract them.

3   A key mechanism of settler colonization is the reframing of inhabited territory as empty, or *nullius*. In doing so, the settler colonial project justifies its existence and expansion, glorifying the violence it does to human and non-human inhabitants of the place cast as empty.

4   Here, "fixing" indexes both stabilization (or emplacement) and repair.

## REFERENCES

Abu-Lughod, Ibrahim, and Baha Abu Laban. 1974. *Settler Regimes in Africa and the Arab World: The Illusion of Endurance.* Wilmette, IL: Medina University Press.

Anand, Nikhil. 2011. "Pressure: The PoliTechnics of Water in Supply in Mumbai." *Cultural Anthropology* 26 (4): 542–64.

———. 2012. "Municipal Disconnect: On Abject Water and Its Urban Infrastructure." *Ethnography* 13 (4): 487–509.

———. 2017. *Hydraulic City: Water and the Infrastructures of Citizenship in Mumbai.* Durham, NC: Duke University Press.

Ballard, Chris, and Gene Banks. 2003. "Resource Wars: The Anthropology of Mining." *Annual Review of Anthropology*, no. 32, 287–313.

Barnes, Jessica. 2014. *Cultivating the Nile: The Everyday Politics of Water in Egypt.* Durham, NC: Duke University Press.

Barnes, Jessica, and Samer Alatout, eds. 2012. "Water Worlds." *Social Studies of Science* 42 (4): 483–631.

Catellino, Jessica. 2015. "The Cultural Politics of Water in the Everglades and Beyond." Presentation at the University of California, Irvine. Irvine, CA, October 1, 2015.

Closson, Damien, and Najib Abou Karaki. 2009. "Salt Karst and Tectonics: Sinkholes Development along Tension Cracks between Parallel Strike-Slip Faults, Dead Sea, Jordan." *Earth Surface Processes and Landforms*, no. 34, 1408–21.

Espland, Wendy. 1998. *The Struggle for Water: Politics, Rationality, and Identity in the American Southwest*. Chicago: University of Chicago Press.

Hastrup, Kristen. 2013. "Water and the Configuration of the Social Worlds: An Anthropological Perspective." *Journal of Water Resource and Protection* 5 (4): 5.

Helmreich, Stefan. 2009. *Alien Ocean: Anthropological Voyages in Microbial Seas*. Berkeley: University of California Press.

Kelman, Ari. 2007. "Boundary Issues: Clarifying New Orleans's Murky Edges." *Journal of American History*, no. 4, 695–703.

Li, Fabiana. 2015. *Unearthing Conflict: Corporate Mining, Activism, and Expertise in Peru*. Durham, NC: Duke University Press.

Limbert, Mandana. 2001. "The Senses of Water in an Omani Town." *Social Text* 19 (3): 35–56.

McLean, Stuart. 2008. "Bodies from the Bog: Metamorphosis, Non-human Agency, and the Making of 'Collective Memory.'" *Trames* 12 (3): 299–308.

———. 2011. "Black Goo: Forceful Encounters with Matter in Europe's Muddy Margins." *Cultural Anthropology* 26 (4): 589–619.

Niemi, Tina M., Zvi Ben-Avraham, and Joel R. Gat, eds. 1997. *The Dead Sea*. Oxford Monographs on Geology and Geophysics. Oxford: Oxford University Press.

Nissenbaum, Arie, and Stephen Buckley. 2013. "Dead Sea Asphalt in Ancient Egyptian Mummies—Why?" *Archaeometry*, no. 55, 563–68.

Norris, Jacob. 2011. "Toxic Waters: Ibrahim Hazboun and the Struggle for a Dead Sea Concession 1913–1948." *Jerusalem Quarterly*, no. 45, 25–42.

———. 2013. *Land of Progress: Palestine in the Age of Colonial De-development, 1905–1948*. Oxford: Oxford University Press.

———. 2014. "Colonialism in Palestine: Science, Religion and the Western Appropriation of the Dead Sea in the Long Nineteenth Century." In *The Routledge History of Western Empires*, edited by Robert Aldrich and Kirsten McKenzie. New York: Routledge.

Novomeysky, Moshe. 1956. *My Siberian Life*. London: Max Parrish.

———. 1958. *Given to Salt: The Struggle for the Dead Sea Concession*. London: Max Parrish.

Ogden, Laura. 2011. *Swamplife: People, Gators, and Mangroves Entangled in the Everglades*. Minneapolis: University of Minnesota Press.

Olson, Valerie, and Lisa Messeri. 2015. "Beyond the Anthropocene: Un-Earthing an Epoch." *Environment and Society*, no. 6, 28–47.

Scaramelli, Caterina. 2018. "Fish, Flows, and Desire in the Delta." *Anthropology News* website. March 12, 2018.

Shahvar, Soli. 2002. "Concession Hunting in the Age of Reform: British Companies and the Search for Government Guarantees; Telegraph Concessions through Ottoman Territories, 1855–58." *Middle Eastern Studies* 38 (4): 169–93.

Shallot, Todd. 2010. *Structures in the Steam: Water, Science, and the Rise of the U.S. Army Corps of Engineers*. Austin: University Texas Press.

Smith, James. 2011. "Tantalus in the Digital Age: Coltan Ore, Temporal Dispossession, and 'Movement' in the Eastern DR Congo." *American Ethnologist* 38 (1): 17–35.

Tawil-Souri, Helga. 2011. "Colored Identity: The Politics and Materiality of ID Cards in Palestine/Israel." *Social Text*, no. 107, 67–97.

Tezçakar, Behice. 2010. *Discovery of Oil in the Minds and the Lands of the Ottoman Empire: Erzurum-Pulk Oil Concessions*. Saarbrücken: LAP Lambert Academic Publishing.

Tironi, Manuel. 2015. "Disastrous Publics: Counter-enactments in Participatory Experiments." *Science, Technology, and Human Values* 40 (4): 564–87.

Yechieli, Yoseph, Daniel Wachs, Meir Abelson, Onn Crouvi, Vladimir Shtivelman, Eli Raz, and Gideon Baer. 2003. "Formation of Sinkholes along the Shore of the Dead Sea: Summary of the First Stage of Investigation." *GSI Current Research*, no. 1, 1–6.

Yiftachel, Oren. 2006. *Ethnocracy: Land and Identity Politics in Israel/Palestine*. Philadelphia: University of Pennsylvania Press.

Zalasiewicz, Jan, Mark Williams, Will Steffen, and Paul Crutzen. 2010. "The New World of the Anthropocene." *Environmental Science & Technology* 44 (7): 2228–31.

LUISA CORTESI

# 3. The Shape of Waterland

## *A Geomorphoanthropological Commentary on Fluvial Infrastructures and Amphibious Environmental Knowledge*

How do we know the landscape? What are the forms of knowledge and knowledge of forms that people summon when referring to it? This essay explores the fluvial topography of North Bihar through a perception of its man-made infrastructure and through the population's perception of its infrastructure. It yields two outcomes, first, that the ecology of knowledge is one of presence as much as absence, and second, that the forms of knowledge matter, quite literally, as knowledge takes forms and forms take knowledge.

This chapter builds on the *ecology of absences* and the *aesthetics of ecology* toward a *geomorphoanthropological* commentary—the world around us is worthy of study through the ways in which the shapes of the world shape our life with it. In other words, the function of the form matters as much as the form of the function. I aim to extract the aesthetic logic of institutionalized practices of fluvial management as juxtaposed with those enacted by riverine societies. By aesthetic logic, I am referencing not beauty and allure but instead appearance in terms of shape, form, and geometrical figure. I posit that people use a form of spatial logic for visualizing, understanding, and reading the material world and interpreting their perceptions of it. In order to prevent deterministic recoil, the discussion concludes by proposing amphibiousness as a reflective, liminal, adaptive modality of knowing the world.

IT WAS A MOMENT OF COLLECTIVE CONCENTRATION. As I handed over a few sheets of paper and responded to a few questions on the exercise "draw your own *chetr*,"[1] an atmosphere of attention took over rather quickly, as if a silent spell had been cast over us. Cross-legged on mats of woven grass, everyone, slowly but simultaneously, leaned forward to start drawing.

I remember that I had intended to make chai for everyone, but I decided to savor the moment of collective purpose instead. I remember observing my eleven colleagues, all rural inhabitants, either Muslim or Hindu, diverse in terms of their caste origins, with uneven but mostly minimal schooling, absorbed in drawing the map of the panchayat where each of them worked; they were silent and still, but for their pencils rasping on the coarse white paper.

I noticed a pattern. Although three men, with longer formal education, first drew cardinal directions as if setting up the map, they then proceeded to sketch the river like everyone else: the main body of water first, in the form of waves, undular movement.

After this, the lines and the borders started. The first was Shamji, my colleague from the only panchayat that included the railways, which he drew together with the two rivers flanking them on either side. Some stood up to reach for a ruler to draw the lines of the fluvial embankments. Some used the edge of their notebooks instead. Yet, these movements in the room did not break the air of concentration — no small talk, no social interaction.

It was only after drawing the embankments that a few started drawing human habitations, sets of houses standing in for a village. Three women focused on their own settlements, sensibly the starting point of their daily movement across the landscape. Everyone else, in their own time, proceeded to outline roads, mostly departing from the embankment, either perpendicularly or in parallel.

It was the unison of the drawing sequence that struck me as unexpected. I would have imagined that some people would start drawing from the main town or their own village. Even if the river was unanimously the most important feature of the waterscape, perhaps the town would come in second? Which led me to think — why do the layers of infrastructure, in a specific order, frame and qualify a territory? The succession of the landscape's components drawn by each person was strangely similar, as if the relative importance of the features had been agreed upon beforehand.

The difference between the maps was as striking as the similarities in drawing sequence, which rendered the latter even more conspicuous. No two drawings of the same physical area were recognizable as such. Each person drew different features. While everyone drew a map with a bird's-eye view, some features were represented symbolically, resulting in drawings combining different perspectives. For example, human settlements were represented through stylized houses seen frontally. Despite their use of the same drawing materials, each person deployed a different scale and personal flair. Some were faster, others more reflective. More precision, or hesitation, in drawing a line. One decided to sharpen their pencil, another their details. But why, I could not help asking, did not a single person set off the drawing from their house, or place of worship, or village, instead of the river?

It was Buddhanji to breach the spell. While drawing roads, he had started to turn, slowly pivoting himself in half a cardinal direction every handful of seconds, like a vault tentatively trying to open itself. It did not take more than three or four turns for another colleague, the ironic Shamji, to reproach him: "Why are you spinning?" The room burst into laughter. I was already accustomed to the whimsicalities of Buddhanji, perhaps noticing that, despite his origins in one of the most discriminated communities, everyone in our group nevertheless appreciated his originality as a sign of his peculiar intelligence. He explained: if the road is turning, he also needs to turn in order to draw it. I recognized that having the road squared in front is the most realistic of situations, also useful for representing what one sees on either side. I would have also "spun around."

Others had a different take on perspective. Sumeetji had a "map in their head," so they did not need to move along the road to know what was there. Champaji commented that things were better seen from afar. How much afar? I asked. Khartikji replied with the Golghar, a large round granary of colonial origin in Patna—if one recognizes that it is a sphere from outside, it becomes clear what one can expect once inside. Sunilji, who had been there, added that the Golghar was far more interesting as an elevation point from which to see the river Ganga nearby. From the top it is easier to see things that are far away. But we always perceive them as flat, added Champaji, while the politicians, from their helicopters, can really see from above. But then, from above, everything would be flat, wouldn't it? Sumeetji asked. That is the beauty of a bridge, added the well-traveled Buddhanji, we all are able to see something from above. We can only see the river, contested Champaji. *Only* the river. What else shall we look at, if not the river?

## THE FLUVIAL AND INFRASTRUCTURAL LANDSCAPE OF NORTH BIHAR

Recalling this ethnographic moment serves to introduce the two key themes of this chapter. First, the ways in which the inhabited riverine terrain (in)forms different understandings of the landscape and the multiple hierarchies that these perspectives entail. Viewpoints on the landscape result from places perceived as features, either as separate objects observed by the standing observer or as things with which people relate and have forms of cognitive engagement. Second, the material forms that such features and cognitive engagements entail and, therefore, the hierarchies to which these forms contribute and are shaped by.

In particular, this chapter is about ways of knowing one's waterland (Cortesi 2022). Conditions of climate change bring to the fore the need for revisiting the epistemic conundrum of knowing our changing habitats. This is specifically true for those who sense their habitat and *modus habitandi* as increasingly loosened by wetness. What are the knowledges mobilized on a wet terrain, and which forms do they take?

This work has developed in a place that, over the last few decades, has been increasingly wet. Known as the land of floods, North Bihar, in India, is the alluvial floodplain of several Himalayan rivers rushing from the mountains in or near Nepal toward the Ganges. In the rural areas in which I work, flooding occurs every year, often multiple times a year. As if going through a form of anticipated climate change, people there have been dealing with floods for a long time, and for a few decades, they have experienced their regular worsening. Thus, during the current times of climate change, Bihar has swollen into a locus of focus: learning from the people of North Bihar, virtuosos in the matter of water, is useful for those of us who are newer to the world's damper circumstances.

North Bihar is also an apt context through which to observe the function and form—and particularly the function of the form—of infrastructure, since its overlapping floods occupy the ecopolitical space of slippage between three types of inundations: (1) physiological floods; (2) infrastructural inundations, or inundations originating in or worsened by the infrastructure that is supposedly meant to control floods; and (3) the more recent, tangible, destructive, yet difficult-to-ascribe consequences of climate change. This is why North Bihar, populated by flood infrastructure as much as by the floods themselves, is a place to investigate how the waterland is lived in and known by its people.[2]

This chapter develops from observing North Bihar's local people depicting the area they traverse, work, and live in daily. It then observes two types of infrastructure impinging on the broader landscape and discusses complementary observations on microfluvial management in North Bihar. From those, it extracts two complementary morphologics, which rest on a set of assumptions and intertwined erasures. I then propose a reflection on what attention shapes can open up conceptually and subsequently suggest an epistemological attitude with political implications.

Longer-term ethnographic fieldwork corroborated the observations of the exercise narrated in the opening of this chapter. The serendipitous order of depiction—river, then embankments and railways, then roads and bridges, then villages—revealed the (superficial) space as understood through mobility infrastructure. When asked to refer to the history of their village, the inhabitants of C, a village on the railway line just north of the Ganga, recounted that even at the beginning of the last century, before the building of embankments, the British initiated the construction of the railway that still runs parallel to the Ganga, from west to east, connecting Patna with Kolkata. From that main railway line, a few minor lines (for example, the one that travels from Mansi to Supaul) were later extended toward the north (see also Yang 1999). Elderly people remember the construction of the first embankments during their childhoods, built to protect the railway from the river where it most often tended to flood. Testimony to the relevance of the railway and embankments, the dates of construction of both are known by heart even by later generations who did not experience their construction firsthand.

The historical layering of mobility infrastructure is also visible on satellite maps. From Google Earth, infrastructure aligns with the Ganges in parallel, perpendicular, and forty-five-degree-oriented lines, building a rectilinear grid that is inclusive of isosceles triangles. This is the case both east of the Kosi, where the river flows from west to east and the grid is thus oriented along the north-south axis, and west of the Kosi, where the Ganges flows thirty degrees southeast, thus making the infrastructural grid similarly inclined. The grid-like pattern reminded me of the geodetic surveys—a set of measurements initiated in the eighteenth century to account for the curvature of the Earth's surface, which reached the subcontinent as the Great Trigonometrical Survey of India and divided the world map into triangles (Edney 1997). Paradoxically, this history of polygon shapes is also referred to in a book that argues that rivers were invented to fit a specific ideal of linear water (da Cunha 2019).

As a student of epistemology, I am reminded of the fallacy about the exactitude of science: the map is never the territory; the representation is never the represented (Borges 1999). What is, then, the represented, and what is the representation? Or is it *me, the interpretant* of the lines and the shapes?

## Embankments

Running along the rivers on both sides, an embankment is a wall of soil that, together with its equivalent on the other side of the riverbed, frames a major river more or less in parallel to its course. The embankment's purpose is to contain the river's watery excess away from habitation, land, and infrastructure (Cortesi 2022). In a river-dense and flood-prone area such as North Bihar, embankments have quickly become the primary structure that configures mobility. First, crossing a river requires either a

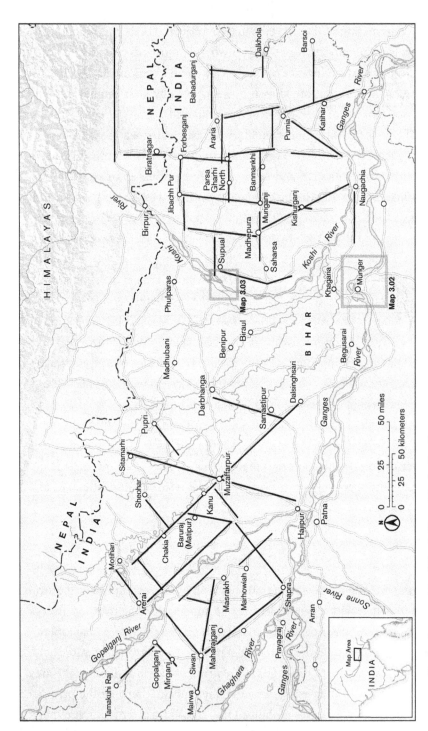

MAP 3.1. The landscape grids of North Bihar. Map by Ben Pease.

large watercraft or a bridge—neither of which has been a common sight in the area—so it is necessary to move along the river to be able to cross it. Vehicles treat the embankment, whether surfaced with tarmac or not, as the road. In a landscape in flux, roads were built consequentially, mostly perpendicularly, or occasionally diagonally, to connect the main frame of railways and embankments.

From day one, Indian embankments were built by erasure. D'Souza's (2006) acute historical analysis shows how the British constructed embankments on the Mahananda to solidify and therefore profit from land, its market, and related schemes of taxation. The British rule had severed the channels of trust that were supplying the previous rulers, and probably would have supplied them, with reliable information on floods. Without that information, and therefore without being able to adjudicate on tax relief, they decided to "secure" rivers instead. Eliminating floods seemed the way to do without flood-related local knowledge.

While a history of fluvial morphology would be a salient contribution to this narrative, Bhattacharyya (2018) points out that embankments were originally developed through experiences with fundamentally different rivers, more stable streams that do not carry as much sediment (see also Mishra 2002; D'Souza 2006; Ivars and Venot 2019). Nonetheless, the history of embankment theory (Cortesi 2021a) shows that rivers with higher sediment loads or with a history of avulsion were considered the perfect patient for the cure. This was because, in theory, by constraining the river, embankments would magnify its erosive capacity and use it to scour its own bed, leading to a much-desired incised channel capable of withstanding flow variabilities. In theory, the erosive capacity would carry sediments downstream to the delta, and the incised channel would stabilize the river once and for all.

In practice, the rivers of North Bihar have proven the theory wrong. In Bihar, embankments have been the multiplicator of, instead of the solution to, floods, aggravating the situation in more ways than we can discuss here (Barry 1998; Oliver 2000; D'Souza 2006; Elvin 2006; Singh 2008) and increasingly accepted even by the Indian bureaucracy (Iyer 2013, 2014). I argue here that embankments, and the understanding of rivers they

84 *Cortesi*

subsume, are built on the erasure of their inseparable fluvial morphology, hydrogeology, and ecology.

The theory of embankments hinges on several inappropriate assumptions, first and foremost on the construction of an abstract essential shape and nature of the river (Lahiri-Dutt 2000), presupposing a fundamental similarity of all riverine spaces that then justifies shared technological responses. In the geometry of embankments, the river—any river—is mapped as a two-dimensional channel of water moving through linear space, considered through its physics and mechanics. In trying to define the channel of the river, embankments alter it and separate it from its surrounding lands, de facto constructing a new channel that is both more unpredictable than the river and in need of constant management.

Embankments are an obstacle to the physiological movement of both sediment and land. The sediments that would disperse into the surrounding floodplain during a physiological flood, or that would have rushed to the delta in the fiction of embankment theory, instead concentrate within the channel. The resulting buildup, and therefore accrual of the riverbed, requires continual construction and elevation of the embankments. An accrued bed impedes the convergence of rivers that are now lower, and therefore either the riverbed needs to be constantly dredged—an unfeasible proposition—or more embankments need to be constructed along the tributaries. And yet, embankments, a self-reproducing technology, constantly need more embankments, higher embankments, better embankments (for a discussion on intensification, see Kockelman 2010). More embankments are built, for example, further inside other embankments to straighten the river or to protect an older embankment. Outer embankments are built to provide a second layer of protection, using the older embankment to protect themselves.

Heavier-than-usual flows that would normally travel into the floodplain instead concentrate and rise within the embankments, causing turbulent whirlpools that breach the infrastructure and thus generate disastrous floods. The trapping of water occurs not only within the enclosed area but also outside the embankment or in between different strata: the structure is an obstacle to the river's ability to drain water, limiting the river's essential function. On some embankments, sluice gates were built for drainage, but the accretion of the riverbed physically impedes the release of water from the lower outer floodplains to the elevated riverbed. This inverted drainage also modifies the water table. As a result of this impeded and altered drainage, the floodplains of North Bihar are extensively water-logged, commonly referred to as "seepage under the embankment." The area, previously overflowed with a shallow layer of nutrient-rich water, is now saturated with stagnant water.

So, the technology of the embankment does not exclude soil from water but still pits one against the other (Cortesi 2021a), and in so doing, it narrows the knowledge of fluvial morphology to the channel, suppressing the larger alluvial landscape. Contrary to da Cunha's idea that the invention of the river is a matter of choosing the line over the rain, the times of reality over the moments of ephemerality (da Cunha 2019), I believe the invention of the embanked rivers occurred by isolating the visible part of the river over the invisible parts of a more complex drainage and ecology (Cortesi 2018).

## Dams

In India and beyond, rivers have been managed not only through em-bankments built *along* the river but also famously through dams built *across* the river. Despite the still unrefuted condemnation of dams by the World Commission on Dams' report (2000) and their unquestionable unprofitability and lack of safety (Pradan and Srinivasan 2022), dams of different types, shapes, extensions, and materials have been the prescribed protocol for irrigation, cooling, drinking consumption, transportation, power generation, recreation, you name it.[3]

Even climate change is poised to be treated with dams, despite all the evidence pointing to their inability to do so (Bloodworth 2021). While rare—in Bihar there are only two, compared to over five thousand in the country—dams are also an important river management technology; "If only there were dams to control rivers, Bihar would not be flood-affected" is a common refrain I heard from government officials, bureaucrats, engineers, and laymen. Given that, from the perspective of Bihar, the geomorphic gradient necessary to build an effective dam is available not in India but in Nepal—a reflection answered with a variation of "If only Nepal would build more dams" or "If only Nepal could manage its dams." I suspect that dams are better as discursive devices than for holding water.

Despite being sophisticated technologies whose design and construction consider a multiplicity of factors and forces, dams are also built on a set of abstractions and erasures. Embedded into dams' inability to account for changes and nonwater flows is a lack of consideration of dynamic hydrogeology, fluvial morphology, and ecology in their modeling. Similarly to embankments, dams construe the river as a channel of water with a certain width, but they also add the dimensions of flow and depth. Each of these dimensions is represented by measurements that capture quantities under ideal conditions. The river and its measurements are mostly static; even though flow is measured, it is treated as a data point rather than a continuous and variable phenomenon. The channel is seen predominantly as a hydraulic gradient to exploit, conceptually emptied of its nonwater contents and removed from its surrounding fluvial waterlands.

Beyond its existence within the river itself, land is also absent from the conceptualization of the dam. Rivers sit atop shifting and often unstable geologies in the Himalayas, making dam building and tunneling risky. For several decades, dams have been known to trigger geological troubles, such as landslides from tunneling (Kohli 2011) and earthquakes from the weight of the reservoirs (Gupta 1992). This known fact is discursively tampered with, as Gergan (2020) explains; rather than blaming the idea of the dam as a solution, Sikkimese hydropower developers fault the landscape, which they depict as antagonistic and unpredictable. Basic hydrological processes are similarly excluded from consideration. A dam diminishes a river's ability to replenish groundwater downstream, leading to its depletion in the long term (Molle and Mamanpoush 2012). The dam and its reservoirs, which purposefully relocate water in an effort to maximize its utility, end up wasting huge amounts of water by creating the ideal conditions for its evaporation.

Dams' aquatic ecosystems often disable the technology from functioning or render it counterproductive, much in the same way as water and sediments trapped by embankments (Carse 2014; de Micheaux, Mukherjee, and Kull 2018; Camargo and Cortesi 2019). For example, the concentration of dead organic materials in reservoirs, where aerobic and anaerobic bacteria decompose them, results in dams emitting large quantities of the very greenhouse gases (carbon dioxide and methane) that contribute to climate change (Rosa et al. 2004).

Although newer dams have shapes that optimize weight distribution and maximize strength, the operation they perform in the landscape is still the perpendicular cutting of the river. As a result, new construction still has not prevented events like the Kerala floods of 2018 and the Andhra Pradesh floods of 2020, two recent examples of reservoirs that overflowed due to amounts of rainfall and sediment unaccounted for by planners or managers. In times of climate change, dams' dangers intensify faster than they improve technologically: as I write this in February 2021, water, mud, debris, and ice fallen from a glacier have breached a dam in Uttarakhand, a tragedy that recalls the terrible disaster of the Vajont Dam in Italy in 1963. Somewhat darkly, I maintain that more will follow, in the global South as much as in the global North. Dams map the river into timeless, placeless gradients, whose discourses are frozen for decades (Khagram 2004), even when conditions are rapidly changing (van Hemert, Rao Polsani, and Ramnath 2021).

The construction of reservoirs, like that of embankments and more in general rivers, also imagines an empty, unpopulated space that is free to be flooded and filled, a view that is inevitably violent to the people and ecosystems already existing there. Dams displace the inhabitants of the river while disproportionately benefiting distant communities through hydropower (Gergan 2020). Their effect on the river and its human communities is also indirectly violent, contributing to climate change that will increase danger to riverine societies (Strang 2013). Despite their ecological consequences and well-documented greenhouse gas emissions, dams are still framed as sources of green energy. These effects not only harm people directly by erasing them, their histories, their habitats, their ways of living, but also have the potential to intensify existing inequalities. The conditions that result from dams impact a wider radius of people, yet disproportionately affect those that are already discriminated against (Baviskar 1999; Joy et al. 2008; also on displacement in India, Ghertner 2014).

## AN ECOLOGY OF ABSENCES

Until this point, I have narrated a waterscape dominated by the infrastructure of mobility, corridors of political and technological power (Williams 1993) that structure people's experience of space (Dourish and Bell 2007). In analyzing two of the contemporary institutionalized infrastructures of discursive and practical fluvial management in India, I am interested in moving the discussion away from considering the (inevitable) ignorance that causes technological malfunction (Pellow 1984) to the ignorance that they need in order to function.

These tangible infrastructures, technological wonders in their own right, are often used to assert human ingenuity and engineering skillfulness. Observing a dam from above or below, for example, can generate feelings of awe, admiration, and reverence. It is undoubtedly huge, grand, imposing. As scholars of science and technology have discussed at length (see in particular Fischer 2007; Scudder 2018; Anand, Gupta, and Appel 2018), these technologies construct their own necessity and related expertise. More than provoking awe because of their effectiveness, for example, their effectiveness is reasoned through the awe they provoke. Such reverence also overshadows the negative consequences they produce, as well as the unfavorable cost-benefit analysis, the outdated timescales, the unaccounted externalities, the epistemic conflicts (Boelens, Shah, and Bruins 2019), and the missing factors upon which they rest.

We should consider these missing factors as knowledge—or ignorance—that is however not a *lack of* knowledge but a specific knowledge comprising epistemic absences—whose aggregate resembles that of an ecology, an *ecology of absences*. Such absences are not simply the result of things being overlooked or carelessness; instead, the existence of these absences is essential for the technology's discursive existence. Further, these ghost knowledges are interconnected and mutually sustaining to the point that they can be read as ecological. They are neither intentional nor coherent, nor can they be proven methodical or organized—meaning they cannot be defined as systematic (for system thinking ecologies, see Hughes 1987). *Ecological* is a better fit to show how they are intertwined, relying on each other, perpetuating their existence in their technological iterations, their whole greater than the sum of their parts. The idea of ecology, different to that of a system, serves to account for the absence of coherence and yet shows a specific set of interactions. For example, dams' calculations consider sediment loads, yet they often ignore the long-term effects of sediment accumulation, which is made possible by deleting the wider landscape, and which also allows the erasure of those sentient and insentient beings who consider it their habitat.

## THE FLUVIAL GEOMORPHOANTHROPOLOGY OF NORTH BIHAR

Among the forms of knowledge that are ecologically elided by those technologies are not only hydrogeology, ecology, fluvial morphology, and, as many commentators have already written (Gruppuso, this volume), the environmental knowledges that local people form and exercise. One of the types of knowledge to which I want to pay attention is a specific form of environmental knowledge that sits in the ways in which a society interprets its landscape. In my narration at the beginning of the chapter, Sunilji, Champaji, Sumeetji, Khartikji, and Buddhanji provoked me to think about points of view and their influence on the shapes of the landscape. In this section, I leverage their contribution to investigate what I call *geomorphoanthropological knowledge*, which I intend as a consideration about how people socioculturally see the shapes of the environment they inhabit.

Water management in India, with its indigenous ethnoforestry, is probably one of most explored topics when theorizing traditional and local knowledge (for an elaborate reflection on this, see Mosse 2003). Yet most of the views on knowledge expressed in that broader literature and its application by several UN bodies and governmental agencies tend to be rather formulaic, content-based, and standardized despite the early warnings by

90 Cortesi

Agrawal (1995). Eschewing the praxis of compiling knowledge and the related risk of misappropriation (see Pottier, Bicker, and Sillitoe 2003; Nagan et al. 2010), in what follows I explore geomorphoanthropological commentaries on how rivers inhabit the landscape as extended by my interlocutors in the riverine areas of North Bihar.

When entering the Terai, where the slope suddenly turns gentle and subtle, the powerful *nadiya* (the plural of *nadi*, Hindi, translatable as river, a feminine word) find themselves freed from the direction imparted by the upper gradients of the Himalayas. Then, the *nadiya* meander, not because they are unsure of where to go, but perhaps because they are enjoying staying, slowing, and deepening their breathing, releasing their sediments where they see fit. Some *nadiya* are shallower yet faster. Others remain shy and idle for a while, till they gush, at full force and without notice. Others are deeper and larger, self-confident and steady. And yet they more joyfully break into a myriad of smaller channels, braiding with each other and designing a lace of sinuous, polychromatic, glittering sparkles.

For those who know these *nadiya* in the flesh—not the occasional visitor who aspires to microimpressions, nor the faraway observer whose body does not get measured with that of the *nadi*—they produce and are produced through curved motions. Meandering and exploring, arching and vaulting, decorating the landscape, hooping on previous or new paths, *nadiya* design new images of themselves, convoluting, as if bowing, around an invisible obstacle, twisting and turning as braids in experienced hands, bending back and winding over lush lands. The rivers of North Bihar, after rushing through as bubbling juveniles, eventually gain sight of each other—they can mingle, exchange their offspring, visit each other's beds, and enjoy each other's gifts.

And then, during the monsoon season, when they swell and inflate, they reach one another, spreading and blending in new, untouched realms. Occasionally, a voluptuous, forceful flush would have everyone run for safety, swiftly untying cattle and reaching for banana trunks to use as boats. But the *nadiya*'s rage would recede as quickly as it had flared up. Most often, only a shallow layer of animate wetness would coat the land, as in a delicate yet encompassing embrace. And then, retreat and respite, before the next irresistible caress.

Or at least that was how it was before — before embankments were set up to separate *nadiya*, to straighten them, contain each of them and their bodily matter. Embankments have restricted the *nadiya*'s ability to explore and exchange with each other. Now that they are tied within, their waters and sediments trapped and adding up, *nadiya* let their turbulent motion build their ire. They release themselves to topple over the embankments, unleash in whirlpools to erode these structures from below and attack their inopportune spurs.

### Embankments

"But Biharis have always built embankments themselves," say *bara log*, the "cultured" ones who distinguish themselves from the "illiterates" of the lower castes and classes. Even if that were the case, those embankments have nothing to do with those of today. The inhabitants of rural flood-affected Bihar, familiar with recurrent overflows that rarely turned threatening, used to build circular embankments, bunds, around their habitations. Those embankments were not meant to oppose the river; they were not a barrier, only an invitation for the river to circumvent it.

How do Bihari build embankments? I ask my interlocutors in C, the village close to the Ganga where the construction of century-old infrastructure represents local historical data to transmit to the new generation. As I accompany them twice a day to check on the river, we discuss their flood preparation strategies. We discuss where to set up the bund. When they begin construction the next day, I notice that they are shaping it circularly. They explain that this way permits them to cover more ground toward the southeast. A circle, I realize, encompasses the largest area under the same perimeter, maximizing construction material.

I was curious as to why they intended to cover the southeast, since the river runs west to east on the south of their village — wouldn't water come in from the southwest? I ask. Water will come in from the plantation on the east, they answer, it always did. This would mean that the water effectively accomplishes a U-turn, something they have observed again and again. If you had more material at your disposal, wouldn't you build a longer embankment? I ask. They struggle to find material, but its availability does not affect their plan; building a longer embankment southward toward the river would be useless, we agree. Building it north would risk locking the people of C in the water because of the railway line, running north of the village and effectively the highest elevation in the area, would likely facilitate a rebounding current U-turning toward the south. Such a current would either stagnate inside the containment or, if strong enough, effectively flush back and knock it down. Nor would they build a bund long enough to reach the railway line, as that would become an obstacle that the water would target and destroy. The goal of the bund that the people of C build whenever facing floods is to slow down the arrival of water into the village, not to oppose it. The purpose of the bund is to buy time, never to modify the water flow. Leveraging their observational collective memory of the river's patterns of movement, they interpret the current scenario by encouraging its circular motion away from their place of habitation.

Physical attempts to straighten and contain the river through embankments and dams are seen by many as unnecessary and counterproductive obstructions both for the river and for their lives and livelihoods in the plains, therein lying disregard for the river's need to drain. The inhabitants of North Bihar used to cut openings in the embankments when they deemed it necessary to release the river from its restraints (see also Mishra 2002, 2003, 2008, 2012). These acts, never the deeds of "seditious elements" but coordinated by large groups of people, have always been rare, and are even more so now given contemporary social sensibilities, because cutting the embankment carries a high risk of being buried alive in the mud of the river that erupts from the breach.

Those who find solace in the presumption of locally built containments ignore that locals see them as very different structures. As compared to the bund, the modern embankment is seen as a process of separation, of division, of pitting one part against the other. *Nadiya* resisted the line. Inherently beings of connection, mobility, and recombination, of change, they do not sit atop or in juxtaposition to their surroundings, say the inhabitants of C (Cortesi 2021a). As they would say in North Bihar—who would tie up a river? Who would cut it with a knife?

## *Dams*

Rivers always find ways to oppose barriers to their flow, as mythology also narrates. The river Kamla was being pursued for marriage by a deceitful and crooked merchant. In order to capture her, he built a perpendicular embankment—a dam—with the idea that once the Kamla Goddess rose on top of it, he would be able to put vermilion on her forehead and thus de facto marry her. The Goddess's helper, from the fisherfolk community, came to her rescue and destroyed the wall. The merchant, however, built another wall made of bones and hides, impure for the fisherman, a Hindu, who could not destroy it even after killing the merchant. The wall remained an obstacle in the path of the Kamla until a local Muslim offered to help and destroyed the wall. In some versions of the myth, the Kamla had to go to Arabia to find him and then offered him and his family the opportunity to settle along her banks.

Asked to comment on this myth, people mention that a perpendicular obstruction to the river is an outrage. While the river is capable of overcoming such obstacles by rising above them, that would not happen without consequences. This myth contradicts the idea that relationships with the river mostly take the form of religious reverence (Sen 2019, among others) and instead refers to a syncretic religion (Burman 1996), where coexistence includes respect for each other's sacredness (Alley 2019; Cortesi forthcoming). Both Hindus and Muslims, the two prevalent communities in the area, share the ontology of the river as a life-giving and shape-making agential creature against which opposition does not make sense. At a more subtle and perhaps even unconscious level, the violence of the infrastructure, its capacity as a manifestation of and medium for structural violence (Rodgers and O'Neill 2012), is perceived at a morphological level.

While embankments develop in parallel to the river and dams as perpendicular to the flow, this is a simplification for two reasons. First,

94 *Cortesi*

because many embankments are armed with spurs, perpendicular to the embankments, built at regular intervals for the purpose of slowing down the water. "They are the first line of defense," says Araav, the state engineer from the Minor Irrigation Department inspecting the status of a particular embankment. "Like the pawns of the army," he unravels the crude metaphor, "they are disposable." My friend Pawan, also an inhabitant of fluvial North Bihar from a discriminated community, instead describes the spur as "a nose, a prying intrusion in the *nadi*'s body, a thorn." It seems, he says, counterproductive—the *nadi* does not appreciate the impingement and often targets a spur head-on. When the *nadi* manages to knock it down, the space that opens between two spurs is conducive to the formation of whirlpools, Pawan explains, a turbulent motion that provokes torsion against the main structure. The rubble of the spur is precisely where the embankment is likely to breach. Had the spurs not been there, Pawan suggests, the *nadi* would be less irritated.

More broadly, it is the straight obstacle to the river flow that causes it to boil over. It is the shape of the structure and its orientation in the landscape that either transforms it into an obstacle, as in the case of the embankment, the dam, and the spur, or that embodies people's intentions to delay, to avoid confining the water or provoking the *nadi*'s ire—as in the case of the bund. As the conversation on viewpoints brought to the fore, shapes are crucial categories in apprehending the landscape.

## THE SHAPES OF THE RIVER

My interlocutors in North Bihar use a form of spatial logic for visualizing, understanding, and reading the material world, as well as interpreting their perceptions of it (Gibson 1979). This theoretical assertion sits between, on one side, the geomorphological idea that the formation of the landscape occurs out there, with living beings variably impacting it (Goudie 2018), and, on the other, studies on environmental knowledge/cognition (among others, Li 2000 and 2003; Dove 2003; Bicker, Ellen, and Parkes 2003; Sillitoe 2009; Descola 2021; Ingold 2021). Rapoport (1994) suggests that the built environment is read through its geometrical design in both "western" and "nonwestern" societies, the latter previously seen as "ritual, symbolic, social in nature" (Littlejohn 1967; Wheatley 1971; Tambiah 1973; Bourdieu 1973; Rykwert 1980, in Rapoport 1994). He then explains how the schemata that constrain people's movements are "as much as temporal as spatial" (Rapoport 1994, 465), as all beings are both organized in space as they organize space, but does not further consider space's geometrical and aesthetic components.

In a time when the paradigm celebrates embodied knowledge away from representation, I move from the figuration of concepts toward the conceptualization of figures. Since Massey (2005) pushed geographers and other scholars to pay enough attention to the concreteness of space, several scholars have also proposed looking into geometries, notably Allen (2011), who explains the topology of proximity and separation in power relations;

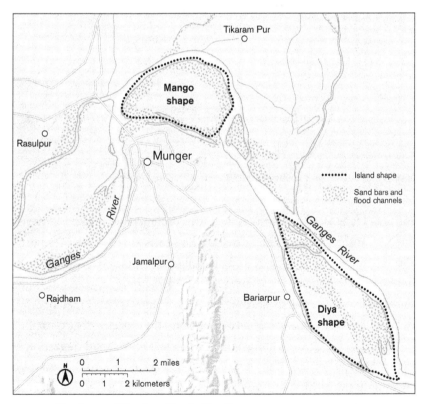

MAP 3.2. The shapes of the river. Map by Ben Pease.

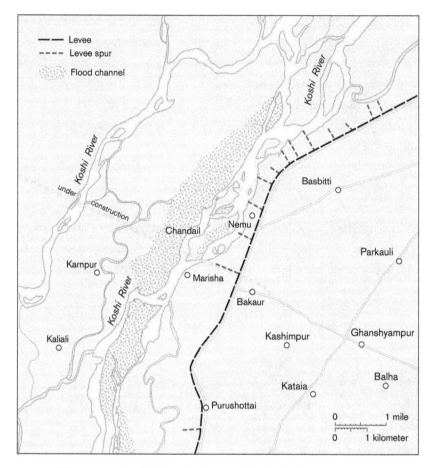

MAP 3.3. The spurs on the fluvial embankments. Map by Ben Pease.

Holbraad (2020), who examines the forms designed by concepts as developed by anthropologists; and Green, who draws shapes with Strathern's social relations (Green 2017) and also engages topology to examine the borders of the Aegean sea (2005) and the overlapping of locations in the same space. While in all these cases, the use of shapes is either metaphorical or figurative—the distances of power relations, the trajectory of a question's motion, the cutting and gluing operated by kinship, the materialization of the immaterial borders of the nation—following Larkin (2013), I aim to go beyond the performative production of "things as space."

I instead propose a geomorphoanthropology for gauging the angles and lines, the shapes and forms, that the rivers and the riverine infrastructure of North Bihar physically encrust on their *waterland* (Cortesi 2022) through the eyes of their inhabitants. We know materiality isn't simply what one can touch, and concepts and social relations have material lives (e.g., Cortesi 2021b). Similarly, I am interested in exploring the possibility that the physical geometry of both infrastructure and rivers has a conceptual life. How does morphology shape knowledge formation?

In my field notes, I find that Jagarnathji argued that a *diyara*, the island of sediments left by the river, is called as such because it is shaped like a *diya*, an earthen vessel filled with oil and used as a candle (see Lahiri-Dutt and Samanta 2013; Cortesi 2018). Its tightly twisted cotton wick rests in its pout, a pointed part of the circle, the union of two minor symmetrical convex curves that disrupt the concavity of the circle. To imitate the shape of the *diya*, Jagarnath unites his index with his thumb, sending his fingertips back a little. For Navrozji, from another district, the *diyara* instead has the shape of a mango, an oval, elongated and round, with a smaller convex bend at one end, only on one side, in delightful asymmetry. Pradeepji (who lives just outside the embankment in yet another district) tells me that the river is *tedha-medha*. A zigzag, I ask him? Initially he agrees, but as I draw the *Z* shape on the sand in front of us, he corrects me. More like an *S*, he says, than like a *Z*. Like a snake. When a neighborhood snake visits to enjoy its amphibious dinner under my bed, I notice how one curve of its reptilian body shortens just as another curve ahead is widening. While I am not fond of snakes, with which Bihar abounds, this makes me think of a rhythmic opening and closing of diameters. The next day Pradeepji and I wait together for the snake, who shows up as expected. The locomotion of the body moves not only forward but also sideways through the curves that widen and shorten. In my writer's imagination, I think about a bent and italicized *S*. That is how the river moves, Pradeepji observes with his calm enthusiasm.

This "morphologics" — a logic of shapes based on the idea that the forms have function as much as the function takes forms — reveals patterns that inform studies that we can call geomorphoanthropology. While it would be worth exploring the cognitive way in which the rigid form conjures authority, for now I interpret my data to show that the rectilinear and cuboidal politics of the confinement structures are strikingly at odds with the shapes and movement they need to contain.

Ignoring this morphologics is part of an ecology of absences that enables certain technologies to thrive by obscuring what they should instead incorporate. Through the technology in form more than in function, this regime of ignorance molds the landscape and, in the wet times of climate change, can turn it into a disastrous one. Geomorphoanthropology instead makes evident that the aesthetic awe the technology culturally provokes has the effect of anesthetizing other morphological sensibilities and geomorphological anthropologies, thus, environmental knowledge. What would it take, instead, to hear them?

## AMPHIBIOUS ENVIRONMENTAL KNOWLEDGE

I suggest the use of a geomorphoanthropological strategy that pays attention to the political signification of ecology and aesthetics.

Confronting a worsening and unpredictable waterscape, the fluvial inhabitants of North Bihar are virtuosos of wet living. Anthropologists have shown since the beginning of the discipline that certain people have sophisticated ways of understanding what is for others unintelligible (see, for one, Evans Pritchard and the Azande, and the related commentary by Holbraad 2020). Biharis are attuned to the water in experiencing, thinking with, enduring, and transforming the shapes of their space; they collectively accumulate formative experiences, infer propositions about the space and its agents, its pasts and possible futures; enact their knowledge into more or less conscious practices, dialogically validating and triangulating their understanding. They know the environment from recurrently measuring themselves, in total and in part, with the multiscalar bodies of the landscape (Cortesi 2018 and forthcoming).

Without establishing causality, a condition of possibility for this knowledge is to *live in* the environment, to have sufficient occasions to develop such knowledge. This mirrors and reverses Ingold's reflection on the trope of the globe understood as the shape of our planet, apparent from space but not from Earth: "It appears that the world as it really exists can only be witnessed by *leaving* it" (2000, 211). Apart from astronauts, even the most seemingly mindless inhabitant of planet Earth never stops actively inhabiting their space. A person driving a car in the apogee of humanly constructed environments, for example, is (literally) alive by virtue of their paying attention to a multiplicity of synchronous movements and assemblages of intervals, transient speeds and accelerating durations, continuities and combinations, chromatic sequences and sonic arrangements, patterns of shapes and their imminent, new and old, transformations.

We, the inhabitants of this newly confusing wetness, whom this book addresses, have plenty to learn, and not only from the riverine people of North Bihar, from the bodymind of those who walk, labor, and sweat wetness, but also from and about technologies, how they amoebically reproduce themselves, and how they are deployed toward a virtually endless intensification of *infrastructural density* (Kockelman 2010, 2022). From and about embankments, agentive infrastructures, we could learn how they organize the topographical space by creating forms. From and about forms, consequential if not agential, we could learn how they take root in the landscape, mingle with hierarchies, communicate, and delete. We could also learn how to subvert them in order to reassess and rebound our epistemology of nature. This reassessment does not call for biomimicry of perceived natural geometry. Rather, we seek to use this reassessment to echo Goldstein and Johnson's question: "What forms of knowing—both embodied and immaterial—do we want to mobilize in our ongoing processes of world-making?" (2015, 77).

I suggest *amphibious knowledge* as a humble way of learning across multiple forms of knowledge. It is not the waterland of North Bihar that makes this knowledge amphibious. Being amphibious means, as Sloterdijk taught us, to be able to change medium, to be flexible in how we think about the world around us, to unchain ourselves from our *umwelt—um* means ring, confinement, and *welt* means world—the ordered arrangement to which Uexküll (2013) and Heidegger (1962) attributed our physical and mental caging (also ten Bos 2009).

Amphibiousness thus indicates the act of bringing to the surface that which was previously unquestioned, the implicit overlapping of shapes, forms, aesthetics, assumptions, missing pieces that have become obvious, the ecology of absences on which technologies rely. It means to treat the obvious—the institutionalized infrastructures of flood control and river management in their function, form, and consequences—as only one of multiple possibilities, another one being the fluvial knowledge shared by the many inhabitants of North Bihar, and being able to move seamlessly between the two. If amphibious living is not simply living with more water, but muddying the water, bringing above what is down there, as well as navigating in and between both, an amphibious epistemology is thus an invitation to reflect on, instead of making assumptions about, the knowledges that are part of a specific setting, digging up those that are missing, living with them physically and conceptually, navigating between them with adaptability and suppleness.

## CONCLUSION

By asking why we privilege the geometries of the technician and the draughtsman, those learned from abstractions and grids, over those learned by living with the river, I mean to suggest not simply a slight adaptation to an existing managerial paradigm but the reconsideration of its very structure. Yet, by juxtaposing local environmental knowledge and the shapes that people see in the river, I am also not proposing that we should combine local environmental knowledge with other forms of knowledge. Much ink has been put to good use for reminding us about the complexity of local knowledge (Agrawal 1995), the impossibility of inserting it into a managerial system (Nadasdy 1999; Goldman and Turner 2011), and the consequences of its neoliberal appropriation (Lave 2012).

Instead, I am arguing for the inclusion of amphibious geomorphological understanding as a political statement. By considering their effectiveness, politics, and assumptions, amphibious knowledge reveals the implicit violent narratives that shape the technical geometries of the river and pushes us to look for alternative ways of knowing spatially and geometrically beyond the oppositional line. Amphibious living entails not simply living with the river or with more water but unlearning the shapes embedded in the hierarchy of the medium and building a new lexicon to live with our wetter world.

If linear geometries of the river technologies are violent, it does not mean that circular forms are inherently inclusive. Spaces ruled by circular geometries can remain viciously oppressive, and riverine societies in North Bihar are certainly not organized around equitable principles. Rather, they mirror the divisiveness of the country along a variety of axes of social differentiation. The community of C, for example, is still ridden with casteism, classism, and gender and religious violence despite its rounded riverine technologies. Let this serve as a warning: neither respecting nor learning from circular inclusiveness is a guarantee for cohesion, equity, or equality.

While local knowledge propositions can be controversial or political, dismissing them is also a political choice. Learning from the riverine communities of North Bihar is not the obvious choice. In India more than elsewhere, the "learned" communities are usually considered to be those of the intellectuals and scientists, with water scientists and water bureaucrats historically trained as civil engineers. Fluvial technologies are an interesting case in this regard; although civil engineers design and construct these infrastructures, those who actually live with them regularly demonstrate a differently rich perspective. And yet it remains unusual to attempt to learn from those who inhabit the most precarious environments, often coincidentally belonging to the most discriminated castes or religions — their knowledge, and the epistemic reflection such knowledge can offer, remaining untapped.

Further, it is not necessary to couple local politics with technologies—"infrastructure both shapes and is shaped by the conventions of a community of practice" (Star 1999, 381). While fluvial technologies are notoriously both artifacts that have politics and politics that have artifacts (Winner 1986; Joerges 1999), politics infects not only the contents of these technologies but also the very shapes that they enact on the land. Both the riverine habitat and the encrusted infrastructure are thus epistemic loci for political visions of the future.

In this chapter, I argued that the ways in which engineers design the landscape through infrastructures of mobility and water management is a learned geometry that operates under aesthetic, cognitive, ecological, and political assumptions and implications. Attending to the knowing means attending also to the ignorance that is produced in between and articulated in what I call an ecology of absences.

Curiously dichotomic to this geometry are the shapes and forms through which the inhabitants of Bihar, accustomed to floods and more or less predictable wetness for generations, have come to understand and interact with the river. Those morphologies, or more specifically morpho-logics, are also operating under aesthetic, cognitive, ecological, and political assumptions and implications, which I suggest ought to be studied through a geomorphoanthropological approach.

A geomorphological or amphibious approach is not invested into assuming what the river does nor engaging in a nature-culture discussion but rather examines how riverine societies have learned from the river and suggesting we should pay it some attention. As amphibious knowledge presumes an environment that requires the flexibility of shifting through elements (see the introduction of this volume), I suggest an amphibious epistemology, or a reflexive, humble awareness of knowledge that can allow the unlearning of entrenched morphologies and the suspension of the taken-for-granted, a goal to whose pursuit the knowledge of the riverine people of North Bihar can be useful.

## NOTES

I am indebted to Wyatt Westerkamp, then an undergraduate student at Cornell University, to whom I taught an individual reading course at Cornell in 2021 and who conducted an internship in my Water Justice and Adaptation Lab. Without his smart enthusiasm and diligent initiative, this chapter would not have been possible.

1   *Chetr* is the field, in this case the area assigned to a team of fieldworkers.

2   Even if we consider the whole north of the state of Bihar, according to Bihar's Water Resources Department, 73 percent of the land and 76 percent of the population experiences flooding (Government of India 2020).

3 In fact, the creation of the World Commission on Dams was in part triggered by the activities of the Narmada Bachao Andolan, a social movement to protect the river Narmada from dams (see Cullet 2007; Baviskar 1999).

## REFERENCES

Agrawal, A. 1995. "Dismantling the Divide between Indigenous and Scientific Knowledge." *Development and Change* 26 (3): 413–39.

Allen, J. 2011. "Topological Twists: Power's Shifting Geographies. *Dialogues in Human Geography* 1 (3): 283–98.

Alley, K. 2019. "River Goddesses, Personhood and Rights of Nature: Implications for Spiritual Ecology." *Religions* 10 (9).

Anand, N., A. Gupta, and H. Appel, eds. 2018. *The Promise of Infrastructure.* Durham, NC: Duke University Press.

Barry, J. 1998. *Rising Tide: The Great Mississippi Flood of 1927 and How It Changed America.* New York: Simon & Schuster.

Baviskar, A. 1999. "A Grain of Sand on the Banks of Narmada." *Economic and Political Weekly* 34 (32): 2213–14.

Bhattacharyya, D. 2018. *Empire and Ecology in the Bengal Delta: The Making of Calcutta.* Cambridge: Cambridge University Press.

Bicker, A., R. Ellen, and P. Parkes. 2003. *Indigenous Environmental Knowledge and Its Transformations: Critical Anthropological Perspectives.* London: Routledge.

Bloodworth, G. 2021. "Tocks Island and the End of the Big Dam Era in the USA." In *Split Waters: The Idea of Water Conflicts*, edited by L. Cortesi and K. J. Joy, 95–116. New Delhi: Routledge.

Boelens, R., E. Shah, and B. Bruins. 2019. "Contested Knowledges: Large Dams and Mega-hydraulic Development." *Water* 11 (3): 416

Borges, J. L. 1999 (1946). "On Exactitude in Science." In *Collected Fictions*, edited by J. L. Borges, translated by A. Hurley. London: Penguin Books

Burman, J. J. R. 1996. "Hindu-Muslim Syncretism in India." *Economic and Political Weekly* 31, no. 20 (May 18): 1211–15.

Camargo, A., and L. Cortesi. 2019. "Flooding Water and Society." *WIREs Water* 6 (5).

Carse, A. 2014. *Beyond the Big Ditch: Politics, Ecology, and Infrastructure at the Panama Canal.* Cambridge, MA: MIT Press.

Cortesi, L. 2018. "The Muddy Semiotics of Mud." *Journal of Political Ecology* 25 (1): 617–37.

——. 2021(a). "The Ontology of Water and Land and Flood Control Infrastructure in North Bihar, India." *Journal of the Royal Anthropological Institute* 27 (4): 870–89.

——. 2021(b). "Water Conflicts: The Social Life of an Idea." In *Split Waters: The Idea of Water Conflicts*, edited by L. Cortesi and K. J. Joy. London: Routledge.

——. 2022. "Dismantling Hydrotopias and Introducing Waterland." *Geoforum*, no. 131, 215–22.

——. Forthcoming. *In Disastrous Water: The Environmental Knowledge and Technologies of Floods, Toxic Drinking Water, and Other Muddy Disasters.*

Cortesi, L., and K. J. Joy. 2021. *Split Waters: The Idea of Water Conflicts.* London: Routledge.

Cullet, P., ed. 2007. *The Sardar Sarovar Dam Project: Selected documents.* Chesterfield, UK: Ashgate.

da Cunha, D. 2019. *Invention of Rivers: Alexander's Eye and Ganga's Descent.* Philadelphia: University of Pennsylvania Press.

de Micheaux, F. L., J. Mukherjee, and C. A. Kull. 2018. "When Hydrosociality Encounters Sediments: Transformed Lives and Livelihoods in the Lower Basin of the Ganges River." *Environment and Planning E: Nature and Space* 1 (4): 641–63.

Descola, P. 2021. *Les formes du visible: Une anthropologie de la figuration.* Paris: Seuil.

Dourish, P., and G. Bell. 2007. "The Infrastructure of Experience and the Experience of Infrastructure: Meaning and Structure in Everyday Encounters with Space." *Environment and Planning B: Planning and Design* 34 (3): 414–30.

Dove, M. R. 2003. "The Life-Cycle of Indigenous Knowledge, and the Case of Natural Rubber Production." In *Indigenous Environmental Knowledge and Its Transformations*, edited by A. Bicker, R. Ellen, and P. Parkes, 213–51. Amsterdam: Harwood Academic.

D'Souza, R. 2006. *Drowned and Dammed: Colonial Capitalism and Flood Control in Eastern India.* New Delhi: Oxford University Press.

Edney, M. H. 1997. *Mapping an Empire: The Geographical Construction of British India, 1765–1843.* Chicago: University of Chicago Press.

Elvin, M. 2006. *The Retreat of the Elephants: An Environmental History of China.* Yale University Press.

Fischer, M. J. 2007. "Four Genealogies for a Recombinant Anthropology of Science and Technology." *Cultural Anthropology* 22 (4): 539–615.

Gergan, M. 2020. "Disastrous Hydropower, Uneven Regional Development, and

Decolonization in India's Eastern Himalayan Borderlands." *Political Geography*, no. 80, 102–75.

Ghertner, D. A. 2014. "India's Urban Revolution: Geographies of Displacement beyond Gentrification." *Environment and Planning A: Economy and Space* 46 (7): 1554–71.

Gibson, J. J. 1979. *The Ecological Approach to Visual Perception*. Boston: Houghton Mifflin.

Goldman, M., and M. D. Turner. 2011. "Introduction." In *Knowing Nature: Conversations at the Intersection of Political Ecology and Science Studies*, edited by M. Goldman, P. Nadasdy, and M. D. Turner, 1–23. Chicago: University of Chicago Press.

Goldstein, J., and E. Johnson. 2015. "Biomimicry: New Natures, New Enclosures." *Theory, Culture & Society* 32 (1): 61–81.

Goudie, A. S. 2018. *Human Impact on the Natural Environment*. John Wiley & Sons.

Government of India, National Remote Sensing Centre Indian Space Research Organisation Dept. of Space. 2020. "Flood Hazard Atlas—Bihar: A Geospatial Approach." Official Document. https://bhuvan.nrsc.gov.in/pdf/Flood-Hazard-Atlas-Bihar.pdf.

Green, S. 2005. *Notes from the Balkans: Locating Marginality and Ambiguity on the Greek-Albanian Border*. Princeton, NJ: Princeton University Press.

Green, S. F. 2017. "Thinking through Proliferations of Geometries, Fractions and Parts: Conclusion and Summary of the Work of Marilyn Strathern." In *Redescribing Relations*, edited by A. Lebner, 197–207. New York: Berghahn.

Gupta, H. K. 1992. *Reservoir Induced Earthquakes*. Amsterdam: Elsevier.

Heidegger, M. 1962. *Being and Time*. Translated by John Macquarrie and Edward Robinson. Malden, MA: Blackwell.

Holbraad, M. 2020. "The Shapes of Relations: Anthropology as Conceptual Morphology." *Philosophy of the Social Sciences* 50 (6): 495–522.

Hughes, T. P. 1987. "The Evolution of Large Technological Systems." In *The Social Construction of Technological Systems: New Directions in the Sociology and History of Technology*, edited by W. E. Bijker, T. P. Hughes, and T. J. Pinch. Cambridge, MA: MIT Press

Ingold, T. 2000. *The Perception of the Environment: Essays on Livelihood, Dwelling and Skill*. London: Routledge.

———. 2021. *Being Alive: Essays on Movement, Knowledge and Description*. Routledge.

Ivars, B., and J.-P. Venot. 2019. "Grounded and Global: Water Infrastructure Development and Policymaking in the Ayeyarwady Delta, Myanmar." *Water Alternatives* 12 (3): 1038–63.

Iyer, R. 2013. "Viewpoint: The Story of a Troubled Relationship." *Water Alternatives* 6 (2): 168–76.

———. 2014. "Interlinking of Rivers: A Plea to the Government." *Economic and Political Weekly* 49 (50): 16–18.

Joerges, B. 1999. "Do Politics Have Artefacts?" *Social Studies of Science* 29 (3): 411–31.

Joy, K. J., B. Gujja, S. Paranjape, V. Goud, and S. Vispute, eds. 2008. *Water Conflicts in India: A Million Revolts in the Making.* New Delhi: Routledge.

Khagram, S. 2004. *Dams and Development: Transnational Struggles for Water and Power.* Ithaca, NY: Cornell University Press.

Kockelman, P. 2010. "Enemies, Parasites, and Noise: How to Take up Residence in a System without Becoming a Term in It." *Journal of Linguistic Anthropology*, no. 20, 2406–21.

———. 2022. *The Anthropology of Intensity: Language, Culture, and Environment.* Cambridge: Cambridge University Press

Kohli, K. 2011. "Inducing Vulnerabilities in a Fragile Landscape." *Economic and Political Weekly* 46 (51): 19–22.

Larkin, B. 2013. "The Politics and Poetics of Infrastructure." *Annual Review of Anthropology*, no. 42, 327–43.

Lahiri-Dutt, K. 2000. "Imagining Rivers." *Economic and Political Weekly* 35, no. 27 (July): 1–7.

Lahiri-Dutt, K. and G. Samanta. 2013. *Dancing with the River: People and Life on the Chars of South Asia.* New Haven, CT: Yale University Press.

Lave, R. 2012. *Fields and Streams: Stream Restoration, Neoliberalism, and the Future of Environmental Science.* Athens: University of Georgia Press.

Li, T. M. 2000. "Articulating Indigenous Identity in Indonesia: Resource Politics and the Tribal Slot." *Comparative Studies in Society and History* 42 (1): 149–79.

———. 2003. Locating Indigenous Environmental Knowledge in Indonesia. In *Indigenous Environmental Knowledge and Its Transformations: Critical Anthropological Perspectives*, edited by A. Bicker, R. Ellen, and P. Parkes. London: Routledge.

Massey, D. 2005. *For Space.* London: Sage

Mishra, D. K. 2002. *Living with the Politics of Floods.* Dehradun: People's Science Institute.

———. 2003. "Life within the Kosi Embankments." *Water Nepal* 9 (10): 277–301.

———. 2008. *Of Deluge, Candles and Matchboxes*. India Water Portal. http://www.indiawaterportal.org/articles/deluge-candles-and-matchboxes.

———. 2012. *River Bagmati: Bounties Become a Curse*. Dehradun: South Asia Network on Dams, Rivers and People; People's Science Institute.

Molle, F., and A. Mamanpoush. 2012. "Scale, Governance and the Management of River Basins: A Case Study from Central Iran." *Geoforum* 43 (2): 285–94.

Mosse, D. 2003. *The Rule of Water: Statecraft, Ecology, and Collective Action in South India*. New Delhi: Oxford University Press.

Nadasdy, P. 1999. "The Politics of TEK: Power and the 'Integration' of Knowledge." *Arctic Anthropology* 36, nos. 1–2: 1–18.

Nagan, W. P., E. J. Mordujovich, J. K. Otvos, and J. Taylor. 2010. "Misappropriation of Shuar Traditional Knowledge (TK) and Trade Secrets: A Case Study on Biopiracy in the Amazon." *Journal of Technology Law & Policy* 15 (1): 9–64.

Oliver, S. 2000. "The Thames Embankment and the Disciplining of Nature in Modernity." *Geographical Journal* 166 (3): 227–38.

Pellow, C. 1984. *Normal Accidents: Living with High-Risk Technologies*. Princeton, NJ: Princeton University Press.

Pottier, J., A. Bicker, and P. Sillitoe, eds. 2003. *Negotiating Local Knowledge: Power and Identity in Development*. London: Pluto Press.

Pradan, A., and V. Srinivasan. 2022. "Do Dams Improve Water Security in India? A Review of Post Facto Assessments." *Water Security*, no. 15.

Rapoport, A. 1994. "Spatial Organization and the Built Environment." In *Companion Encyclopedia of Anthropology: Humanity, Culture and Social Life*, edited by T. Ingold, 460–502. London: Routledge.

Rodgers, D., and B. O'Neill. 2012. "Infrastructural Violence: Introduction to the Special Issue." *Ethnography* 13 (4): 401–12.

Rosa, L. P., M. A. dos Santos, B. Matvienko, E. Santos, and E. Sikar. 2004. "Greenhouse Gas Emissions from Hydroelectric Reservoirs in Tropical Regions." *Climatic Change*, no. 66, 9–21.

Scudder, T. 2018. *Large Dams: Long-Term Impacts on Riverine Communities and Free-Flowing Rivers*. Singapore: Springer.

Sen, S. 2019. *Ganges: The Many Pasts of an Indian River*. New Haven, CT: Yale University Press.

Sillitoe, P., ed. 2009. *Local Science vs. Global Science: Approaches to Indigenous Knowledge in International Development*. Vol. 4. London: Berghahn.

Singh, P. 2008. "The Colonial State, Zamindars and the Politics of Flood Control in North Bihar (1850–1945).” *Indian Economic & Social History Review* 45 (2): 239–59.

Star, S. L. 1999. “The Ethnography of Infrastructure.” *American Behavioral Scientist* 43 (3): 377–91.

Strang, V. 2013. “Going against the Flow: The Biopolitics of Dams and Diversion.” *Worldviews* 17 (2): 161–73.

ten Bos, R. 2009. “Towards an Amphibious Anthropology: Water and Peter Sloterdijk.” *Environment and Planning D: Society and Space*, no. 27, 73–86.

Uexküll, J. 2013. *A Foray into the Worlds of Animals and Humans: With a Theory of Meaning*. Minneapolis: University of Minnesota Press.

van Hemert, M., J. Rao Polsani, and M. Ramnath. 2021. “The Negation of Change as a Narrative Strategy of Control: The Case of the Polavaram Mega-Dam in India. In *Split Waters: The Idea of Water Conflicts*, edited by L. Cortesi and K. J. Joy. London: Routledge.

Williams, R. 1993. “Cultural Origins and Environmental Implications of Large Technological Systems.” *Science in Context* 6 (2): 377–403.

Winner, L. 1986. “Do Artifacts Have Politics?” In *The Social Shaping of Technology: How the Refrigerator Got Its Hum*, edited by J. Wacjman and D. Mackenzie, 26–37. Milton Keynes, UK: Open University Press.

World Commission on Dams. 2000. *Dams and Development: A New Framework for Decision-Making*. Earthscan: London.

Yang, A. 1999. *Bazaar India: Markets, Society, and the Colonial State in Bihar*. Oakland: University of California Press.

PART II

# In the Damp

PAOLO GRUPPUSO

# 4. Keeping the Land Wet
## *"Wet Lands" and the Rise of "Wetland Literacy"*

On December 20, 2011, I was driving through the Agro Pontino trying to meet my research interlocutors to wish them a happy Christmas. Around 5:30 p.m., I went to visit Gaetano, who at the time was a buffalo farmer in the Fogliano wetlands, within the Circeo National Park, in Italy. After a quick greeting, we started, as usual, to speak about the Circeo National Park's policy with regard to farming and about his difficulties of working within the National Park. In that context, and maybe for the first time, I heard him pronounce the expression *zona umida* (wetland) but in an ironic way in regard of the national park's policy: "This is a wetland, [and] you cannot do anything there because this is a wetland," he said. This small, unexpected episode piqued my interest in this particular word, *wetland*, which I was taking for granted as an unproblematic term used to identify a natural entity. In Gaetano's phrase, instead, *wetland* pointed to a different meaning, related to environmental ethics and regulations, and ultimately to the politics involved in defining the legitimate criteria to identify an environment and to establish its boundaries. In the life experience of Gaetano, rather than identifying an entity pertaining to the natural state of things, *wetland* was the reflection of a "Nature State" (Hardenberg et al. 2017): a historical formation resulting from top-down political decisions concerning what is natural and how to manage it.

As I later discovered in my studies, the history of the term *wetland* points precisely to the same meaning. It is the outcome of landscape policy and environmental ethics that emerged in the 1950s. Earlier, there were no wetlands: "They were swamps, mires, morasses, unruly and troubled geographies that required reclamation" (Sutter 2021, xi). It is in that period that the loss of wet landscapes caused by the worldwide activity of draining and reclamation started to be perceived as a problem in ecology and environmental sustainability, and wetlands emerged as an object of political, ethical, and environmental concerns. In this sense, wetland science and conservation, the definition of wetlands and the politics of it, are deeply connected (Mitsch and Gosselink 2007, 26). This point is highlighted by ecologists William J. Mitsch and James G. Gosselink in their seminal book *Wetlands*, where they argue:

> The definition of a wetland and by implication its boundaries . . . became important when society began to recognize the value of these ecosystems and began to translate that recognition into laws to protect itself from further wetland loss. However, just as an estimate of the boundary of a forest, desert or grassland is based on scientifically defensible criteria, so too should the definition of wetland be based on scientific measures to as great a degree as possible. What society chooses to do with wetlands, once the definition has been chosen, remains a political decision. (Mitsch and Gosselink 2007, 26)

It is critical to understand that wetlands, rather than being natural entities, are the result of a particular literacy that by means of scientific criteria and measures identifies and defines wetlands against a wider environment. Following Dilip da Cunha's argument on rivers (2018), I call this literacy *wetland literacy*. This reflects global environmental policies, ethics, and contingencies, thus making clear ontological relations between wetlands and the political agenda that raise important anthropological questions. The first one concerns political and epistemological processes: What are the legitimate knowledges used to identify and define wetlands? The second one concerns the agency of wetlands: What actions do wetlands empower?

These questions resonate with Gaetano's argument and relate to the process of naturalization that the term *wetland* and its literacy seem to imply, and to the politics that they involve. I reflect on these questions by adopting an analytical distinction between two different categories. I use the one-word *wetlands* to refer to particular areas identified by local, national, and international environmental treaties or laws. I use instead the two-word expression *wet lands* to indicate places specifically thought of as wet, within the frame of a holistic and relational understanding.[1] Far from being theoretical overinterpretation, this distinction is one I encountered during my fieldwork in Agro Pontino, Italy, where I explored environmental conflicts between farming and conservation in protected wetlands. In this context, I noticed that the expression *zona umida*, the equivalent of *wetland* in Italian, was mostly used as a normative term by conservationists and environmentalists. Farmers instead used to speak about *wet land* (*terra umida*), referring to the land (*la terra*) in relation to the material qualities of the soil and to the agricultural activities performed to keep the land wet (see Gruppuso 2017). The former is the outcome of a *wetland literacy*, which looks at the environment as an array of measurable physical features. The latter, instead, relates to what I call an *amphibious literacy*, which highlights the historical and phenomenological experiences of people who inhabit "wet lands" and who engage within the environment understood as an array of particular practices.[2]

Such a distinction echoes the discussion on English wetlands by Gearey, Church, and Ravenscroft, who reflect on "the relationship between knowing a wetland and *knowing* a wetland" (2020, 20), respectively in epistemological and ontological terms. The authors refer to the "epistemologies of wetlands" as "the forms of knowledge building and sharing" involved in identifying wetlands as "landscape types." They use instead the expression *ontologies of wetlands* to point out "the ways in which wetlands are incorporated into our life courses' habits and behaviours" (2020, 21). Without addressing the theoretical quagmire of the relations between ontology and epistemology, this chapter explores the tensions between the normative approach used to identify "wetlands" and the ways in which instead wet lands emerge in the life activities of those who inhabit them. It does so by discussing scientific literature on wetland ecology and conservation and by presenting historical and ethnographic materials drawn from my research in Agro Pontino.

## THE AGRO PONTINO: FROM LAND RECLAMATION
## TO WETLAND CONSERVATION

Agro Pontino is a region seventy kilometers south of Rome on the Italian west coast. This area housed one of the largest marshlands in Italy, the Pontine Marshes, affected by several projects of land reclamation since ancient times. Far from aiming at the complete drainage of the marshes, these projects must be framed within typical Mediterranean rural economies, as ordinary forms of water management that served the purpose of integrating agricultural activities with fishing, hunting, and gathering of plant materials (Traina 2002). It is in the eighteenth century that land reclamation assumes the modern meaning of social, economic, and cultural progress expressed through "exerting control over the fluid and ephemeral materials of nature" (Gruppuso 2022, 54), and ultimately through the complete drainage of marshlands read in terms of social, sanitary, and moral disorder (Gruppuso 2014). In Agro Pontino, this ideological approach was embraced first at the end of the eighteenth century by the Papal State and then in the 1930s by the fascist regime, which implemented one of the most iconic processes of land reclamation in the Mediterranean.

With this process, named Bonifica Integrale (wholesome reclamation), the regime drained the Pontine Marshes, perceived as a remote and sparsely inhabited wasteland (Gruppuso 2014). The Bonifica Integrale conveyed strong social implications that resulted in a massive process of colonization by which the fascist regime replaced the local people who lived in the marshes with settlers brought from the north of Italy, hence starting a huge project that transformed the Agro Pontino into one of the most important agricultural districts in Italy. The Bonifica Integrale also involved the construction of three "new towns," Latina, Sabaudia, and Pontinia (Mariani 1976; Folchi 2000) and the foundation of the Circeo National Park in 1934.[3]

It is important to understand that at the time of its establishment, the national park was not intended to preserve a tract of the Pontine Marshes. On the contrary, like the rest of the region, the territory included within its boundaries underwent a severe process of transformation that was the expression of the same productivist paradigm that underlay the overall

Bonifica Integrale. This approach to the management of the national park continued even after the fall of fascism, leading to the overall ecological degradation of the area. It was in the 1970s that the productivist paradigm started to change, pivoting on the category of wetland that at the time was emerging in the global scientific and conservationist arena, as a result from a process of revaluation of previously despised environments, such as the Pontine Marshes. This process of revaluation recognized the fragility and ecological salience of wet landscapes on a political level and at different scales.

Such a process has raised questions about how to identify and define wetlands in order to protect them and to prevent their further loss (Mitsch and Gosselink 2007, 26). In this regard, the Convention on Wetlands of International Importance Especially as Waterfowl Habitat, signed in Ramsar, Iran, in 1971, is particularly significant (Ramsar Convention 1994). Beyond being the first and most important intergovernmental treaty devoted to the protection of wetlands, the convention is significant because it provides a widely shared definition of wetlands as "areas of marsh, fen, peatland or water, whether natural or artificial, permanent or temporary, with water that is static or flowing, fresh, brackish or salt, including areas of marine water the depth of which at low tide does not exceed six metres" (Ramsar Convention 1994).

This broad definition identifies a variety of environments that barely resemble each other, thus making clear that "it is not self-evident what constitutes wetland" (Huijbens and Pálsson 2009, 299). However, it is the most popular definition adopted on a global level, and most importantly, it mirrors the inspirational value of the Ramsar Convention, which conveyed and promoted an ethical and aesthetical shift in understanding wet landscapes, "rebranding diverse watery topographies as worthwhile" (Sutter 2021, 12). As anthropologist Caterina Scaramelli observes, "The category of wetland has been a semantic sponge, absorbing changing environmental preoccupations throughout the twentieth and twenty-first century" (2021, 6). In this sense, "wetland" is a metaconcept (Cavallo 2014, 2) used to make connections between different kinds of places in order to bring about political ends, namely, the conservation and appreciation of previously

116  *Gruppuso*

despised wet landscapes (O'Gorman 2021, 147). The Ramsar Convention also plays an important symbolic role in the conservationist milieu, as it is the first international treaty devoted to specific ecosystems (Matthews 1993), and its very nature points out the entanglement between science and political agenda (Schiappa 1996).

The following section explores how this process of revaluation reverberated in Agro Pontino, and particularly in the history of the Fogliano area, a wetland complex that is nowadays part of the Circeo National Park.

## FOGLIANO AND THE RISE OF "WETLAND LITERACY"

Fogliano is a coastal area in the province of Latina, composed of three lakes and wet pastures that are divided from the sea by a thin dune cordon. Before the Bonifica Integrale, the three lakes of Fogliano, Monaci, and Caprolace constituted the most important economic complex in the marshes, whose administrative center was situated around the Fogliano lake. There was a primary school, a medical office, a small general store, and more importantly, many people worked there in fishing, farming, gamekeeping, gardening, and housekeeping (see Busatto 2005). All these people worked for the Caetani, one of the most powerful noble families of Italian history (Pitkin 1998, 59), who owned the whole area until the 1930s, when the property was acquired by Gioacchino Mecheri, a deputy of the fascist government (Alvisi 2005, 4; Cecere 1989).

Like the rest of Agro Pontino, Fogliano was also strongly modified by the Bonifica Integrale, which changed most of its ecological features. The marshy areas were drained through the construction of new channels; the three shallow lakes were deepened; the surrounding pools filled, and the lakes' perimeters were eventually modified with the creation of artificial banks.[4] In addition, an array of structures was created in order to modernize and improve the traditional practice of fishing in the lakes (Priolo 1999). Despite these transformations, Fogliano maintained a strong continuity with the Pontine Marshes' cultural and economic context. In fact, unlike the larger part of the reclaimed Pontine territory, which during the Bonifica Integrale was colonized with people from northern Italy, Fogliano was still inhabited by local people, who continued to work and live there as tenant farmers involved in agriculture, fishing, and hunting management.

Such an economy based on activities traditionally implemented in the marshes characterized Fogliano until the 1970s, when the owners decided to sell the area to a northern property company. This aimed to transform the lakes and the surrounding pastures into a big private housing estate for tourists at the expense of the ecology of the area and of the tenant farmers (Sottoriva 2005; Priolo 2005), who went to court against the owners, in order to defend their job and dwelling. Also, public opinion campaigned against the overbuilding project and for safeguarding the aesthetic value of the coastal landscape in Agro Pontino, at the time well-known as a tourist destination for the Roman upper class. These campaigns aimed to stop the overbuilding project and to transform the area into a green public space for leisure and for a different kind of tourism based on the enjoyment of the landscape beauty, of which Fogliano became a symbol at the local and national level. At the same time, the Circeo National Park reacted to the overbuilding project, although the Fogliano area at the time was just outside its boundaries. By standing against the project, the national park aimed to preserve the integrity of the coastal environment, while redeeming its reputation as a state institution devoted to the protection of the environment. At the time, in fact, the Circeo National Park was described as a "joke" (Cederna 1970) whose ecology was in a "desperate and shameful situation" (Cederna 1967), because of the long-lasting productivist management initiated during fascism and implemented for many decades.

Although based on different motivations, these reactions reached the goal of stopping the overbuilding project at Fogliano. The whole area was included in the Circeo National Park in 1975, and in 1976, the three lakes and pastures were designated as Wetlands of International Importance under the Ramsar Convention. This was a critical moment in the history of Fogliano and the Circeo National Park, as emphasized in the speech that the president of the park delivered in 1975, during a public conference:

The coastal lakes of Fogliano, Caprolace, and Monaci, which constitute in Italy one of the most important stopping places of migratory birds for wintering and nesting, are excluded from the national park because of an inexplicable and strange decision. . . . They constitute a unique and extraordinary lacustrine system, and it is absurd to think that we are not able to protect it, whereas all over the world, people are concerned about residual wetlands [*zone umide*], and in some cases people are studying how to restore wetlands [*zone umide*] that were previously drained. The inclusion of the Fogliano area within the national park, which is something that many international organizations wish for, would resolve an absurd situation by increasing the park's scientific value, but it could also represent a new and interesting attraction for visitors and tourists. (Ente Provinciale per il turismo di Latina 1978, 212–13, translation by the author)

In this speech, the president of the Circeo National Park introduced, arguably for the first time in Agro Pontino, the term *wetland*. This quote unveils the importance of this category, which, far from being a neutral term used to identify a geographical formation, is instead very charged with political and ideological connotations that involve a specific "wetland literacy," which is the capacity to see and to identify a "wetland" in the landscape through a particular lens that emphasizes certain features over others. Particularly, the president of the Circeo National Park emphasized the importance of Fogliano's coastal lakes "as stopping places for migratory birds." Far from being an element idiosyncratically highlighted by the Circeo National Park's president, "birds" are the basic constituents of "wetland literacy." In fact, the number of birds, in terms of individuals and species, is critical to define and to identify a "Wetland of International Importance" under the Ramsar Convention (Ramsar 1971).

In the context of Agro Pontino, the introduction of "wetland literacy" represented a new discovery of Fogliano's ecological value that epitomized a wider trend in the conservation context of that time. At the same time, "wetland literacy" purified Fogliano from its historical, political, agricultural, and social connotations, emphasizing certain features, such as avian, scientific, and recreational values over other values, such as the farming, hunting, fishing, and agriculture that characterized the area until the 1970s. Between the late 1960s and early 1970s, Fogliano, which until then was an agricultural company, changed status by becoming a *zona umida* (wetland), an area symbol for the protection of the Italian coastal landscape.

This process led to the purchase of Fogliano by the state, which, in the 1980s, evicted the owner and the tenant farmers who lived and worked there, entrusting the management of the area to the State Forestry Corps.[5] On the one hand, the expropriation process prevented any further threat to Fogliano, and on the other hand, it resulted in a long legal battle between farmers, government, and the Park Authority. A few farmers, and among them my main interlocutors, are still working in the Fogliano area, where they are considered illegal occupiers. In this context, conflicts between farming and conservation concern not only the ownership of the land but also different understandings of what a wetland is or should be, and concomitantly different understandings of how the relations between wet and dry, water and land, need to be managed.

Until the 1970s, Fogliano has been characterized by an economy based on fishing, hunting, and farming deeply rooted in the social and cultural history of the Pontine Marshes. This economy resisted the transformation caused by the Bonifica Integrale but was disrupted by the conservation policy of the national park. In this sense, the designation of Fogliano as a "wetland" and the introduction of a "wetland literacy" meant the end of a culture and economy—a different literacy—grounded in the marshes. Beyond the end of this cultural and economic legacy, this process also affected the ecology of the area, which was deeply related to peculiar activities that had historically shaped that particular landscape.

The next section focuses particularly on buffalo farming, which epitomizes the environmental relations that characterized the Pontine Marshes and Fogliano before the Bonifica Integrale. Buffalo still roam at Fogliano, although since the 1980s, farming has been very much contested because of the new conservation regime, introduced along with the category of "wetland."

## THE PONTINE MARSHES:
## THE "CULTIVATION OF THE BOG"

In spite of the fascist propaganda, which portrayed a long-lasting representation of the marshes as a wasteland, the Agro Pontino before the Bonifica Integrale was an inhabited, rich, and productive landscape (e.g., Gruppuso 2014, 2018b, 2022). Italian geographer Letizia Cavallo used the term *amphibious* to describe the Pontine Marshes as an environment "where the prevalence and the changing nature of the liquid element determined an unstable structure, variable during the long periods of geomorphological processes, during the seasonal cycles, and sometimes even during a single day" (Cavallo 2011, 116, translation by the author). This peculiar environment coevolved along with an "amphibious economy" that was effectively summarized by the French intellectual Edmond About with the expression *cultivation of the bogs* (1861, 206). Although About did not clarify what he meant by using the term *bogs*, this phrase condenses the typical economy that characterized Mediterranean rural landscapes until the nineteenth century, when he was traveling along the Pontine Marshes. Such an economy was based on the integration of extensive agriculture (i.e., wheat, rye, and maize production), with forestry, animal husbandry, hunting, and fishing (see Folchi 1996; Traina 1988; Horden and Purcell 2000).

By highlighting the array of activities performed in the wet lands of the region, the expression *cultivation of the bogs* lets us imagine the relations between the people and the environment of the Pontine Marshes. This expression defines a taskscape, "an array of related activities" (Ingold 1993, 158) performed to keep the land wet and to nurture the marshes. This pattern of agricultural practices involved humans and nonhumans, which shaped the land through the process of inhabiting that particular environment. This aspect emerges strongly with regard to activities such as the buffalo farming that has characterized the Agro Pontino since before the Bonifica Integrale.

Buffalo were farmed in the coastal areas of Agro Pontino, and particularly at Fogliano, where they were described in exotic tones by travelers as being "like hippopotamuses" (Strutt 1842, 8) or "living fossils" (About

1861, 207), giving "an altogether un-European aspect to the scene" (Bagot 1911, 218; see also Gruppuso 2018b, 403–4). Buffalo were considered as the utmost expression of the marshes as an amphibious environment. They moved between land and water, corresponding with the environment in which they dwelled and built, in turn, by digging pools where they could "plunge into the mud up to the neck, and go to sleep" (About 1861, 196).

Beyond representing a "tourist attraction" *ante litteram*, buffalo farming was considered "the specialty of the province" (Nobili Vitelleschi 1883, 259), economically important for the production of milk and meat (Stanga 1921, 1). Moreover, the buffalo played a paramount role in managing the ecology of the marshes, thus highlighting the contribution of nonhumans in making that particular landscape. Buffalo were considered potentially dangerous for the hydraulic system in the marshes, as they used to pasture in the channels, destroying their banks and thus flooding the surrounding areas. The local reclamation authority took advantage of the buffalo's hydrophilia to clean the Pontine channels of aquatic plants. With this goal in mind, buffalo were led into the channels, where their supervised bustling was supposed to eradicate aquatic plants in order to prevent their overgrowth, which would otherwise obstruct the water flow, flooding the surrounding fields (Barra-Caracciolo di Basciano 1902, 14).

Buffalo farming, with other activities such as fishing (Gruppuso 2022), represented a major influence on the flow of water and its stagnation, thus contributing significantly to shaping the Pontine wet landscape. For the engineers who worked on the reclamation of the Pontine Marshes between the late eighteenth and the early twentieth centuries, it was clear that the squelchy landscape of the region was not the result of predetermined hydrogeological features; it was rather related with the behavior and the activities of the local communities, who "did everything they could in order to frustrate the reclamation" (Nicolai 1800, 140), by "cultivating the bog" and nurturing the marshes.

The expression *cultivation of the bog* is significant because it articulates an amphibious literacy that highlights an economy and an environment where water and land, wet and dry, do not appear as distinctive and opposite categories but rather emerge along with the multiple activities carried out by human and nonhuman beings in their daily lives (see also Krause, this publication). This aspect leads me to consider the usefulness of the concept of amphibious when describing this kind of social and environmental context at the "confluence of land and water" (Gagné and Borg Rasmussen 2016).

## AMPHIBIOUS IN-BETWEENNESS

The word *amphibious* comes from the Greek word *amphibios*, composed by two different words, *amphi* (on both sides) and *bios* (life), literally meaning "living on both sides" (see also ten Bos 2009, 75).[6] Thinking of the Pontine Marshes, Marcus Terentius Varro coined the term *ambivium* to indicate the peculiar bivium (crossroad) between a land route and a waterway (Traina 1988, 81). This term recalls the way of life in the Pontine Marshes, where humans and nonhumans inhabited an environment performing an economy at the "confluence of land and water" (Gagné and Borg Rasmussen 2016), aptly summarized by the expression *cultivation of the bogs* (About 1861, 206).

As I have already indicated, this expression defines a taskscape, a pattern of human-environment relations based upon particular practices and activities. Likewise, I suggest reading the concept of amphibious not as an adjective describing a being "living on both sides," between wet and dry, but as a literacy that characterizes a modus vivendi, a pattern of environmental relations based on water and land understood not as distinct social realms but as one ecological unit. This ecological unit is the field of relations comprehending the biotic and abiotic spheres that constitute the *oikos* of human and nonhuman beings. In this kind of ecology, organism and environment have to be understood not as in relation to each other, but as constituting one indivisible totality (Ingold 2000; see also Descola and Pálsson 1996, 14). The amphibious here is a constellation of social practices and ecological processes emerging along with, or in between, the shapes of the land.

This amphibious literacy challenges the traditional idea of liminality associated with marshlands and wet landscapes in general (e.g., Andrews and Roberts 2012) and recalls the reflections by Ingold on the concepts of between and in-between (2015). The former, Ingold suggests, is liminal, transitory, and marginal; the latter instead is arterial, central, and unending. Ingold writes, "'Between' articulates a divided world that is already carved at the joints. It is a bridge, a hinge, a connection, an attraction of opposites, a link in a chain, a double-headed arrow that points at once to this and that. 'In-between,' by contrast, is a movement of generation and dissolution in a world of becoming where things are not yet given—such that they might then be joined up—but on the way to being given" (Ingold 2015, 147).

Accordingly, I argue that wetland is between wet and dry; it is a category emerging from a literacy based upon the discrimination of hydrological features, such as water and land. Wet land, instead, is in-between, and it emphasizes practices and activities performed to keep the land wet. In wetland literacy, *amphibious* is an adjective that denotes the quality of a being living between water and land. But in the literacy that wet land implies, being amphibious is not a quality, nor an adjective, it is rather a process that reflects the experience of living in-between and corresponding with a particular environment. The tension between wetland and wet land is outlined in greater detail in the next section, where I contrast these categories and their literacies, focusing on three aspects. I first explore the maintenance of "wetlands," in relation to the activities aimed at keeping the land wet. Subsequently, I explore two different kinds of human-bird relations that reflect the distinction between wetland and wet lands.

## WET LAND: KEEPING THE LAND WET

Wetland scientists Mitsch and Gosselink (2007, 26) explain the importance of defining wetlands and their boundaries in order to provide laws to protect these ecosystems, which are nowadays considered among the most important on Earth, at the core of the hottest debates on global environmental matters like climate change, desertification, biodiversity, water management, and sustainability. However, "the diversity of these environments prevents a single, universally accepted definition of wetlands"

(Meindl 2005, 244). One can certainly argue that the main attribute of wetlands is the presence of a certain level of water or wetness in the land, even if in small quantities or for short periods of time in a year (Meindl 2005, 244). But water as such is a tricky element if used as a classificatory item, since these environments are associated with different water regimes (Tiner 2002, 234). Positing water and wetness as the main common attributes of wetlands, indeed, makes the already difficult task of defining these ecosystems harder, since "the most constant 'quality' of water is that it is not constant, but is characterised by transmutability and sensitivity to changes in the environment" (Strang 2004, 49). The same point is stressed by Rod Giblett, who, with regard to the mutability of these environments, argues that "wetlands are the space of mutability. . . . Wetlands constantly change" (Giblett 1996, 141).

In order to deal with this changeability, scientists treat "wetland ecology" as "a distinctive field of study" (Mitsch and Gosselink 2007, 18) and refer to wetlands as ecotones: "transitional spatial gradients between adjacent aquatic and terrestrial environments. . . . As ecotones, wetlands usually interact strongly to varying (allogenic) forcing functions from both ends of the ecotone. These forces may push a wetland toward its terrestrial neighbour if, for example, regional water levels fall, or toward its aquatic neighbor if water levels rise" (Mitsch and Gosselink 2007, 234). This transitionality means that "allogenic forces" can easily and quickly turn wet lands into completely aquatic or terrestrial ecosystems. Such a transformation is connected with the process of ecological succession that is known in wetland ecology as hydrosere, which is the transitional process that transforms wet lands into shrubby fields and eventually into woodlands. This means that a variety of actions must be performed to intervene in this process of ecological succession in order to maintain the transitional nature of wet lands.

This issue was very salient during my fieldwork, with particular regard to contestations concerning the management of the protected wetlands in the Fogliano area. One of the reasons behind these controversies has to do with the different understandings of the role that agriculture, and in particular buffalo farming, should play in the maintenance of the wet landscape. On the one hand, conservationists aim for a substantial reduction, if not the complete banning, of buffalo from the coastal wetlands; they argue that the number of heads has increased in recent years, causing problems of overgrazing and animal waste management in some areas. On the other hand, farmers defend their right to work in these areas, complaining that the national park's institutional bodies do not allow for the construction of structures for waste management or stables for keeping animals inside (see Gruppuso 2018b). The bureaucratic difficulties due to the contested ownership of the land resulted in a failure to address the problem and, most importantly, led to a general lack of management, hence a failure in maintaining these "wetlands."

The former head of the State Forestry Corps in the Fogliano area, who is now retired, stressed this point. I met him in order to better understand the situation related to the management of the wetlands in the park, so he took me for an interesting and revealing walk in one of the strict nature reserves of the park. During our walk, among reeds, brushes, and ponds, my informant told me something that I did not expect from him:

> Among these groves of reeds, one should dig proper ponds with tractors to keep wetlands . . . because the vegetation in a few years will fall on the ground, and then there won't be water anymore; the ground rises, and it becomes grassland . . . the grove of reeds advances. One has to manage the wetland . . . by giving the right quantity of water . . . with buffalo grazing . . . with their bustle, buffalo turn over the soil and delay the advance of reeds . . . you can't just say 'leave the wetland. . . .' Wetland does not survive on its own. . . . These areas need to be managed. If they are supposed to be wetlands, they need to be managed . . . if the national park wants to grow woodland . . . they can ban grazing, and the wood comes on its own. (August 26, 2014, translation by the author)

My interlocutor was very critical of the current policy of the national park, which in his understanding is neglecting those areas. He is the only conservationist I met who argued for the importance of farming and managing the "wetland" in order "to keep the land wet." He certainly used the term *wetlands* (*zone umide*) to mean the protected areas within Circeo National Park, but he described them through an amphibious literacy, pointing out not a set of predetermined ecological features but an array of activities and practices that I have called "wet land."

The same literacy emerges in other words by one of my interlocutor-farmers, Gaetano, who highlighted the importance of buffalo in keeping the national park alive:

> I am convinced that if they remove the buffalo, this park, which is an important site for migratory birds, will be ruined. It would become so dirty and overgrown with weeds, this area would become completely overgrown with rushes and brambles and then all the animals that now use the ponds, where would they go? It's a park that would die in a few days. Because buffalo attract these animals . . . for example the duck eats where it finds the worm, the widgeon needs the pasture, it leaves the lake and it goes to eat grass, and then the ponds attract the teal and other animals. If you remove the buffalo, the animals disappear; they no longer have territory. (March 28, 2011, translation by the author)

Like the former head of the State Forestry Corps, Gaetano argues that the park, hence the "wetlands," do not survive on their own. They need to be constantly kept alive through farming, which, by intervening in the process of ecological succession, maintains wetlands in between wet and dry. This particular understanding recalls the "cultivation of the bog" that characterized the Pontine Marshes, and it resonates with my description of "wet land" as opposed to "wetland." The point addressed by my informants is significant in wetland conservation, and it is paramount to the sustainable management of these environments.

## WETLAND: A PLACE OF QUIET FOR THE ANIMALS

An interesting aspect concerning the use of the word *wetland* among farmers is the association between this notion and the normative vocabulary of bureaucrats and conservationists. Let me illustrate this point with a story that has to do with one of my main interlocutor-farmers, Guglielmo, who was born and grew up in the Fogliano area, where he still keeps a small herd of cows. For several years, he led as president a historical reenactment group, named Cavalcanti dell'Agro Pontino (Agro Pontino's Cowboys), which staged several events in the Fogliano area connected with the traditional pastoral and rural activities that people used to carry out in the old marshes and in the Fogliano area before the Circeo National Park acquired it.

During one of our meetings, the conversation fell on the concerns expressed by the national park's president in giving him permission to organize an annual event in the Fogliano area. On that occasion, Guglielmo told me:

> I went several times to the Circeo National Park's president, and at the beginning he was a bit unwilling, a bit scared. He told me, "You know, Fogliano is defined as a wetland, as a quiet area, like this and like that," and I replied, "Look, it is an area where I am going to repeat nothing else than the traditions and the customs of the Pontine Marshes." [ ... ]
>
> Then one day I got worked up, and I told him, "Doctor, you have to excuse me. I don't understand why you don't want to accept this, because I was born and bred in Fogliano . . . that's all." And then he replied, "Mr. Guglielmo, this is a wetland, a place of quiet for the animals." But then I said, "The animals, Doctor, have always been there. The wild ducks and the mallards, you see them now, but I was born among them, I remember them from when I was a kid." Then, he gave us permission, and I received a letter that I still remember. It reads, "Attention, if a branch falls, you will be charged . . . this is not to be ruined . . . caution with fire . . . the association will be considered responsible for everything." For goodness' sake! (April 13, 2011, translation by the author)

From what I remember during my fieldwork, Guglielmo used the word *wetland* (*zona umida*) only on specific occasions, when he switched from a familiar to an official-bureaucratic linguistic register, the vocabulary of conservation, which implies a wetland literacy. When Guglielmo used the word *wetland*, it was the Circeo National Park's president who was speaking.

This story addresses an important issue related to correct behavior, hence to the "moral geography" (Matless 1994) of wetlands: wetlands are supposed to be a "place of quiet for the animals" that does not afford human inhabitation, places for animals and not for human beings. In the conversation that Guglielmo had with me, this aspect is emphasized with regard to a particular group of animals, namely birds. Birds, in fact, play an important role in the local imaginary of wet lands, but as I already mentioned, birds are also the basic constituents of wetland literacy, as they are used as a criterion for identifying "wetlands of international importance" (Ramsar 1971).

In what follows, I explore this tension, describing two different approaches to birds that I have experienced during fieldwork. I will contrast the approach adopted by a local group of environmental interpreters with Guglielmo's imaginary of birds.

### BIRDS

During fieldwork, I attended introductory sessions of birdwatching in the Fogliano area organized by a local group of nature guides. During these sessions, we stayed in one place with a telescope and a field guide; of course, we walked to get to the right place, and in the right season, but that approach to birds seemed to me completely disjointed from the complexity of the whole landscape, disjointed from its history and from my experience of that environment. With the farmers, the experience of birds was completely different. As an example, I will describe a stroll I had with Guglielmo along the Fogliano's bank, when we were looking for a particular plant that I had asked him to show me.

From Guglielmo's reserve, we were approaching the bank of the lake, walking through a path surrounded by thick vegetation, mainly reeds. Immediately out of the thicket, Guglielmo saw the plant we were looking for, but suddenly a lot of birds took flight, and the focus of our attention changed from plants to birds. Looking at the flight of birds, he said excitedly, "Eeh! Coots [*folaga* — *Fulica atra*] . . . look. . . . Look, look, there are not only coots, also wigeons [*fischione* — *Anas penelope*], tufted ducks [*morettoni* — *Aythya fuligula*]. . . . They were called white hunt and black hunt" (January 13, 2012, translation by the author). Then we returned to the plant, and Guglielmo briefly told me about the old use of *giuncarella* (*Juncus acutus*).[7] After this, we continued to walk along the banks, and our conversation focused mainly on birds. Our walk almost changed into a sort of imaginary hunt for birds: sometimes we stopped behind a bush in order to watch them, and when possible, we tried to approach the water to have a closer look at the animals, without being noticed by the birds, and to "surprise them," as Guglielmo told me.

These two experiences, respectively with nature guides and with Guglielmo, could not have been more different; they highlight different literacies that correspond with different approaches to Fogliano's wet environment. With the environmental interpreters, the sense of sight was strongly underlined by the high-powered view of the telescope. A focused and discriminating attention was at work, aimed at detecting and recognizing specific objects, namely birds (see Macdonald 2002, 54). This approach resonates with the visual literacy that Dilip da Cunha (2018) associates with the invention of rivers, as outcomes of a cartographic imagination. For Guglielmo, instead, looking at birds was not related to the recognition of specific taxa; it was not something he used to do every day, a kind of "ornithophilia" (Bonta 2003), nor did it reveal a particular fascination for birds. Guglielmo noticed and recognized the birds with an act of remembrance through which he "re-collected" the landscape within his life history and with the history of that specific place, where people were used to hunting birds until the national park acquired the area. Indeed, while looking at birds, Guglielmo started narrating to me hunting stories that his father used to tell him, intertwining them with his ideas about the conservation policy of Circeo National Park. Unlike the guides, for whom birds were objects to detect, for Guglielmo, birds were clues to follow. Our attention, in fact, was not focused on birds; instead it floated, roaming the landscape, following the birds.

130 *Gruppuso*

These different approaches recall the distinction between decoding and revelation drawn by Ingold (2000, 13–26). The former is based on the detection of objects, decoded by means of specific keys, knowledge, and tools, represented in my case by field guides. The latter is a process of revelation grounded in the practices of inhabiting a particular place: Guglielmo "discovered" birds and started to follow them as a hunter would, with animals' clues. In the first case, the birdwatchers adopted particular and specific visual practices, moving in "wetlands" as in an "open air laboratory" (Macdonald 2002, 73). In the second case, Guglielmo followed traces and joined with the birds along the wet pastures of Fogliano's banks. He moved in a "wet land," retracing the steps of the previous hunters who used to hunt at Fogliano (see Gruppuso 2018a).

The differences between these approaches reflect the distinction between "wetland" and "wet land" as characterized by different human-bird relations that reflect different literacies. The former is a visual literacy by which birds are detected and admired from a distance by visitor-birdwatchers. The latter is a haptic literacy that sees the lives and movements of birds join and mingle with the historic lives of inhabitant-hunters, as they move through Fogliano.

## CONCLUSION

In this chapter, I have discussed historical and ethnographic materials by emphasizing a tension between "wetland" and "wet land." The former is a normative term used to identify generic areas characterized by specific features and designated by particular environmental laws and universal knowledge. The latter is an expression that emerges along the historical practices that human and nonhuman inhabitants perform to keep the land wet. These categories correspond with different literacies. What I named "wetland literacy" is based upon scientific and measurable features, such as the number of birds, in terms of species and individuals. The literacy implied in wet land, that I would call "amphibious literacy," emphasizes processes, stories, and activities that make "wet lands" as environments of life for human and nonhuman beings.

This distinction recalls the origin of the term *wetland* in the ancient Mediterranean world, and particularly in ancient Greece, where, according to archaeologist Giusto Traina, two words were mostly used to identify a wetland: *helos* (ἕλος) and *limne* (λίμνη) (1988, 54–59). The former was grounded in a naturalistic intuition, and it was also related to the literary and cultural imaginary of these environments (1988, 60–61). *Helos* indicated a holistic understanding of wetlands as complex environments, made of plants, animals, and human inhabitants. It also implied an economic understanding, in relation to the people who inhabited and used these environments. In this sense, *helos* corresponds to "wet lands," as they emerge in the life activities of the inhabitants.

The term *limne*, instead, pointed to a completely different meaning. It was a normative term embedded within geometrical thought (Traina 1988, 60), indicating a precise geographical space defined by the presence of water and by its relations with land (1988, 56). Furthermore, *limne* had an affinity with the Latin word *līmĕn* (1988, 56), meaning border, boundary, frontier. *Limne* corresponds with "wetland" as an environment seen from an outsider, according to a cartographic rationality. After the Classical Age, the term *helos* ended up coinciding with *limne*, referring to the cartographic demarcation of particular areas defined by external observation for descriptive necessities (1988, 56). Similarly, the introduction of wetland literacy has transformed wet lands into wetlands: artifacts of objectifying classification, divorced from their history and from their sociocultural and symbolic connotations.

The history of Agro Pontino demonstrates that wetland literacy is an outcome of the same modernist logic that characterized the fascist Bonifica Integrale and the coeval establishment of the Circeo National Park. Even though based on different ethical, aesthetical, and scientific approaches, they are facets of the same "Nature State" (Hardenberg et al. 2017). They created new environments implementing processes of purification, simplification, and abstraction of the land that disentangled the landscape from its historical and cultural dimensions. The notion of wetland, like the act of reclamation, has emptied wet lands of their history, of the cultural and social efforts aimed at keeping the land wet, or cultivating the bog. The notion of wetland has frozen the mutability of wet lands within the defined boundaries of natural protected areas. In the rhetoric of global conservation, these environments are described as "ecotones," places between land and water (e.g., Mitsch and Gosselink 2007), but all the activities geared to maintaining these areas in between, to "keeping the land wet," disappear, naturalized in the notion of "wetland."

This is the result of a "logic of inversion" that, according to Tim Ingold, "turns the pathways along which life is lived into boundaries within which it is enclosed" (2011, 164). Such a logic transforms the amphibious in-betweenness of wet lands, characterized by ongoing social practices of correspondence with a particular environment (see Ingold 2018), into wetlands, understood as liminal and transitional spaces between adjacent aquatic and terrestrial environments (see Mitsch and Gosselink 2007, 234). In order to reverse this inversion, I challenged the traditional interpretation of *amphibious* as an adjective that links two distinct realms, suggesting instead an alternative understanding of this concept as a modus vivendi, a constellation of environmental relations. These are based on a literacy that understands water and land not as distinct realms but as one ecological unit.

"Wetland" and "wet land" are certainly simplifications. However, this distinction maintains a heuristic value, which is particularly important in our age of environmental crisis. Wetlands are, in fact, considered key to sustain life on Earth and to mitigate the effects of climate change (Smith et al. 2022). Nevertheless, two-thirds of European wetlands have been lost in the last century, and they are still the most threatened ecosystems in Europe despite the fact that they are now protected. The problem lies in what I called wetland literacy, which is based on universalist knowledges and global conservation policies that understand these environments in terms of measurable features and protect them accordingly by drawing a line that divides them from their historical and social contexts. To overcome this problem, we need, instead, to look at wet lands, and to switch our attention from scientific criteria and measurable standards to practices, tasks, and ecological processes that, by keeping the land wet, preserve "wetlands" with their invaluable ecology.

## NOTES

1 This expression was first used in 1928 by ecologist Percy Viosca with regard to the biological, conservationist, recreational, and educational values of the Louisiana wet lands in the United States (Viosca 1928). Viosca's article, published in *Ecology*, is considered the first scientific paper aimed to "extoll the values of wetlands as natural resources and to dispell the ill-conceived public notion of wetlands as wastelands" (Tiner 2002, 5).

2 Ingold and Kurttila draw a similar distinction between weather and climate in northern Finland (see Ingold and Kurttila 2001, 187).

3 Latina was originally founded with the name of Littoria and renamed after the fall of fascism in 1945. Latina, Sabaudia, and Pontinia were established in 1932, 1934, and 1935, respectively.

4 See the Information Sheet on Ramsar Wetlands for each lake, accessed January 2025, https://rsis.ramsar.org/.

5 In 2016 the State Forestry Corps (Corpo Forestale dello Stato) was absorbed by the Carabinieri and named Command Unit for the Forestry, Environmental and Agrifood Protection (Comando Unità per la Tutela Forestale, Ambientale e Agroalimentare).

6 Vocabolario Etimologico della Lingua Italiana di Ottorino Pianigiani, accessed May 2016, http://www.etimo.it/?term=anfibio&find=Cerca.

7 The leaves of this plant were used, until few decades ago, to make short strings, particularly for use in viticulture or for basketry.


## REFERENCES

About, E. 1861. *Rome of Today*. New York: James O. Noyes.

Alvisi, M. 2005. "Dear Old Fogliano: 'Storie di famiglie nobili e luoghi nobilitati.'" In *Villaggio Fogliano: Di storia in storia, naturalmente . . .* , edited by R. Busatto, 31–47. Cisterna di Latina: Associazione Villaggio Fogliano.

Andrews, H., and L. Roberts, eds. 2012. *Liminal Landscapes: Travel, Experience and Spaces In-Between*. London: Routledge.

Bagot, R. 1911. *My Italian Year*. New York: James Pott.

Barra-Caracciolo di Basciano, G. 1902. *L'allontanamento delle erbe acquatiche nei canali di bonifica della Palude Pontina*. Roma: Tipografia Cooperativa Sociale.

Bonta, M. 2003. *Seven Names for the Bellbird: Conservation Geography in Honduras*. College Station: Texas A&M University Press.

134 *Gruppuso*

Busatto R., ed. 2005. *Villaggio Fogliano: Di storia in storia, naturalmente.* . . .
Cisterna di Latina: Associazione Villaggio Fogliano.

Cavallo, F. L. 2011. "Terra: Acque, Macchine." *Geografie della bonifica in Italia tra Ottocento e Novecento.* Reggio Emilia: Diabasis.

———. 2014. "Valori geoculturali e turisticità delle zone umide costiere italiane." In *Wetlandia. Tradizioni, valori, turismi nelle zone umide italiane,* edited by F. L. Cavallo, 1–19. Lavis: Cedam.

Cecere, C. 1989. *La Villa Caetani a Fogliano: Il Luogo—L'Architettura—La Storia.* Roma: Fratelli Palombi Editori.

Cederna, A. 1967. "Prima Carta dell'Italia da Salvare." *Abitare.* July 1967. https://www.archiviocederna.it/pdf//articoli/630/00630_05_001.pdf.

———. 1970. "Il Parco Nazionale in Agonia: Le ultime carte del Circeo." *Corriere della Sera.* September 3, 1970. https://www.archiviocederna.it/pdf//articoli/672/00672_01.pdf.

da Cunha, D. 2018. "River Literacy and the Challenge of a Rain Terrain." In *Critical Humanities from India: Context, Issues, Futures,* edited by D. Venkat Rao, 177–204. London: Routledge.

Descola, P., and G. Pálsson. 1996. *Nature and Society: Anthropological Perspectives.* London: Routledge.

Ente Provinciale per il turismo di Latina. 1978. *Memoria sui problemi del Parco Nazionale del Circeo.* Latina: Ente Provinciale per il turismo di Latina.

Folchi, A. 1996. *L'Agro Pontino 1900–1934.* Roma: Regione Lazio.

———. 2000. *I Contadini del Duce: Agro Pontino: 1932–1941.* Roma: Pieraldo Editore.

Gagné, K., and M. Borg Rasmussen. 2016. "Introduction—An Amphibious Anthropology: The Production of Place at the Confluence of Land and Water." *Anthropologica* 58 (2): 135–49.

Gearey, M., A. Church, and N. Ravenscroft. 2020. *English Wetlands: Spaces of Nature, Culture, Imagination.* Cham: Springer.

Giblett, R. 1996. "Postmodern Wetlands." *Culture, History, Ecology.* Edinburgh: Edinburgh University Press.

Gruppuso, P. 2014. "Nell'Africa tenebrosa alle porte di Roma." *Viaggio nelle Paludi Pontine e nel loro immaginario.* Roma: Annales Edizioni.

———. 2017. "Geologic and Historical, Surface and Depth: Entanglement of Water and Temporality in a Contested Wetland of Agro Pontino." *Archivio Antropologico Mediterraneo* 19 (2): 69–79.

———. 2018a. "Vapours in the Sphere. Malaria, Atmosphere and Landscape in

Wet Lands of Agro Pontino, Italy." In *Exploring Atmospheres Ethnographically,* edited by S. A. Schroer and S. B. Schmitt, 45–60. London: Routledge.

———. 2018b. "Edenic Views in Wetland Conservation: Nature and Agriculture in the Fogliano Area, Italy." *Conservation & Society* 16 (4): 397–408.

———. 2022. "In-between Solidity and Fluidity: The Reclaimed Marshlands of Agro Pontino." *Theory, Culture and Society* 39 (2): 53–73.

Hardenberg, W. G., M. Kelly, C. Leal, and E. Wakild, eds. 2017. *The Nature State: Rethinking the History of Conservation.* London: Routledge.

Horden, P., and N. Purcell. 2000. *The Corrupting Sea: A Study of Mediterranean History.* Oxford: Wiley Blackwell.

Huijbens, E. H., and G. Pálsson. 2009. "The Bog in Our Brain and Bowels: Social Attitudes to the Cartography of Icelandic Wetlands." *Environment and Planning D: Society and Space* 27 (2): 296–316.

Ingold, T. 1993. "The Temporality of the Landscape." *World Archaeology* 25 (2): 152–74.

———. 2000. *The Perception of the Environment: Essays on Livelihood, Dwelling and Skill.* London: Routledge.

———. 2011. *Being Alive. Essays on Movement, Knowledge and Description.* London: Routledge.

———. 2015. *The Life of Lines.* London: Routledge.

———. 2018. *Anthropology and/as Education.* London: Routledge.

Ingold, T., and T. Kurttila. 2001. "Perceiving the Environment in Finnish Lapland." *Body & Society* 6 (3–4): 183–96.

Macdonald, H. 2002. "'What Makes You a Scientist Is the Way You Look at Things': Ornithology and the Observer 1930–1955." *Studies in History and Philosophy of Biological and Biomedical Sciences* 33 (1): 53–77.

Mariani, R. 1976. *Fascismo e "città nuove."* Milano: Feltrinelli.

Matless, D. 1994. "Moral Geography in Broadland." *Ecumene* 1 (2): 127–55.

Matthews, G. V. T. 1993. *The Ramsar Convention on Wetlands: Its History and Development.* Gland: Ramsar Convention Bureau.

Meindl, C. F. 2005. "Wetland Diversity: The Limits of Generalization." *Journal of Geography* 104 (6): 243–56.

Mitsch, W. J., and J. G. Gosselink. 2007. *Wetlands.* New York: John Wiley.

Nicolai, N. M. 1800. *De' Bonificamenti delle Terre Pontine.* Roma: Stamperia Pagliarini.

Nobili Vitelleschi, F. 1883. *Atti della Giunta per la inchiesta agraria sulle condizioni della classe agricola.* Vol. 11. Tomo I. Provincie di Roma e Grosseto. Roma: Forzani e C., Tipografia del Senato.

O'Gorman, E. 2021. *Wetlands in a Dry Land: More-Than-Human Histories of Australia's Murray-Darling Basin*. Seattle: University of Washington Press.

Pitkin, D. 1998. *La ruota gira: Vita a Sermoneta 1951–1952*. Milano: Franco Angeli.

Priolo, M. 1999. "Il valore delle aree demaniali del Parco." In *Il Circeo, Parco della realtà e dell'immaginazione*, edited by Parco Nazionale del Circeo, 61–82. Pomezia.

———. 2005. "Un luogo monumentale: L'esproprio: Una storia che parte da lontano." In *Villaggio Fogliano: Di storia in storia, naturalmente . . .* , edited by R. Busatto, 49–55. Cisterna di Latina: Associazione Villaggio Fogliano.

Ramsar. 1971. "The Ramsar Sites Criteria: The Nine Criteria for Identifying Wetlands of International Importance." Ramsar. http://www.ramsar.org/sites /default/files/documents/library/ramsarsites_criteria_eng.pdf.

Ramsar Convention. 1994. *Convention on Wetlands of International Importance Especially as Waterfowl Habitat*. Ramsar, 2.2.1971. As Amended by the Protocol of 3.12.1982 and the Amendments of 28.5.1987. Paris.

Scaramelli, C. 2021. *How to Make a Wetland: Water and Moral Ecology in Turkey*. Stanford: Stanford University Press.

Schiappa, E. 1996. "Towards a Pragmatic Approach to Definition: 'Wetlands' and the Politics of Meaning." In *Environmental Pragmatism*, edited by A. Light and E. Katz, 209–30. London: Routledge.

Smith, P., A. Arneth, D. K. A. Barnes, K. Ichii, P. A. Marquet, A. Popp, H. Portner, A. D. Rogers, R. J. Scholes, B. Strassburg, J. Wu, and H. Ngo. 2022. "How Do We Best Synergize Climate Mitigation Actions to Co-benefit Biodiversity?" *Global Change Biology*, no. 28, 2555–77.

Sottoriva, P. G. 2005. "Quando Fogliano rischiò di diventare un cantiere: Le vicende del Parco nel Piano regolatore." In *Villaggio Fogliano: Di storia in storia, naturalmente . . .* , edited by R. Busatto, 57–67. Cisterna di Latina: Associazione Villaggio Fogliano.

Stanga, I. 1921. "Zootecnia di Palude." *Il Circeo: Settimanale dell'Agro Pontino* 1 (2): 1.

Strang, V. 2004. *The Meaning of Water*. Oxford: Berg.

Strutt, A. J. 1842. *A Pedestrian Tour in Calabria e Sicily*. London: T. C. Newby.

Sutter, P. S. 2021. "Foreword: Entangled Agencies." In *Wetlands in a Dry Land. More-Than-Human Histories of Australia's Murray-Darling Basin*, by E. O'Gorman, ix–xiii. Seattle: University of Washington Press.

ten Bos, R. 2009. "Towards an Amphibious Anthropology: Water and Peter Sloterdijk." *Environment and Planning D: Society and Space* 27 (1): 73–86.

Tiner, R. W. 2002. *In Search of Swampland. A Wetland Sourcebook and Field Guide.* New Brunswick, NJ: Rutgers University Press.

Traina, G. 1988. "Paludi e bonifiche del Mondo Antico." *Saggio di archeologia geografica.* Roma: L'Erma di Bretschneider.

———. 2002. "Uso del bosco e degli incolti." In *Storia dell'Agricoltura Italiana,* edited by G. Forni and A. Marcone, 225–58. Firenze: Polistampa.

Viosca, P., Jr. 1928. "Louisiana Wet Land and the Value of their Wild Life and Fishery Resources." *Ecology* 9 (2): 216–29.

FRANZ KRAUSE

# 5. Situating Wetness in Soomaa, Estonia

When I visit Ulvi at her farm, I always leave the car at the edge of the forest and walk the last few hundred meters along the riverbank, across the meadow, and past the paddock to her house. This is a nice way to get into the mood for this place, listening to the sounds of the birds and the river, inhaling the smells of moist earth and horse stables, and watching the farmstead appear and grow as I approach it. But this is not the reason for me walking. I am doing this because Ulvi asked me to. She is not keen on people driving across her land, since that ruins the track leading to her house. For most of the year, the ground is so wet that the cars' tires leave deep marks in the ground. Only rarely does she use her own truck to get in and out; only when the ground is frozen in winter, or during a dry period in summer, is it safe to drive across the land. "There is no use in building a gravel road, either," Ulvi says with a dismissive gesture. "The next flood would just wash it out again."

When the water runs high in the river and soaks the meadows around, Ulvi rather walks to the village; not along the road, however, which is built on high ground and in a nine-kilometer detour across a faraway road bridge, but along the riverbank, often through knee-high floodwater. She has to know where to step and where not to step — occasional ditches, where the water is much deeper, are invisible through the water. Once I accompanied her on this walk along the flooded bank, but I soon excused myself and turned back, since I was not confident in making the return walk on my own. In March, the water is still very cold, and the nights dark — not a particularly inviting combination for stumbling around on the bank of a flooding river. Ulvi, in her sixties but much fitter than me, seemed to first think I was joking but finally let me go.

Ulvi's brother Harri walks to the village center almost every day. The man, in his eighties, is keen on reading the newspaper that gets delivered to their letter box on the main road, and on Wednesdays, the only day in the week that a bus comes to the village, he takes the bus to town, shopping and socializing. However, he finds the walk along the riverbank too long; instead, he uses a small raft, tied to the riverbank in front of their house, and paddles across the river. When the water is particularly high, the riverbank may still be dry, but the meadow beyond is also inundated. Harri has prepared a second raft for these times, which he keeps in the meadow in dry times, and which takes him to the forest edge during higher floods. Further along the path toward the letter box and bus stop is a deep ditch, which most of the time is almost dry but occasionally can run so high with water that crossing it becomes impossible even in rubber boots. Using wood from the forest around, Harri has built a makeshift bridge across the ditch, further flood-proofing his daily walk. Beyond the ditch begins a forest road, and beyond the forest are the old schoolhouse and the bus stop. He stores his rubber boots in the former school's cellar before changing into his city shoes.

Ulvi and Harri live in a part of Estonia that has become known as Soomaa: "marsh-land" in literal translation. Its history is characterized by waves of population and depopulation, of economic development and abandonment, and currently only a few people live in Soomaa permanently. It is associated with large tracts of bogs, on the one hand, and with spectacular floods at the confluence of a number of rivers, on the other. Every year, Estonian media reproduce images of flooded meadows and forests in Soomaa, washed-out roads, animals seeking higher ground, and water encroaching on people's homes. And even in the absence of such impressive events, the ground is wet in many places at many times, hindering plant growth and tractor mobility. For many people, including Ulvi and Harri, this abundance of water is a challenge; for others, whom I will introduce in the following pages, it figures very differently in their life projects, as a distinguishing feature of place and subjectivity, for instance, or as a spectacle that invites visitors and income. The predicaments, assets, and dilemmas that Soomaa presents to its inhabitants could be approached through a number of vantage points, including postsocialism, rural-urban migration, or tourism—although I

140  *Krause*

am not aware of any such studies. Here, I am approaching them through an attention to wetness in people's lives. I thereby treat life in Soomaa as amphibious, that is, an ongoing negotiation of both water and land, without a certain and stable recourse to either one of them. I use *wetness* as a term to explore the interconnectedness and simultaneity of land and water in people's lives, and—conversely—I use people's different encounters with, and performances of, wetness to illustrate how wetness itself is multiple, and more than an objective measure of the degree of water in an otherwise-dry medium. Wetness can be considered as one of the principal vectors of the amphibious, as outlined in the introduction to this book. As a character-istic of the lived world, wetness is central to the processes that make and unmake amphibious lives, narratives, and environments. But wetness is not synonymous with amphibiousness. Where the amphibious refers to lives lived in between water and land, or wet and dry, wetness is a shorthand for the experiences of, and stories about, the ground people inhabit and work. A practice can be understood as amphibious but not wet; the land can be experienced as wet but not amphibious.

This chapter explores some aspects of people's relationships with wetness in Soomaa, as well as some of the contexts in which people experience wetness. Here, wetness is not a given but emerges as a phenomenon in people's lives, sometimes as dilemma and sometimes as asset, in line with their particular life projects. This means not taking wetness for granted, as an objective quality, but rather becoming attentive to the ways that specific social, cultural, and economic arrangements make wetness into what it seems to be so self-evidently most of the time. In other words, specific places emerge as wet in relation to particular practices and imaginations at particular times, and for particular people. Furthermore, the wetness that such differently situated people encounter is multiple—it is not the same phenomenon for all of them, but these different kinds of wetness are still linked by some of the relations that give rise to them. Treating wetness as multiple is not to dematerialize it or deny the biophysical characteristics and processes that configure wetness; quite on the contrary, this wetness is nothing if not material, the very materiality in which amphibious life in Soomaa unfolds. However, it is more than just a physical measure of water content or degree of malleability, as it is fundamentally shaped by the people's specific land uses, economic standings, and future prospects, among other factors. I propose this approach to wetness as produced by relationships between materially situated people as an amphibious-anthropological alternative to the false assumption that wetland life consists of social and cultural adaptations to a given hydromorphology.

## MULTIPLE WETNESS

With this argument, I am developing recent work that has formulated ways of understanding water as multiple—not as the universal substance $H_2O$, as which we get to know it in science class and global water scarcity discourse, but as differently situated and enacted waters that matter precisely because of their plurality. Although I am here concerned with wetness—which is not to be mistaken for a measure of water content—much of what has been written about the multiplicity of water is relevant for my argument. Geographer Jamie Linton (2010), for example, argues that "modern water," that is, the version and image of water that characterizes policy discourses, development planning, and the framing of the global water crisis, is the product of a long history of separating an assumed essence of water from the host of social and ecological relations in which it is entangled in real life. In Linton's analysis, this process of "abstraction" has been fueled by, and plays into the hands of, large-scale and state-centered management efforts that seem best placed to handle such abstract(ed) water. Linton, however, illustrates that these efforts cannot be the cure for the world's ever-escalating water problems but are rather integral parts of these problems. Tackling them would require, analytically as well as practically, "applying a relational-dialectical approach" (Linton 2010, 241) to water issues, or in short, practicing "hydrolectics." This involves identifying not only the different social and ecological contexts in which water comes to matter to particular people and in particular places but also recognizing the different waters that emerge from these contexts. Only if water is pluralized, Linton concludes, can we begin to understand and solve the hydrosocial conundrums we face today.

Recent work inspired by science-and-technology studies also emphasizes the multiplicity of water (e.g., Barnes and Alatout 2012). In these analyses, different waters are enacted in specific assemblages of social organizations, expertise, management paradigms, technologies, governance regimes, and ecologies, which produce these waters while simultaneously being transformed by them. Anthropologist Maria Louise Bønnelykke Robertson (2016), for example, explains how different technologies for obtaining drinking water on the Pacific island of Tarawa are entangled with different moralities and social arrangements, and through these entanglements produce different kinds of water. The water from the traditional, shallow wells is therefore not the same as the water piped into people's homes or that pumped from water reserves on the far end of the island, especially because of the strong moral links between fresh water and family-controlled land in Tarawa. Similarly, anthropologist Mandana Limbert (2010) reports how water in the arid country of Oman, imbricated in different infrastructures, religious practices, and ideas of ownership, is a multiple substance. Where pumped irrigation and piped drinking water have superseded animal draught-powered wells, open channels, and shared bathing houses, the essence of water has morphed, too, from a public substance that could be measured in allocated time to a private good measured in quantity. The oil export–driven social and economic transformations in Oman since the 1970s have enabled infrastructural developments bringing water directly into people's homes, which has in turn unsettled ideas and practices of sharing and communally using water.

In this chapter, I am also concerned with multiplicity, but not with that of water itself. In fact, people encounter water in many different guises and, perhaps, most often not in the form of pure, liquid, flowing water at all, but through various kinds of wetness—humid air, damp walls, soaked firewood, slippery surfaces, spongy vegetation, soggy ground, saturated soils, wet lands (e.g., Jerstad 2014; McLean 2011; Richardson 2016; Soentgen 2012; Walker et al. 2011; da Cunha 2019). It is often precisely because water is not present in its pure form that such kinds of wetness may be judged as uncanny, dangerous, or waste, as environmental humanities scholar Rod Giblett (1996) argues for wetlands. These judgements are couched, according to Giblett, in a patriarchal, Western, and modernist framework of control, order, and categorical separations. Studies of wetlands in Icelandic cartography (Huijbens and Pálsson 2009) and Estonian folk traditions, memories, and current attitudes concerning mires (Pungas and Võsu 2012; Pungas-Kohv et al. 2015) confirm the pervasiveness of the imaginary of wetlands as liminal, marginal, and transgressive. The incommensurability of the wetlands' wetness with Western legal and political aspirations has led colonial governments to initiate large-scale, but often futile, efforts to separate water and land in order to render the colonies productive. Geographer Kuntala Lahiri-Dutt (2014), for instance, suggests that British concerns in land tenure and revenue collection have fueled the engineered transformation of Bengali floodplains into supposedly distinct patches of fluid watercourses and solid ground, the latter to be listed in land registers and taxed accordingly. The physical reengineering of the landscape went hand in hand with a legal reform in land tenure and a societal transformation into a "land-based community" (Lahiri-Dutt 2014, 521).

These accounts all bear witness to how problematic wetness is for a conventional understanding of landscapes. Water as freely flowing substance can be understood in opposition to solid land, but wetness is more difficult to grasp, since it elides common images of water and land. Anthropologist Stuart McLean (2011, 609) suggests that even the term *wetland* "conveys too an unmistakable partiality for terra firma and a concomitant desire to reduce liquidity and wetness to predicates of the solid substance of dry land. What the term wetlands simultaneously references and seeks to contain is precisely the volatility of substance that characterizes such land–water admixtures, their existence betwixt and between clearly differentiated states of matter." The wetness of wetlands is indeed more than an attribute, among many others, of a basically unaffected, solid substrate land (see Gruppuso, this volume). As I will illustrate in the following pages, wetness can be a defining feature of a place, but it is clearly a multiple phenomenon: different wetnesses emerge from people's differently situated projects, histories, and hopes. For tracing wetness as multiple, I take an approach of phenomenological ethnography, attempting to convey the particular experiences and practices that constitute wetness for people in Soomaa, based on intermittent fieldwork between 2012 and 2014, the ethnographic "now" of this text. By paying particular attention to lived experience rather than focusing on symbols, categories, and rules, phenomenological ethnography (see Jackson 1996; Katz and Csordas 2003) is particularly apt to explore how wetness is not a pre-given, objective feature but emerges differently in relation to people's concrete life projects. I shall expand on Ulvi's wetness and then contrast it with the wetness that matters to two other Soomaa inhabitants: Rait, a relative newcomer with a vision, and Algis, who is making a living from tourism.

Addressing amphibious anthropologies through these juxtapositions, I hope to show that in studying lifeworlds between wet and dry, we must not take wetness (and, by extension, dryness) to be a mere physical given. Rather, wetness as a quality of water, as much as of land, is a phenomenon produced relationally in the context of particular people's practices and imaginations. What wetness is, as well as what it means, how it is dealt with, and what it, in turn, does to those encountering it, should not be assumed in a mechanistic understanding of amphibious life. For example, we must not presume that grounds with a higher water content, or more frequent flooding, result in social consequences that can be known beforehand. Instead, the relationships of wetness, sociality, and meaning must be studied as an integral part of research on human life at the interstices of water and land.

## CHALLENGING WETNESS

In Soomaa, wetness is often considered a dilemma, but of course, people have found ways of dealing and living with it. Ulvi's and Harri's strategies for traveling to and from their home are just a couple in a much larger array of such ways. For instance, hay used to be stacked for drying not on the ground but on raised wooden platforms constructed on the meadows. It is risky to make silage on the fields, since it would be ruined by possible floods; therefore, farmers maintain relationships with other farmers whose fields lie outside of the flood-prone area and buy silage off them. Buildings, especially farmsteads, are usually built in higher places, and fields are lined with drainage ditches. While all these techniques make small-scale farming in Soomaa possible, many techniques of dealing with wet ground and recurrent flooding require additional labor and can be incompatible with current economies of agricultural production in Europe, based on small labor and high technology inputs and large scales of land acreage and animal numbers (see Palang and Printsmann 2010).

For example, a part of the reason why Ulvi's land is so wet is that it is poorly drained. Often, a large section of the paddock is covered in water, which also soaks into the adjacent meadows. Ulvi explains that when the farm used to be in better shape, a wooden pipe drained that area into the river. Ever since she has been running the farm on her own, she has been in constant shortage of labor and has not managed to keep up with all the necessary repairs and maintenance, so the pipe clogged up, and the ground is soaked. In addition, the ditches and brooks that used to drain the water away from her land have grown shallow and stagnant. Ulvi is not sure how this happened; perhaps it is linked with the state-sponsored drainage works in the forests around. What she is sure about, though, is that she has neither the means nor the time to restore the former drainage capacity properly. In fact, Ulvi has more than enough work in looking after her horses and cow and maintaining the hay meadows, which provide her with fodder for the animals and some financial support from a landscape conservation program. She just about makes a living from these sources, but not only does she feel poor in relation to the former wealth of the farm; she must also fear for the sustainability of her livelihood, which does not produce enough income for any meaningful investments. For making hay, Ulvi uses the small Soviet tractor from the 1960s that has been on the farm since the time of the kolkhoz, and each summer she hopes that it will not break apart just yet.

Ulvi stores part of her hay in a rather new shed at a small distance from her farm. This, she tells me, had been built as a shelter for cattle owned by an agricultural entrepreneur, who rented local meadows for grazing and haymaking. The entrepreneur, along with his cattle, left Soomaa when he noticed that his business model did not work out, leaving behind the shelter and some unpleasant memories with Ulvi. "His tractor was huge," she exclaims, "like an elephant! It damaged the fields! And the big machinery he used to cut hay left such long stubble that the storks never went there to look for food; they all came here, even though my own fields are much smaller." She explains to me that the wet ground is too soft for such heavy machinery, an appraisal that I repeatedly heard in Soomaa: large tractors both compact the ground and damage the surface, which compromises the quality of the hay.

I enjoy the smell of the hay on the farm, but Ulvi dismisses my enthusiasm. First, she claims, it is not the right kind of grass; in wet years like the previous one, only inferior grasses thrive on the meadows. Second, it has been harvested too late in the year; the landscape conservation program, in which she participates for a little income, prohibits haymaking before midsummer, apparently to protect ground-nesting birds. However, the grass has begun to grow seeds at that stage and lost most of its nutritional value. Lowering her voice, Ulvi confides to me that some of the meadows she is meant to maintain for this program she has not mowed for years. The summers have simply been too wet, and she did not want to get stuck with her little tractor in the soft ground. Furthermore, some of this land is located on the opposite side of the river, and its inferior-quality hay would not warrant the long tractor trips across the next bridge she would have to make in order to harvest it.

When I ask Ulvi why she does not leave Soomaa, sell her land and move into an apartment in the next town, as so many others have done before her, she first presents a string of economic arguments: low real estate value in the park, high living costs in town, little chance to find adequate employment with her background. On another occasion, however, she speaks of her reasons to remain on the farm in quite a different register, which may be as relevant to her staying put as the monetary explanation: now she speaks of the sounds that surround her in Soomaa, the howling wolves and singing birds, and the wonderful silence that engulfs her during high water. Wetness makes part of Ulvi's appreciation of the area's everyday beauty, as much as it features in her list of local challenges.

Indeed, wetness belongs centrally to the narrative of decline that characterize Ulvi's understanding of Soomaa. Her family farm functions as a constant reminder of these developments. The farm's name is Venesauna, which translates as "Russian cabin" and derives from a place a bit into the forest, where a deserter from the tsarist army is said to have lived in the eighteenth century, when Estonia became part of Russia. Local lore has it that during this period, the impassable Soomaa wetlands provided refuge for various people escaping the authorities, including those running away from the quasi-serfdom under the feudal landlords in the agriculturally more productive parts of the country. Before the 1919 land reform that redistributed agricultural land to those having fought in the war of independence and to the former laborers on estates owned by the German-speaking landholding class, there was only sparse agricultural and forestry activity in Soomaa, as the feudal landlords concentrated their labor force in the more productive, drier lands. Alongside the runaways and few peasants, who tried their luck in this peripheral area, a number of families were forcibly settled in a part of Soomaa by a landlord from a nearby estate, eager to develop this wet frontier.

When Ulvi's grandfather founded their farm in the 1860s, this was a remarkable feat in the era before the 1919 land reform, when most Estonian peasants did not own their land. As was to be expected, during the first years, he and his family were struggling with recurrent floods that ruined their crops, but they managed to transform the place into a successful farm with a sizable dairy herd, horse breeding, a smithy, and a mill on the river, with over twenty people living and working in Venesauna. Ulvi emphasizes that the land is rather fertile because of the recurring floods, which means that not only hay but also grain, potatoes, and vegetables grow very well—if only the summers are not too wet. Another villager remembers Venesauna as the largest farm in this part of the village still in the late 1930s, with its own bridge across the river. During the 1920s and 1930s, when Estonia established itself as an independent country, Soomaa experienced somewhat of an economic boom fueled by state forestry and small-scale dairy farming; the village had around 280 inhabitants in 1939, its own school, library, post office, and shop, a cooperative and clubs, and two dairies (Tetsmann 2011, 11–16)!

Then came the Soviet and German occupations during the Second

World War, and the subsequent incorporation of Estonia into the Soviet Union. Ulvi's father, along with many other Soomaa inhabitants, was deported for allegedly resisting the Red Army, or simply for owning a larger farm. Luckier than many others, and probably because he spoke Russian, Ulvi's father survived and returned to the farm in 1955. In the next year, Ulvi was born. By that time, Venesauna had been integrated into the kolkhoz system of compulsory collective farming (see Miljan 2015) and specialized in horse breeding, since horses were still used a lot in agriculture. After a fire devastated the farm in 1956, the farmstead was quickly rebuilt with help from the kolkhoz. The mill and other functions, however, were never rebuilt, as they had become redundant in the kolkhoz division of labor. In spite of these and other drawbacks associated with Soviet rule, Ulvi remembers the kolkhoz period as an enjoyable time. Of course, there was a lot of manual work to do, but at least there was work, and there were people, too, both to work with, for instance in communal haymaking, and to socialize with in meetings and celebrations.

Nevertheless, in successive steps of enlargement of collective production units and divestment in the less accessible areas, people drained out of the peripheries like Soomaa into "centralized villages" (see Annist 2011) and other developing centers with their factories, amenities, and social life. Whereas the early kolkhoz days still had room for horse-drawn agricultural equipment and small-scale, if collectivized, production, the later decades were characterized by ever larger equipment and more centralized forms of production, typical of the high-modernist aspirations of the Soviet economy (see Scott 1998, chapter 6). In the process, Soomaa—where soils were not as productive, large equipment had difficulty operating, and transportation infrastructure was vulnerable, all due to its wetness—was relegated to a peripheral role of hay supplier or calves' nursery for the new production centers. By the time Estonia regained its independence in 1991, few people were left in the village year-round, many of them elderly. Some farms were being used as summer houses; many others were abandoned and decaying or had already collapsed. Similar trends were discernible across the Estonian countryside (see Palang and Printsmann 2010), but areas like Soomaa were particularly hard-hit, not only because the agricultural productivity was compromised by its wetness but also because its floods eroded buildings and infrastructures. The inauguration of the Soomaa National Park in 1993 brought short-lived hopes for local income from tourism (see Tooman and Ruukel 2012), but the little that has materialized has totally bypassed Ulvi. For a while, her personal ambitions lay with the plans, driven by a local NGO, to refurbish the old schoolhouse into a hostel and seminar complex. Dependent on external funding and political priorities, however, this project proceeds only slowly. Furthermore, the road embankment that improved the access of motorized vehicles to the area in the 1970s has changed the local hydrology in a way to channel more water toward the schoolhouse, which has been damaging its foundations and jeopardizes its structural integrity, further complicating the refurbishment plans. Ulvi is not expecting anything from this project before she reaches legal retirement age. In the meantime, the village keeps emptying—in 2014, its population was around ten people.

Wetness, for Ulvi, is foremost a challenge. It is the materialization of her farm's peripheral location and an index of the decay of her village's social life. Wetness includes foregone agricultural income and increased labor and capital inputs. Wetness is a challenge that can be met by collaborating, resolute people, but it can also cause disinvestment, population loss, and abandonment. Amphibious life in wetness-as-challenge means constantly struggling with disadvantageous, even if cherished, conditions.

## DISTINGUISHING WETNESS

One of the ten current inhabitants of the village is Rait, who has lived in and around Soomaa since 2005, when he worked in a hostel close to the park. Interested in local history, he initiated what became known as the Memory Landscapes project to record names and stories of the many places in Soomaa that once bustled with activities, but today are overgrowing with bushes and forest. In the process, he became a heritage specialist for the park, but he left the state service a few years later to start an alternative enterprise together with his friend Anu, another newcomer to Soomaa. Having bought Mardu, an abandoned farm, Rait and Anu are in the process of refurbishing parts of it into studio spaces for visiting designers in residence. Rait, himself a designer by training, enthusiastically tells me how inspiring Mardu has been for him, and how he envisages other designers benefiting from a creative stay at the farm, too. Moreover, he hopes that the designs created during the residences will be made available to craftspeople in the surrounding towns and villages, to complement their technical skills with attractive designs that have, as he calls it, "a sales argument also outside of Estonia." People in the surroundings would benefit from new ideas and designs, and visiting artists would benefit from the particular atmosphere in Soomaa—quiet, empty, natural, and wet. Especially the last attribute sticks out as a distinguishing feature of this place, which is evident both in Rait's verbal descriptions and in the images he regularly posts on Mardu's Internet representations: damp forests, flooded meadows, frozen overflow. There is a lot of beauty in these descriptions and images but also a sense of achievement and stamina.

Like the schoolhouse project on the other side of the village, realizing the Mardu vision is a long work in progress, negotiating funding applications, loan agreements, wood prices, and personal projects. So much needs doing at Mardu, and new issues come up constantly. One winter, Anu and Rait spent a lot of time working on a campaign against large-scale felling in the state forests of the park; before that, they successfully lobbied for renewing the decaying electricity line supplying the village. And of course, Rait is also struggling with wetness. He has bought sheep to graze the meadows around the farm, and he is planning to get a light tractor to work the land—both of these, he says, are suitable for the soft ground. Hay for livestock rearing might be the only crop that his land will produce in the near future, without the risk associated with grain or potato cultivation. Moreover, the tractor still needs financing, and the sheep still live with their previous owner, since Rait has not yet managed to construct a wolf-proof fence at Mardu. In the meantime, he hires one of the other farmers to mow the meadows, but has already noticed how their heavy tractors damage the ground.

Rait is passionate about Mardu, the residency project, and reanimating local heritage. In contrast to Ulvi's farm, the main road across the park passes right in front of Mardu, but Rait is still concerned about wetness. In part, this is because of that very road: built in the 1970s, it repeatedly cuts through the course of a local stream; in some places, the water passes the road embankment through a culvert; in many others, the embankment acts as a dam and creates stagnant pools of water. It completely upsets local hydrology, Rait explains to me, and it creates perfect conditions for beavers that in turn block the drainage ditches on his land so that some of it is much more wet now than it probably used to be fifty years ago. They used to grow rye on those fields, he elaborates; presently, some of them are hardly dry enough to produce hay.

Wet ground and stagnant pools are also perfect breeding grounds for Rait's nemesis in Soomaa—mosquitoes. In the summer, when the water warms up, mosquitoes and other blood-sucking insects are nearly impossible to evade, and they annoy many a human being, particularly those who have moved there from the city. This goes far beyond life in Soomaa and is known to many an anthropologist, at least since Evans-Pritchard's fieldwork among the Nuer on the floodplains of the upper Nile, during which he was "continuously tormented by insects . . . especially by the common black fly and the mosquito" (1940, 67). A Soomaa inhabitant once told me that on warm summer days, when city folk flock the countryside, she and her family rather visit town, where it is possible to sit peacefully outside without constantly fighting off nagging insects. Rait has developed some strategies for decreasing the mosquito density around Mardu, such as cutting back bushes and other vegetation, so that the wind would blow more around the farmstead and keep the insects away. However, with the wet ground all around, he has come to accept mosquitoes as an inevitable part of life in the wetland. In fact, he has developed a humorous stance toward this aspect of Soomaa life: for the fourth year in a row, he and other Soomaa newcomers have been organizing an event in early summer, which they call the "beginning of the mosquito hum concert," celebrating the tragic beauty of wetland summers. The concert has brought various musicians, pop-up restaurants, and microbreweries to Soomaa; the visitors seem to be mostly young families and people from urban, middle-class backgrounds. I have had the chance to attend two of these events, which

I enjoyed very much, not least because of their unique juxtaposition of urban hipsters with a rural setting.

While these visitors come for a day and night and then depart again for their insect-proof homes, Soomaa inhabitants have to get on with the wetness and its mosquitoes. Rait believes that only those people who can arrange themselves with such discomforts can make it in Soomaa; other people would never have come to live here or would have left long ago. He confesses to me that only recently has he parted with his nostalgic perspective on Soomaa. Researching for the Memory Landscapes project, and witnessing the general demise and depopulation of the park, he had long shared the view of many, that the area had seen its heyday in the early twentieth century and had been declining ever since. Now, however, he sees that the area has gone through different phases of denser and sparser population in its history. He explains that around two thousand years ago, the banks of the local rivers had been rather densely populated. Later, during the fourteenth century, people displaced by the crusaders came to live in this area, but the population dropped again with wars and plagues. Around 1900, economic progress and population growth throughout Estonia brought another wave of immigration, which receded after the war and with deportation, industrialization, and urbanization during the Soviet period. The resulting void, in turn, makes it attractive to people like Rait and Anu, their prospective artists-in-residence, and a number of other newcomers with urban backgrounds. This attractiveness, in Rait's understanding, comes through the distinction that living in this place bestows upon its inhabitants. Not everybody has the stamina to do the extra work required to maintain fields and buildings in a wet context, and not everybody can live through summers filled with mosquito hum.

Wetness, for Rait, is a distinguishing feature of Soomaa and its people, setting them off from ordinary rural Estonia and its denizens. It is an environment characterized by solitude and inspiration. Unlike Ulvi's wetness that relentlessly undoes her prospects of social and economic inclusion, Rait's is a wetness that enables creativity, discovery, and focusing on the essential, undisturbed by the crowds of people populating the larger cen-

the agricultural productivity was compromised by its wetness but also because its floods eroded buildings and infrastructures. The inauguration of the Soomaa National Park in 1993 brought short-lived hopes for local income from tourism (see Tooman and Ruukel 2012), but the little that has materialized has totally bypassed Ulvi. For a while, her personal ambitions lay with the plans, driven by a local NGO, to refurbish the old schoolhouse into a hostel and seminar complex. Dependent on external funding and political priorities, however, this project proceeds only slowly. Furthermore, the road embankment that improved the access of motorized vehicles to the area in the 1970s has changed the local hydrology in a way to channel more water toward the schoolhouse, which has been damaging its foundations and jeopardizes its structural integrity, further complicating the refurbishment plans. Ulvi is not expecting anything from this project before she reaches legal retirement age. In the meantime, the village keeps emptying—in 2014, its population was around ten people.

Wetness, for Ulvi, is foremost a challenge. It is the materialization of her farm's peripheral location and an index of the decay of her village's social life. Wetness includes foregone agricultural income and increased labor and capital inputs. Wetness is a challenge that can be met by collaborating, resolute people, but it can also cause disinvestment, population loss, and abandonment. Amphibious life in wetness-as-challenge means constantly struggling with disadvantageous, even if cherished, conditions.

## DISTINGUISHING WETNESS

One of the ten current inhabitants of the village is Rait, who has lived in and around Soomaa since 2005, when he worked in a hostel close to the park. Interested in local history, he initiated what became known as the Memory Landscapes project to record names and stories of the many places in Soomaa that once bustled with activities, but today are overgrowing with bushes and forest. In the process, he became a heritage specialist for the park, but he left the state service a few years later to start an alternative enterprise together with his friend Anu, another newcomer to Soomaa. Having bought Mardu, an abandoned farm, Rait and Anu are in the process of refurbishing parts of it into studio spaces for visiting designers in residence. Rait, himself a designer by training, enthusiastically tells me how inspiring Mardu has been for him, and how he envisages other designers benefiting from a creative stay at the farm, too. Moreover, he hopes that the designs created during the residences will be made available to craftspeople in the surrounding towns and villages, to complement their technical skills with attractive designs that have, as he calls it, "a sales argument also outside of Estonia." People in the surroundings would benefit from new ideas and designs, and visiting artists would benefit from the particular atmosphere in Soomaa—quiet, empty, natural, and wet. Especially the last attribute sticks out as a distinguishing feature of this place, which is evident both in Rait's verbal descriptions and in the images he regularly posts on Mardu's Internet representations: damp forests, flooded meadows, frozen overflow. There is a lot of beauty in these descriptions and images but also a sense of achievement and stamina.

Like the schoolhouse project on the other side of the village, realizing the Mardu vision is a long work in progress, negotiating funding applications, loan agreements, wood prices, and personal projects. So much needs doing at Mardu, and new issues come up constantly. One winter, Anu and Rait spent a lot of time working on a campaign against large-scale felling in the state forests of the park; before that, they successfully lobbied for renewing the decaying electricity line supplying the village. And of course, Rait is also struggling with wetness. He has bought sheep to graze the meadows around the farm, and he is planning to get a light tractor to work the land—both of these, he says, are suitable for the soft ground. Hay for livestock rearing might be the only crop that his land will produce in the near future, without the risk associated with grain or potato cultivation. Moreover, the tractor still needs financing, and the sheep still live with their previous owner, since Rait has not yet managed to construct a wolf-proof fence at Mardu. In the meantime, he hires one of the other farmers to mow the meadows, but has already noticed how their heavy tractors damage the ground.

Rait is passionate about Mardu, the residency project, and reanimating local heritage. In contrast to Ulvi's farm, the main road across the park

ters. Amphibious inhabitation of wetness-as-distinction means going back to the roots in an environment that defies urban lifeways and comforts.

## SPECTACULAR WETNESS

The fact that so many people have indeed left Soomaa during the twentieth century also turns a visit to the area into an inviting "wilderness experience," a slogan that one of the most active tourism operators in the park uses. One of the co-owners of this tourism company is Algis. Together with his wife and two children, he lives next to the Soomaa visitor center in a part of the park that, like the area around Mardu, used to be its own village but, with the population declining, has been incorporated into the same huge village. Driving from Ulvi's farm to Algis's place takes half an hour or more, even if the roads are in good shape. Algis grew up in the area, came to live and work in the park when it was establishing its infrastructure, and earned some extra money as a tourist guide. After a while, he became a partner in the tourism company that sells wilderness experience in Soomaa. The company's main products are bog walks and canoe trips; both of them hinge on local wetness. For the guided tours across the raised bogs in the park, they provide their customers with light snowshoes that keep them from sinking in. Thereby, they facilitate access to a half-land, half-water environment that bears an exotic appeal to the visitors. Algis also encourages visitors to swim in the bog pools, the dark water of which can get rather warm even in Estonian summers.

I have come across many commentaries on the snowshoes that Algis's and other tourism companies use to provide access to the bogs. On the one hand, Soomaa inhabitants recognize an old tradition of snow- and "bog-shoes," so-called *räätsed*, that can be made from a few sticks and bits of rope; every so often, one of the visitor centers or companies in the area organizes a workshop where people are taught how to assemble their own. On the other hand, I have not met a single Soomaa inhabitant who uses such bog-shoes when moving across the bogs, for instance when picking berries. They all assure me that they simply know where to step and where not to; the wetness of some parts of the bog does not mean

## 154 *Krause*

that they would get their feet wet when traversing a familiar landscape. It is only for outsiders that these places are wet wilderness.

The bogs as wilderness are not only beautiful in tourist eyes (see Pungas-Kohv et al. 2015) but also fit well the current ecological imagination of Estonian environmental administrators. Whereas large-scale drainage projects, built mostly during the second half of the twentieth century, had aimed to dry some parts of the bogs in order to extend forestry, the current majority in government and environmental organizations believes in the merits of restoring the bogs to their former wetness by blocking the drainage ditches. Part of this change in attitude can perhaps be linked to the defiance of some of these wetlands to transform into forests through drainage. However, the logic of the national park also plays a role, where wetlands inside its borders are considered worthy of conservation and even restoration, while wetlands elsewhere in Estonia are harvested for peat production. Furthermore, the fact that recalcitrant bogs are no longer drained in futile attempts to turn them into forests does not mean that state forestry is on the wane. Quite to the contrary—Anu, Rait, and a group of other Soomaa inhabitants have recently put a lot of energy into a campaign to temporarily halt large-scale felling plans throughout the park. Their argument was not that there should be no forestry at all in the park but that such major operations should not be executed without a prior study of the area's ecology. Since forestry operations in state forests are contracted to large companies, those in charge of felling trees and laying tracks will have no knowledge of the specificities of the forests; degrees of wetness are an important part of these local specificities. Often, state forest management is blind to such variations, as it divides forests into patches lined by straight access tracks and drainage ditches. And drainage is crucial, even on land that is dry enough to produce economically viable forests. Concerns and conflicts about drainage and waterlogging in Soomaa mirror those about streamflow and beaver dams in California as discussed by Woelfle-Hazard and Sarna-Wojcicki (this volume). When I speak to a family of Soomaa inhabitants who manage some forest, they complain about the great success of beaver reintroduction and conservation in the park. Their main concern is that the beavers are building dams across forestry ditches, which can kill sizable parts of forest as the ground becomes waterlogged. Every now and then, one of them claims, he would take a chainsaw to the forest and purge the beaver dams he would come across.

When I talk with Ulvi about bog restoration, she sounds like she would not mind doing the same with the dams that conservationists have constructed across the former bog drainage channels in the park. These areas, too, are foregone forest plots, she explains. If the drainage schemes have been unsuccessful so far, it does not mean that they are futile; they only needed more time and effort to succeed. Estonia, in her opinion, is too small and poor a country to exclude large areas of potentially fertile land for nature conservation. She looks straight at me and asserts, "Just because they have drained most of the bogs in Germany does not mean that we now have to conserve ours!" I feel that behind this national rhetoric there is a more local concern: Ulvi sees Soomaa as a landscape of work and livelihoods, of economic activity and social interaction, and is critical of all developments that seem to further displace these practices from the park. Rait, on the other hand, is more enthusiastic about bog restoration. He is content that a recent pilot project has proven successful, and that the activities will be extended throughout the park, including the large drains through the bog behind Mardu. For him, wetness on the bog is an asset; only wetness on his farm is a problem.

Algis's, Ulvi's, and Rait's different positioning vis-à-vis wetness brings to mind anthropologist Laura Ogden's (2011) work on the "gladesmen," as she calls the white inhabitants of the Everglades swamps in southern Florida, USA. Life in the Everglades, as Ogden vividly describes it, entails the development of a "mangrove logic" that conforms to the "minor" key and a "rhizomatic" structure of the philosophy of Deleuze and Guattari (1987). This logic, and the gladesmen's essence of wetness implicated by it, is situated in the relative freedom and illicit activities but also the dangers that the Florida swamps afford, and always in tense relationships with state projects of reclamation and conservation. The urban and scientific fascination with the Everglades provides simultaneously a set of opportunities and a series of threats to gladesmen lives. In the Everglades as in Soomaa, wetness emerges from people's various engagements with the landscape, materially and semiotically, and thereby becomes specific things and fosters specific subjectivities.

But let us return to Algis and the other main product of his tourism company—canoeing trips. On the bigger rivers in Soomaa, canoeing is possible for the larger part of the year, that is, when they are not frozen. Algis tells me that during the early years of the national park, many Estonians were quite interested in canoeing through the park, and the business went well. Subsequently, however, this activity became old for many customers, and visitor numbers decreased. Furthermore, the economic downturn with the financial crisis in 2008 meant that business clients—groups visiting the park in the course of well-funded company trips—became sparse, too. It was the floods that helped the company recover, Algis says. The year 2010 and the three subsequent years brought exceptionally high spring floods that caused big media coverage and an exponential growth in visitor numbers. Algis experimented with new canoeing routes, not along the rivers—as many of them were still covered with ice during the highest period of the flood—but through the flooded forests. The exceptionally high water inspired a new slogan for Soomaa as a tourism destination, "the Estonian Amazon" (see Krause 2022). Although the individual floods lasted for only a couple of weeks each, and many potential visitors could not make it to Soomaa since Estonians tend to work and attend school when the area floods in March and April, images and stories about the park and its waters spread. When I talk to Algis in late spring of 2015, he reports that this had been the busiest May since he has worked in tourism, even though there had not been any substantial spring floods since 2013. The image of flooded Soomaa keeps visitors coming, even in drier years.

Wetness, for Algis, is an asset. Wetness materializes in exotic bogs and spectacular floods that attract tourists from all over the country, and indeed the world. Related to tour guiding, renting out equipment, and organizing excursions in Soomaa, wetness means business, the more out of the ordinary, the better. Amphibious work in a tourist destination characterized by spectacular wetness implies anticipating the uncertain dynamics of flooding, freezing, and thawing in relation to the desires and timetables of potential customers from elsewhere.

## CONCLUSION

Ulvi, Rait, and Algis live and work in a landscape that is characterized by different kinds of wetness. It is not only the amount of water on or in the ground that differs in Soomaa. It is the very phenomenon of wetness that varies according to people's activities and outlooks. Wetness can be an asset and a dilemma, challenging progress, forming character, breeding annoyance, or attracting customers. How exactly wetness materializes in people's lives is situated in their particular practices and imaginations, which in turn resonate with current, and often conflicting, societal, political, and economic dynamics. More than an absolute measure of water content, wetness is therefore a relational and emergent phenomenon.

People perceive, judge, and respond to wetness in the context of their particular life projects. For Ulvi, it is part and parcel of her narrative of decline regarding the farm and the village community. For Rait, wetness affords an inspirational environment and a struggle with blood-sucking insects. Finally, for Algis, it distinguishes his tourism destination as the Estonian Amazon. What is more, the kind, timing, and degree of wetness that matter for these three people differ too. Algis, an enthusiastic amateur hydrologist, has defined Soomaa floods as a situation when the one gauge in the park measures a water level of 150 cm or more in one of the rivers. At that level, some meadows are flooded, but it requires a measurement of 300 cm or more before it is possible to paddle through the forest. Ulvi, for her part, is not bothered by a couple of weeks of flooding in spring, even if they inundate her yard. But it is the sustained wetness in her poorly drained ground and the lack of direct access to her neighbors that frustrate her. And while Rait deplores how the road has messed up the hydrology around Mardu, he is keen on the rewetting of the nearby bog.

It may seem apposite to map these tensions onto established categories of social and cultural research. We could, for instance, distinguish wetness in terms of productive activities such as agriculture and consumptive activities such as tourism (cf. Ingold 1992; 2011 for a production-consumption critique), or we could differentiate it according to the perspectives of insiders, who live in Soomaa, and outsiders, who come for visits or appreciate the idea of restored wilderness (cf. Narayan 1993 for an insider-outsider critique). However, Ulvi, Rait, and Algis are all insiders, who also participate in outsiders' discourses, and they are all producing their livelihoods in and through Soomaa, while also consuming its beauty. Therefore, I propose to situate wetness not in such sweeping categories, but in the more concrete social and material relationships through which people come to know and to experience the world. These relationships are directly linked to people's livelihoods, their access to capital, their ability to move, and their preferences and imaginations, as well as to the wider geomorphologies, ecologies, and historical interventions that cultivate particular kinds of wetness. Furthermore, these relationships are necessarily temporal and shift along with the abundance or scarcity of water.

Like water itself, wetness is material but much more than its abstract physicality and emerges as multiple through people's specific encounters with it; rather than predominantly about the comparative mix of water and land, wetness must therefore be understood as a phenomenon relative to people's lifeworlds. I suggest to engage wetness as a lens to transcend explicit or implicit binaries between water and land in approaches to wetlands (see Lahiri-Dutt 2014). Wetness is here to be understood neither as a term in opposition to an assumed "dryness" nor as an attribute of otherwise dry land (see McLean 2011; da Cunha 2019) but rather as an emergent quality linked to particular activities and prospects. As hydrologies are dynamic, and people's activities, too, fluctuate, wetness is a deeply temporal phenomenon, its rhythmicity influenced by the weather as much as by changing and often cyclical human projects (see Krause 2013; Krause 2022). Wetness is not objective but experienced, and this experience is necessarily relational—it can be felt as excessive wetness, poor wetness, or "right" wetness. All of this is material wetness, of course, and necessarily experienced as a biophysical reality with all its characteristics of ground malleability, water content of soil, et cetera. In sum, I propose that wetland life, work, and imaginaries can be better grasped as encounters with wetness than as the juggling of water and land.

Amphibious anthropologies that take this understanding of wetness to heart will not run the risk of framing their object as social and cultural adaptations to an external hydromorphological reality but will cultivate an attention to the relationships that produce different kinds of wetness for differently situated people. An understanding of wetness is key to explorations of amphibious lifeworlds also because it provides an idiom for transcending implicit binaries of land/water or dry/wet. Finally, approaching wetness as situated brings analysis closer to the experiences and challenges of those who make an amphibious living in wet environments and helps us describe and appreciate their particular relations that frame their opportunities, understandings, and dilemmas. In sum, while wetness constitutes a relationally emergent materiality, the people constituting and inhabiting various forms of wetness lead amphibious lives, and researchers may follow suit by approaching wetness through amphibious analysis, as outlined in the introduction to this volume.

Soomaa is definitely wet, and this wetness differs in kind for variously positioned people. As I have illustrated through juxtaposing some of the engagements and attitudes of a few Soomaa inhabitants, the wetness of this land is not a given, objective quality, but multiple and situated in their individual projects and activities, as well as historically manufactured through specific works, technologies, and rationalities. The wetness of wetlands emerges from their relationships with concrete and changing practices and imaginations.

### NOTE

I am indebted to Ulvi, Rait, Anu, Algis, and other Soomaa people for sharing their time and knowledge with me. Earlier versions of this chapter have been presented at the Nordic Geographers Meeting in Tallinn, Estonia, June 2015, and at the conference of the Association of Social Anthropologists in Durham, UK, July 2016; I am grateful for feedback I received in these contexts. This final version has benefited from comments by Hande Ozkan, Alejandro Camargo, Luisa Cortesi, Jason Cons, and Caterina Scaramelli. Fieldwork in Soomaa and drafting of the chapter have been supported by the grants ERMOS146 and PUT 690 from the Estonian Research Council (ETAG) and revising the text by the project number 276392588 of the German Research Foundation (DFG).

## REFERENCES

Annist, A. 2011. *Otsides Kogukonda Sotsialismijärgses Keskuskülas: Arenguantropoloogiline Uurimus*. Tallinn, Estonia: Tallinn University Press.

Barnes, J., and S. Alatout. 2012. "Water Worlds: Introduction to the Special Issue of Social Studies of Science." *Social Studies of Science* 42 (4): 483–88.

da Cunha, D. 2019. *The Invention of Rivers: Alexander's Eye and Ganga's Descent*. Philadelphia: University of Pennsylvania Press.

Deleuze, G., and F. Guattari. 1987. *A Thousand Plateaus: Capitalism and Schizophrenia*. Minneapolis: University of Minnesota Press.

Evans-Pritchard, E. E. 1940. *The Nuer: A Description of the Modes of Livelihood and Political Institutions of a Nilotic People*. Oxford: Oxford University Press.

Giblett, R. 1996. *Postmodern Wetlands: Culture, History, Ecology*. Edinburgh: Edinburgh University Press.

Huijbens, E. H., and G. Pálsson 2009. "The Bog in Our Brain and Bowels: Social Attitudes to the Cartography of Icelandic Wetlands." *Environment and Planning D: Society and Space* 27 (2): 296–316.

Ingold, T. 1992. "Culture and the Perception of the Environment." In *Bush Base: Forest Farm. Culture, Environment, and Development*, edited by E. Croll and D. Parkin, 39–56. London: Routledge.

———. 2011. *Being Alive: Essays on Movement, Knowledge and Description*. London: Routledge.

Jackson, M., ed. 1996. *Things as They Are: New Directions in Phenomenological Anthropology*. Bloomington: Indiana University Press.

Jerstad, H. 2014. "Damp Bodies and Smoky Firewood: Material Weather and Livelihood in Rural Himachal Pradesh." *Forum for Development Studies* 41 (3): 399–414.

Katz, J., and T. J. Csordas. 2003. "Phenomenological Ethnography in Sociology and Anthropology." *Ethnography* 4 (3): 275–88.

Krause, F. 2013. "Seasons as Rhythms on the Kemi River in Finnish Lapland." *Ethnos* 78 (1): 23–46.

———. 2022. "Rhythms of Wet and Dry: Temporalising the Land-Water Nexus." *Geoforum*, no. 131, 252–59.

Lahiri-Dutt, K. 2014. "Beyond the Water-Land Binary in Geography: Water/Lands of Bengal Re-visioning Hybridity." *ACME: An International Journal for Critical Geographies* 13 (3): 505–29.

Limbert, M. E. 2010. *In the Time of Oil: Piety, Memory, and Social Life in an Omani Town*. Stanford, CA: Stanford University Press.

Linton, J. 2010. *What Is Water? The History of a Modern Abstraction*. Vancouver: UBC Press.

McLean, S. 2011. "Black Goo: Forceful Encounters with Matter in Europe's Muddy Margins." *Cultural Anthropology* 26 (4): 589–619.

Miljan, T. 2015. "Collectivization of Farming." In *Historical Dictionary of Estonia*. 2nd ed. Lanham, MD: Rowman and Littlefield.

Narayan, K. 1993. "How Native Is a 'Native' Anthropologist?" *American Anthropologist* 95 (3): 671–86.

Ogden, L. A. 2011. *Swamplife: People, Gators, and Mangroves Entangled in the Everglades*. Minneapolis: University of Minnesota Press.

Palang, H., and A. Printsmann 2010. "From Totalitarian to Democratic Landscapes: The Transition in Estonia." In *Globalisation and Agricultural Landscapes: Change Patterns and Policy Trends in Developed Countries*, edited by J. Primdahl and S. Swaffield, 169–84. Cambridge: Cambridge University Press.

Pungas, P., and E. Võsu. 2012. The Dynamics of Liminality in Estonian Mires. In *Liminal Landscapes: Travel, Experience and Spaces in-Between*, edited by H. Andrews and L. Roberts, 87–102. London: Routledge.

Pungas-Kohv, P., R. Keskpaik, M. Kohv, K. Kull, T. Oja, and H. Palang.. 2015. "Interpreting Estonian Mires: Common Perceptions and Changing Practices." *Fennia-International Journal of Geography* 193 (2): 242–59.

Richardson, T. 2016. "Where the Water Sheds: Disputed Deposits at the Ends of the Danube. In *Watersheds: The Poetics and Politics of the Danube River*, edited by M. Bozovic and M. Miller, 308–37. Brighton, MA: Academic Studies Press.

Robertson, M. L. B. 2016. "The Affects of Water: The Materialized Morality of Wells, Pipes, and Pumps in Tarawa, Kiribati." *Society & Natural Resources* 29 (6): 668–80.

Scott, J. C. 1998. *Seeing like a State: How Certain Schemes to Improve the Human Condition Have Failed*. Yale Agrarian Studies. New Haven: Yale University Press.

Soentgen, J. 2012. "An Essay on Dew." In *People at the Well: Kinds, Usages and Meanings of Water in a Global Perspective*, edited by H. P. Hahn, K. Cless, and J. Soentgen. Frankfurt am Main: Campus.

Tetsmann, J. 2011. *Mis Oli, Mis Tuli. Meenutusi 1950–1990-Ndatest Aastatest Viljandis Ja Kõpu-Tipus, Vaadetega Ka Pisut Taha- Ja Ettepoole*. Viljandi: Johannes Tetsmann.

Tooman, H., and A. Ruukel. 2012. "Sustainable Development of a Remote Tourist Destination: The Case of Soomaa National Park, Estonia." In *Sustainable*

*Hospitality and Tourism as Motors for Development: Case Studies from Developing Regions of the World*, edited by P. Sloan, C. Simons-Kaufman, and W. Legrand, 276–95. London: Routledge.

Walker, G., R. Whittle, W. Medd, and M. Walker. 2011. "Assembling the Flood: Producing Spaces of Bad Water in the City of Hull." *Environment and Planning A* 43 (10): 2304–20.

CLEO WOELFLE-HAZARD / DANIEL SARNA-WOJCICKI

# 6. The Hyporheic Imaginary in Multispecies Watershed Governance

## *How Beaver Collaborations Remix Patterns of Wet and Dry in Northern California Streams*

Over the last decade, United States federal, state and Tribal agency biologists, conservation NGOs, landowners, and grassroots salmon activists have come together around the potential of beavers to recharge groundwater systems, recuperate habitat for salmonids, and support resilient watersheds (Castro et al. 2017). Informal networks of self-titled "beaver believers" have begun assembling at conferences such as the Salmonid Restoration Federation conference in California and the State of the Beaver conference in the Pacific Northwest. The promotion for their documentary, *The Beaver Believers*, sums up their credo: "If we can learn to see beaver as a fabulous partner, rather than a nuisance or a pelt, they can help us restore our watersheds and prepare for climate change, one stick at a time" (Koenigsberg 2018). In this chapter, we consider how collaborations with beavers are reshaping rural livelihoods squeezed in between wet and dry in California communities along two watercourses: the Scott River, in Siskiyou County, in the far north of the state, and Salmon Creek, in Sonoma County on the central coast.

In both basins, groundwater depletion has disrupted streamflows, prompting cascades of ecological changes that then ripple back into human lives via imperiled fisheries, upstream-downstream conflicts, and regulatory debates. Tracing evolving relations between people, salmon, beavers, and water, we explore the emergence of a "hyporheic imaginary"—from the Greek *hypo*, below, and *rheos*, flow—as distinct from yet related to the concept of the amphibious. The hyporheic zone extends from the streambed to the water table under the surface of a stream or river. In this zone of water-saturated sediment, water flows between surface and subsurface, nutrient exchanges occur, and some species live. The hyporheic concept makes visible the connections between groundwater and surface water that support amphibious life and multispecies assemblages along rivers, floodplains, and riparia. Scientific attention to these hyporheic flows has both shaped and been shaped by attempts to enlist beavers as restoration partners to restore salmon habitat, recharge aquifers, and support lush riparian ecosystems.

Thinking with beavers and their amphibious multispecies worlds, we theorize a "hyporheic imaginary" as an articulation of a particularly amphibious environmental imaginary (after Peet and Watts 2002) that is emerging in response to the social and ecological effects of the hyperseparation of rivers and floodplains. In this imagined interspecies amphibious community, people see individual and collective subjectivities as coconstituted with ecosystem dynamics and waterscape materialities. In other words, as they become aware of subsurface flows that connect their aquifers to local streams, some people form relations with more-than-human entities—plants, animals, microbes, gravels, and sediment—that transpire, drink, filter, swim, or are transported through those waters. These relations then shape people's identities, affinities, social relations, and water-use practices. We explore the potential of a beaver-inspired hyporheic imaginary to guide modes of interspecies watershed restoration, and we explore how livelihoods attentive to patterns in the timing and spatial distribution of wet/dry in California waterscapes might be considered "amphibious."

In drawing out a beaver-inspired hyporheic imaginary to think with the amphibious as a multispecies network of relations, we bring together theory from anthropologists, feminist scholars of science and technology, and scholars of Indigenous-settler relations. We draw on our respective collaborative research engagements over the last decade in watershed governance in the Klamath River and Salmon Creek River basins and on extended interviews and participant observation that we conducted around Oregon and California from 2012 to 2014. We trace the different ways Tribal members, activists, scientists, and ranchers mobilize hyporheic imaginaries as they participate in multispecies watershed governance.

In framing this exploration, we ask how beavers can help rural human communities maintain agricultural livelihoods while also stewarding aquatic ecosystems in the face of increasingly extreme cycles of wet and dry. Inspired by Jessica Weir's (in Weir and Murray 2009) analysis of how binaries characterize and constrain Australian settler irrigation projects, we explore how beavers' dam-building activities transgress the sets of binaries underlying California settler groundwater and floodplain management. In this chapter, we argue that beavers transgress and reconfigure a set of constitutive binaries that underpin Western water governance, including wet/dry, surface/subsurface, channel/floodplain, human/nonhuman, terrestrial/aquatic, and the chronopolitical now/later. We then trace recent developments in hydroecological science related to salmon recovery projects and explore the potential of human-beaver collaborations to foster a relational view of watersheds, as made of and by a "manifold commons" of more-than-human beings (Bresnihan 2013). We ask, in conclusion, how these relational perspectives enter into water governance practices and speculate what ecohydrosocial transformations may result.

## RETHEORIZING FLOODPLAINS: SETTING THE STAGE
## FOR AMPHIBIOUS LIVELIHOODS

In California, as throughout the American West, boosters and engineers in the late nineteenth century saw the region's unpredictable precipitation, dry summers, and periodic megafloods as unruly and unproductive. Boggy riparian valleys were considered particularly ripe for reclamation as farm fields. Massive water diversion projects eventually dried up Tulare Lake, California's largest freshwater lake, by 1899, while levees and pumps dried up marshy islands in the Sacramento–San Joaquin Delta (~1861–1973) and "reclaimed" their messy, tangled floodplains for agriculture and urban development (Worster 1985).

In service to agriculture, industry, and urban development, hydraulic engineers from the late nineteenth century to the mid-twentieth century designed physical and regulatory infrastructures to control water's spatial and temporal unruliness and make wet land dry and dry land wet. River valleys were flooded to create reservoirs, deserts were irrigated to create fields and lawns, marshes were drained to create pasture for livestock, and rivers were channeled, diked, and leveed to secure space for human development. As efforts to control unruly floods, these projects exemplify what Tsing (2012b) calls stories of human exceptionalism that emphasize human control of nature, rather than interdependence among species. These river engineering interventions interrupted amphibious lifeways that depended on seasonal flooding, by removing or drying out floodplain wetlands that slowed and held water from winter storms through the long dry summer. Weir and Murray (2009, 14) similarly found that settlers rejected Indigenous understandings that productive multispecies relationships depended on amphibious landscapes created by floods: "Indigenous people speak about water as a web of relations within which life, spirit, and the law are connected, whereas the moderns have created a far narrower vision of water as a resource to be stored, regulated, and allocated for human consumption and economic production." Current water management debates in California arise from tensions around conflicting demands for water against the uneven spatial distributions and temporal rhythms of wet and dry, distributions that are now sedimented into California's dams, levees, and governance structures. As mentioned in the introduction of this volume, with climate change "the wet and the dry are out of control" now in California due to reduced overall precipitation, shorter rainy seasons, reduced snowpack, higher average temperatures, and more extreme heat days (Grantham et al. 2018). One crux of these debates has long been to what extent human water-use practices and infrastructure in such a transformed waterscape can accommodate aquatic species and riverine ecosystems in the face of a changing and unpredictable climate.

Let's consider for a moment how floodplains work. They store water outside of the river channel and, over time, create organic soils that act as sponges. Floodplains facilitate the exchange of water, sediment, and nutrients between land and water, providing warm, shallow, nutrient-rich environments that produce abundant algae that feed productive food webs. By expanding rivers laterally, floodplains increase seasonal habitat for aquatic and terrestrial species. In some sense the floodplain itself is an important part of the river, alternatingly wet and dry on the surface but sustained underneath by constant hyporheic flow.

In the floodplain, water plays one of its most dynamic and vital roles. The channel migration zone (or geomorphic floodplain) is the area across which, over time, flowing water will reconfigure river channels, sediment, and vegetation, creating a dynamic mosaic of wet and dry habitats through time. Floodplains are thus quintessentially amphibious, emerging through dynamic ecohydrosocial relations, brought into being and constantly recreated and transformed by interactions among water, sediment, and numerous species (including humans) (Naiman, Johnston, and Kelley 1988).[1] However, the way floodplains have been managed over the last century of settler colonial management to separate wet and dry for human land/water use excludes multispecies assemblages that depend on particular spatial and temporal (re)mixings of wet/dry. Many floodplains are no longer amphibious because they are separated from their rivers by levees, stream downcutting, or groundwater pumping that dries up the floodplains. Some of the commonness mediated by water is no longer active in these separated floodplains. Rewetting these floodplains and reconnecting them to their streams thus reactivates the hyporheic zone, which in turn reanimates the multispecies commons in amphibious habitats along riverscapes.

Although not amphibians, beavers live amphibious lives, swimming through water to the submerged entrances of their lodges, then passing through water to the dry chamber inside. They depend on water to transport food and building materials and for protection from predators and thus reshape dry land by building dams that create ponds and digging channels between them. These actions, especially in the arid western United States, create more movement between land and water, more swampy zones that blur the sharp boundary between water and land. Therefore, in addition to leading amphibious lives, beavers cocreate amphibious landscapes/waterscapes that remix patterns of wet and dry and support floodplain ecosystems in which a multitude of human and nonhuman watershed inhabitants can also live "amphibiously."

Beavers' amphibious ambitions have the potential to counter human-centered hydraulic engineering in the western United States. As Woelfle-Hazard and Cole (Woelfle-Erskine and Cole 2015) have argued, human waterworks have had the opposite aim of beavers': to separate water from land and river channels from their floodplains, to extirpate marshy indeterminacy and replace it with productive irrigated farmland and efficient channel networks for flood control. Settler colonial water engineering works were founded on a misrecognition of swamps, marshes, and floodplains as a barrier to civilization by settlers who were blind to, or simply did not value, the fundamental ecological productivity of amphibious landscapes. We argue that recent collaborative experiments with beavers open up new ways of understanding and managing the hyporheic zone relationally as a multispecies commons. Similar to the "third space of wetness" referenced in the introduction of this volume, the hyporheic zone offers a space of experimentation with beavers and the multispecies assemblages their river works support, suggesting new possibilities for stewarding rivers and floodplains and redrawing the boundaries of wet/dry in the face of climate change and ecosystem collapse.

## THINKING/ACTING WITH BEAVERS TO BUILD AMPHIBIOUS MULTISPECIES WORLDS

Of all watershed inhabitants, beavers have been most often cast as ecosystem engineers by ecologists and anthropologists and in the popular imagination (e.g., Naiman, Johnston, and Kelley 1988; Wright, Jones, and Flecker 2002; Burchsted et al. 2010; Apple et al. 1985). Among anthropologists, Lewis Henry Morgan was famously infatuated with beavers, especially the relationship between their river engineering works and their social relations (Morgan 1986/1868). From 1855 to 1870, Morgan, along with Ojibwa guides including interpreter Jack La Pete, carefully studied the communities of beavers living near Marquette, Michigan (Feeley-Harnik 1999, 249; Morgan 1986). Gillian Feeley-Harnik (1999; 2001, 55) notes how Morgan's research on beavers' zoogeomorphology and sociality significantly shaped his human kinship research, in particular through the problematic figure "channels of blood," which equated the blood coursing through bodies of living creatures with the rivers flowing through the earth (Feeley-Harnik 2001, 60, citing Morgan 1871/1997 [Morgan 1868/1986], xxiii).

Through years of closely watching beavers rework sediment, vegetation, and river flows to create favorable riverine habitat and homes across generations, Morgan noticed the tightly coupled relations between beavers' riverworks—their dams, lodges, and canals—and beavers' family structures. With the help of his Ojibwa guides, Morgan began to see beaver works and their redistributions of water and land as "articulated semantically" through particular sets of social relations and constructed through generations of beaver families. This eventually led him to posit an interspecies kinship between humans, beavers, and all other life forms in their shared existence as earthy/watery mixes, or temporary tangles of land and water, "bodily articulations of the very earth and water in and through which they lived" (Feeley-Harnik 1999, 256).

Here we hope to contribute to an amphibious multispecies ethnography (Kirksey and Helmreich 2010) that departs from Morgan's investigations in important ways but shares an interest in understanding interspecies relations among beavers and humans and the works, worlds, and ecosystems they collectively create through reworking the boundaries between land and water. Like Feeley-Harnik, we are cautious of Morgan's attempts to transpose a vision of beavers "improving" land and water flows through their everyday engineering activities onto the "cultivation and improvement" of humanity through better breeding and social engineering (Feeley-Harnik 2001, 78–80). Morgan's matter-of-factness in killing beavers for photographs showed that his recognition of beavers as fellow "dividers and gatherers of the water" went only so far (Morgan 1986, 252). However, it was ultimately Morgan's attention to beavers that led him to question "the redemptive value of the deadly appropriation of vital flows of earth, water, and blood" and to develop an alternative "analysis of the intimately entwined fates of human and other creatures" (Feeley-Harnik 2001, 80).

Attentive to the dangers of Morgan's slippery transpositions between beaver and human lives along the land/water interface, we think that critical multispecies ethnography can provide fertile grounds for a more "amphibious anthropology" of more-than-human relations and dynamic interspecies watershed repair practices. Inspired by Laura Ogden's ethnography of beavers in Tierra del Fuego, we see beavers embedded in shifting multispecies assemblages composed of "animals, humans, infrastructure, technology and related discursive logics" and caught up in colonial projects of empire building, territorialization, and global market-making (Ogden 2018, 76). Whereas, in Tierra del Fuego, beavers were introduced to ecosystems as a project of empire building in the mid-twentieth century, in the Scott River and Salmon Creek basins, beavers were eradicated throughout the nineteenth century in order to feed global markets in beaver fur and accomplish settler colonial projects of territorialization. In both cases, colonial attempts to manage beavers caused shifts in multispecies assemblages in local ecosystems and global diasporas of humans and nonhumans, resulting in cascading changes in ecosystems and nonhuman communities alongside shifts in human livelihood practices and social relations. In Tierra del Fuego, eradicating beavers as an "invasive species" has become a top priority for international conservation agencies based on the logic and discourse that beavers are a threat to the forest (Ogden 2018, 72–74). In contrast, in the Scott River and Salmon Creek basins, conservation discourses and strategies have converged over the last decade around putting beavers back into streams.

We look to multispecies ethnographies such as Anna Tsing's (2012a, 2012b, 2014) and Donna Haraway's (2008, 2015) to help us theorize relational multispecies conceptions of watersheds that emerge from the beaver moment and to argue against the human-centric instrumentalization of beavers and their dams we spot in both Morgan's seminal multispecies anthropology and in some contemporary beaver collaborations and conceptualizations of the hyporheic. Against beaver instrumentalism, we argue for seeing the hyporheic zone as what Woelfle-Hazard (Woelfle-Erskine 2014) terms a "multispecies commons," emerging through people's recognition of their shared dependence—along with salmon and other aquatic species—on stream and spring flows. Woelfle-Hazard's interlocutors saw their streams as commons that should be shared among humans and other species; they considered groundwater a hidden connective fluid that connected people to other species via their wells and springs. We demonstrate how, by partnering with beavers to manage the hyporheic zone, human participants are negotiating the wet/dry boundary and challenging what queer theorist Mel Chen terms "animacy hierarchies" (Chen 2012). By reconsidering beavers as "architects" and "engineers" of floodplain ecosystems, discourses of beaver collaboration subvert these hierarchies and can challenge discourses of settler exceptionalism and river-control paradigms (Woelfle-Erskine and Cole 2015).

Rather than promoting instrumentalist appropriations of beaver dams to engineer "better" rivers and/or societies, we highlight the potential of beaver collaborations to open the rich multispecies tangles of living and dying that compose the hyporheic zone. As opposed to command and control approaches that attempted to control the boundary between the wet and dry through rigid infrastructure throughout the twentieth century, we remain attentive to the amphibious abilities of beavers and the humans that work with and learn from them in attempts to restore rivers, reconnect floodplains, and revitalize riparian areas. However, we also wish to remain attentive to power imbalances embedded in different ways of knowing about, relating to, or caring for different species and assemblages of species and habitats. With Ogden, we see these shifting multispecies assemblages emerging relationally within the continuous play of history, culture, and power (2018, 67), always political and entangled with historically constituted ways of knowing and ordering the world. In the context of settler colonial and Indigenous relations, it is particularly important to interrogate the ways multispecies commons are composed and the distributions of benefits and burdens resulting from different configurations of watershed relations and spatiotemporal distributions of wet and dry. Practices of care in the hyporheic space in between the wet and dry along rivers and in floodplains must grapple with histories of colonialism and legacies of dispossession related to resource extraction and remain attentive to the cascading losses that accompany emergent patterns of wet/dry in this age of climate change, ecosystem collapse, and mass extinction. In beaver engagements of the hyporheic zone, we seek new ethical and political frameworks to guide practices of "stewarding the earth in a time of loss" (Ogden 2018, 63) through forging resilient multispecies assemblages in the interstitial spaces and temporalities in between wet and dry (Ogden 2018, 63–64; Woelfle-Erskine 2014).

## CASE STUDIES: BEAVERS AND THE HYPORHEIC ZONE IN SCOTT AND BODEGA BAY WATERSHEDS

### *Scott Watershed*

The Scott River drains a rural five-hundred-thousand-acre watershed in Siskiyou County in Northern California. After leaping out of steep drainages, the Scott tributaries pour into a broad floodplain valley and disappear into coarse alluvium. These subsurface flows recharge a massive groundwater aquifer that provides the main source of well irrigation for hayfields and feeds streamflows that support downstream fish populations. The Scott Valley is home to around eight thousand people and contains around thirty thousand total irrigated acres (Foglia et al. 2013). The Scott River also provides spawning and rearing habitat for endangered coho and spring Chinook salmon, which are an important cultural food for downstream tribes. The six-hundred-acre Quartz Valley Indian Reservation is located within Scott Valley, while the Karuk, Yurok, and Hoopa Tribes' territories are located downstream. Settler and Indigenous livelihoods and resource management practices are positioned in conflict as a result of histories and legacies of colonialism, resource extraction, and land and water management policies that have separated the Scott River from its floodplain and watered cattle ranches and hay pastures at the expense of fisheries (Sarna-Wojcicki 2015). Beavers have emerged as a "boundary object" for translating between different ways of knowing, valuing, and managing the Scott watershed to incorporate a range of cultural values and ecosystem functions into the management of floodplains (Star and Griesemer 1989).

Previously, within the territory of the Shasta Tribe, the Scott Valley has gone through numerous social and ecohydrologic shifts following waves of European settler colonialism and resource extraction. The Scott was first a rich source of beaver pelts during the fur rush (1820s–40s) and then gold during the gold rush (1850s–70s). Many miners who remained in the valley later turned to ranching and logging. The economy of the Scott Valley is now centered on cattle ranching and alfalfa exports. Scott Valley lies squarely within Siskiyou County and the "State of Jefferson," a separatist region in Northern California and Southern Oregon allied around ranching and farming economies, libertarian political culture, and belief in the sanctity of private property.

Historically, each shift in the resource-base of Scott Valley rural livelihoods and political economy brought about a shift in the ecological and hydrologic conditions. From ~1823 to 1841, the Scott Valley was on the periphery of the Hudson's Bay Company's "fur desert policy," a strategy for rapidly trapping out beavers to dissuade American, Russian, and Mexican settlers from encroaching on their fur empire north of the Columbia River (Ott 2003). Hudson's Bay fur brigades extended their reach into the Klamath Basin beginning in their 1826–27 southern expeditions. Hudson's Bay trappers who deliberately created fur deserts noticed immediate effects on rivers and riparian areas, remarking in their notebooks when achieving their goals of "ruining the rivers" and the resulting ecological degradation to riparian vegetation and animal habitats (Ott 2003, 179). Beavers and rivers in the Scott were thus enlisted in colonial projects of empire building, territorialization, and global market-making in the frontier regions of the Pacific Northwest (see also Ogden 2018, 75, and Wolf 2010).

Fur trapper Stephen Meek, who entered the valley in 1836 with Thomas McKay's fur brigade for the Hudson's Bay Company, remarked that the valley was "the best place for beaver I ever saw" (Wells 1881, 80). The valley was described by the brigade as "all one swamp, caused by the beaver dams" (Wells 1881, 44). So abundant were beavers that trappers named it Beaver Valley and the creek that ran through it Beaver Creek. However, the cultural and economic relationships between fur trappers, beavers, and the amphibious worlds that brought them together were organized exclusively around the creation of a fur desert buffer zone of beaver death to protect a burgeoning colonial territory and the rapid extraction of furry wealth via beaver pelts. The attempts to create a fur desert were successful, for when John Scott discovered gold in the valley in July 1850, the beavers had been mostly trapped out, and the place became known from then on as the Scott Valley.

In addition to a new political economy centered on mining and ranching, the transition from Beaver Valley to Scott Valley was accompanied by a massive ecological and hydrologic shift from a swampy marsh and meadow mosaic to a network of incised channels, many of which dried up by the end of the summer. In the Scott, as in many other basins around California, hydraulic mining and gold dredging scoured floodplains away or buried them twenty meters deep in tailings. During the mining era, the creeks of the Scott were dammed, diverted, and rechanneled. Their beds and banks were sluiced away and deposited hundreds of yards from their former channels. Many river channels in the watershed are still separated from their floodplains due to mining-era river engineering, depriving salmon and steelhead of critical habitat and refugia.

Following devastating floods in the 1930s, the US Army Corps of Engineers straightened portions of the Scott's mainstem, removed vegetation, and built levees for flood control. The flood control networks fixed the boundary of the river and facilitated development and ranching in the floodplain. Ecologically, this resulted in channel simplification and incision, reduced habitat heterogeneity, disrupted flow regimes, and created barriers to fish passage. Groundwater withdrawals for pasture irrigation dramatically increased in the second half of the twentieth century. As Van Kirk and Naman (2008, 1046) describe, irrigation withdrawals increased 115 percent and irrigated land area increased 89 percent from 1953 to 2001, with most of the increased supply coming from groundwater resources (3 percent in 1953 vs. 80 percent in 2001). As a result of wells drilled into the valley alluvium, base flows in the Scott mainstem have declined significantly, and sections of the river now dry up completely in the low-flow periods of late summer, stranding salmon and steelhead, depleting oxygen, and eliminating the drift of insect prey from upstream.

## Bodega Bay Watershed

The Bodega Valley, formed by upthrust seabeds dating to the Cretaceous, is underlain by a faulted mélange of rock types that create extreme water scarcity on some ridgetops and valley floors, while in other areas springs flow abundantly from sandstone aquifers. Ridgetop redwoods capture coastal fog, while on lower slopes, Indigenous Pomo and Miwok people's cultural burning created a patchwork of oak savannah, prairie, and chaparral. Indigenous inhabitants and beavers managed riparian corridors for different purposes: people burned riparian forests periodically to keep them open as travel corridors, while beavers coppiced alder and willow trees to favor the new green growth they eat.[2] The Pomo and Miwok in this area signed no formal treaties during the 1800s but were recognized in the 1920s, when land was set aside for a small settlement. After undergoing legal termination of Indigenous status in the 1950s, the Federated Indians of Graton Rancheria fought until 2000 to regain Tribal status. They currently comanage several state- and county-owned lands in Sonoma County, though none lie within Bodega Valley. Italian immigrants bought up large ranches around the turn of the twentieth century and then sold off parcels of cut-over redwoods to newcomers beginning in the 1960s. In the coastal ranges, loggers stripped redwoods from the steep hills and dragged or sent them barreling downstream on floodwaters. Valley bottoms were parceled out into smaller ranches, and cattle grazing denuded many riparian corridors.

Several ranches were sold to wealthy hippies in the late 1960s and became important centers of the San Francisco counterculture; three of these properties are still extant, and their residents translate between their rancher neighbors and newer urban and retiree residents and have been instrumental in the local land trust, watershed council, and conservation initiatives. In the Bodega Valley, with only a shallow aquifer, pastures remained unirrigated, but subdivisions on cut-over redwood forest ridges (and a few ranches) tapped sandstone aquifers or spring-fed tributaries.

## THE ECOHYDROLOGY AND POLITICAL ECONOMY
## OF BEAVERS IN CALIFORNIA

By the 1840s, the fur rush had stripped many of the watersheds of California almost entirely of their ecosystem engineers, successfully transforming it into a "fur desert" (Wolf 2010). Early settlers were blind to the ecological value that beaver dams created for their companion species, such as salmon hiding in backwaters during El Niño floods and staying cool in deep pools during the hot summer. Salmonid populations managed to thrive in tune with the region's extreme annual swing between massive flood and harsh drought. The beaver's hyporheic interventions had buffered highly variable flows, and people and other animals ate well from the lush riparian landscape, including Tribal members and trappers who hunted and fished their way through beaver valleys. But with the beavers trapped out, and their dams dynamited or sluiced away, floodwaters scoured out the rich meadow soils and riparian willow forests, eroding gravelly streams into deep gullies.

Beavers' lives unfolded very differently in the Scott and Bodega Valleys. In the Scott, some beavers eluded trappers by hiding out in a slough in the valley, where they were found by the California Department of Fish and Wildlife (CDFW) agents in the 1930s (Tappe 1942). Recognizing that streams downstream of these beaver dams flowed longer into the summer, wildlife agents imported more beavers from the nearby Shasta River during the 1930s to raise water tables depleted by drought and pumping (Tappe 1942). These early beaver translocations employed beavers strategically and instrumentally to support human needs for late-season irrigation for pasturage. Beavers continued to expand their ranges in the valley in the 1930s, but were stymied by drought, flash floods, and active trapping by ranchers, who considered them nuisances when their dams blocked irrigation canals or flooded fields.

In Bodega Valley and nearby coastal watersheds, beavers did not escape the more intensive trapping and agricultural development. Post–European contact, no wild beavers inhabited any creek in Sonoma County until the mid-1990s, when they swam up the Napa River into Sonoma Creek, further to the east. The Bodega Valley is thus typical of most parts of coastal California and the Sierra Nevada, in that few people knowingly share river valleys with beavers. Most see gravelly, meandering streams as natural, rather than as scars of systematic beaver removal, deforestation, and cattle grazing. Beavers are only slowly recolonizing landscapes transformed by their absence; as they return, they encounter a more regulated riverscape whose management is largely determined by a hydrologic science that, until recently, has not accounted for beavers' activity as hydrologic agents.

The regulatory policy around beavers in California in the first half of the twentieth century oscillated between protecting beaver populations from extirpation and mitigating what were perceived as their negative effects on property (Sarna-Wojcicki 2015). Currently, beavers are listed in California as both fur-bearing mammals and nuisance species, meaning that trapping and killing is allowed for recreational and commercial purposes at certain times of the year. In addition, if a landowner can demonstrate that beavers are damaging their property, a CDFW trapper will come to their property and trap, remove, and kill the "nuisance" beaver. In the Scott Valley, where the beaver population is still fairly low, only a handful of beavers are killed each year. In Salmon Creek, where some people desire more beavers in their backyards and streams, current regulations forbid beaver translocations due to other people's fear of property damage and disease transmission; this policy is being actively contested by "beaver believers" in the region. In the Sacramento–San Joaquin Delta, where beavers are seen as direct threats to agricultural production, thousands of beavers are killed each year (California Dept. of Fish and Wildlife 2009).

## BEAVERS, BEAVER BELIEVERS, STOCHASTICITY, AND HYPORHEIC FLOWS

Salmon science, spurred by precipitous declines in salmon runs after the mid-twentieth-century dam building craze, laid the groundwork for the flourishing of beaver ecology studies that catalyzed the turn to beavers among scientists, activists, policymakers, and landowners. Over the last forty years in California, landowners' rights to use water for irrigating pasture and growing cattle has been severely curtailed by court decisions regarding Tribal fishing rights, endangered species listings, water right adjudications, and regulatory policy related to water quality and streambed alterations. Courts and state and federal water and wildlife agencies try to find a balance between requiring minimum flows to sustain fisheries and supporting irrigation-dependent agricultural economies. However, this balance between water for crop and pasture irrigation and water for in-stream ecological use has proved tenuous, and numerous legal and regulatory conflicts have ensued.

This inability to strike a balance between farms and fisheries has inspired us to theorize ways in which rural livelihoods in California can become more amphibious—similar to Fals Borda's amphibious cultures, or "material-semiotic assemblages of ecologies, technologies, practices, and beliefs" (see introduction to this volume and Fals Borda 1979) that are both more resilient to extreme wet/dry cycles and more enabling of timings and distributions of wet and dry that support resilient aquatic ecosystems. We, along with many beaver believers, hydrologists, ecologists, and zoogeomorphologists, see how beavers can help farmers and ranchers live more amphibiously and better buffer the ecological damage caused by rural livelihoods.

Shifts in hydrological and ecological science over the twentieth century were coconstituted with shifts in how scientists and land managers thought about and acted toward beavers. The first shift was from furbearer to habitat maintenance tool (e.g., Ruedemann and Schoonmaker 1938; Beard 1953). In the 1930s, wildlife agencies restricted trapping and reintroduced beavers into desiccated Dust Bowl landscapes (sometimes by airplane) to combat erosion and raise water tables (Heter 1950). The second shift—from instrumental tool to ecosystem engineer—arose from a shift in how ecologists understood landscapes. Whereas midcentury biologists saw beavers as an erosion control tool that could promote game and sustain grazing in a static habitat mosaic, for late-century ecologists, beavers had become "ecosystem engineers" that could be enlisted (without pay) to rehabilitate stream and riparian habitats and reconfigure networks of interspecies relations (e.g., Naiman, Johnston, and Kelley 1988; Wright, Jones, and Flecker

2002; Burchsted et al. 2010; Apple et al. 1985). Beaver dams' rerouting of hyporheic flows became central to this new conception, as scientists who were studying the new field of groundwater–surface water interactions encountered beavers in the field and noted how their dams slowed down and spread out stream discharge, thereby allowing water to infiltrate into the subsurface, only to reemerge downstream cooler and with life-supporting mixtures of carbon and nutrients after its passage through the substrate.

In studies of habitat for salmon and other riverine species, hydrologists and ecologists have tracked beavers' profound introduction of dynamism and stochasticity into streamflow patterns: as beaver dams fill with sediment or blow out, an ongoing play of shifting floods, pools, and bars redistributes water and sediment (e.g., Naiman, Johnston, and Kelley 1988; Benda et al. 2004; Stanford, Frissell, and Coutant 2005; Burchsted et al. 2010). Beavers began to be seen as reknitting watershed relationships that had unraveled after their brutal removal. These relationships include other species, like the salmon, trout, and lamprey eels that died in droves at the base of human-made dams, blocked from reaching their spawning grounds, as well as terrestrial animals such as deer, elk, and migratory birds that forage, calve, nest, and make homes in the riparian vegetation around beaver dams.

As these two concepts—hyporheic flows and stochasticity—have circulated within scientific discourse and percolated out into lay science and advocacy communities/networks, they have shifted people's sense of relation to beavers, salmon, and even water itself. Through a process similar to what Peet and Watts (2002) termed the formation of an environmental imaginary, individual and collective subjectivities are reimagined in relation to other species and waterscapes. Elsewhere, Woelfle-Erskine and Cole (2015) explored the implications of a "stochastic imaginary" infecting engineers with beavers' river-engineering logics. Here, we do the same for the "hyporheic imaginary," drawing on two distinct cases of local groundwater governance that have enlisted beavers as hyporheic stewards and change-agents.

Coming face-to-face with beavers emerged again and again in our conversations with beaver enthusiasts as a pivotal moment in the reshaping of relations between particular people and their local beavers. Through field trips at conferences and chance encounters during fieldwork, scientists and advocates came face-to-face with beavers and saw beaver ponds full of young steelhead and coho salmon, challenging fish biologists' orthodoxy that beaver dams block spawning salmon. Meanwhile, a few Scott ranchers had noticed that in years when they did not destroy beaver dams, streams flowed through the fall. One rancher who did not have time to tear out a beaver dam one year noticed that the stream stayed wet downstream. From then on, the rancher "pretty much let 'em do their thing."

In this moment of recognition, some people related to beavers as family-oriented creatures or as nonmonogamous queer kin-makers, others because of their industrious dam-building, and still others at a more visceral level, describing their soft fur, bright eyes, and sleek dives. These encounters were then communicated, via photographs, stories, and videos on websites and at conferences to other beaver enthusiasts and translated into a potential for interspecies relations. This potential resonated for people living in beaverless landscapes like Salmon Creek as a kind of Edenic return to a wilder and more stochastic landscape. For people living among beavers, including our Scott Valley interlocutors, the story of coming face-to-face with beavers often involved rerecognition of earlier watershed states and processes and a renewed perspective on the human role in stewarding land and water for nonhuman others. However, landowners, watershed councils, and federal and state agencies continue to debate the benefits and downsides of beavers in relation to human property and livelihoods through knowledge conflicts and regulatory policy debates.

## THE "BEAVER TURN" IN SCOTT AND BODEGA WATERSHEDS

### Scott Watershed

In the midst of heated regulatory battles between fisheries advocates (who wanted more water in stream) and ranchers (who wanted more water on their pastures), collaborations with beavers emerged as an alternative way of producing knowledge and managing groundwater in the Scott Valley. In 2011, the Groundwater Advisory Committee, made up of Scott Valley ranchers and landowners, invited Michael Pollock (an ecosystem analyst and beaver expert at the NOAA, the National Oceanic and Atmospheric Administration) to give a presentation. One interviewee described the Pollock presentation as a "wow" moment for the community and a turning point in Scott Valley landowner interest in beavers.

On May 7, 2013, some beaver believers presented to the Siskiyou County Board of Supervisors on how beavers could assist stream restoration efforts in the Scott watershed. At the meeting, the chairman of the watershed council advocated for beavers by referencing Beaver Valley: "Scott Valley owes their wonderful soil and everything else to beaver. It was Beaver Valley before it was the Scott Valley." However, at the same meeting, a trapper from the US Department of Agriculture voiced concerns about the potential negative impacts of beaver dams due to bank erosion and the possibility that "beaver populations [would] get too big and need to be thinned" (Bowman 2013). These discussions about the moral and legal status of beaver were in many ways directed through the prism of human interest. For example, one County Supervisor remarked that they were "skeptical of the effectiveness of beavers as a watershed tool" because they "heard negative stories from several people about the animals interfering with irrigation ditches and other agricultural operations" (Bowman 2013).

While the politics of beaver-based restoration were being debated by county supervisors, beaver advocates set up field experiments and developed hydrologic models to try to demonstrate beavers' hydroecological and social benefits. Beginning in summer 2014, the Watershed Council and Groundwater Advisory Committee partnered with Pollock and designed an adaptive field experiment in the Scott. Their "Beaver Dam Analogue" (BDA) project creates a remarkable material-semiotic technology, experimental infrastructure, and multispecies assemblage through pounded posts to help beavers set up dams at sites in the Scott where impacts on groundwater level, water temperature, fish habitat, and sediment retention are being monitored by multiple instruments (Charnley 2018). Preliminary results show dramatic increases in habitat size and juvenile salmonid abundance

(3,000 percent on average), but efforts to build more BDAs have been slow due to onerous permitting regulations and lack of funding (Charnley 2018).

In August 2016, we visited Sugar Creek, a tributary of the Scott River that flows through kilometers of deep mine tailings and frequently goes dry in late summer. There we met a motley crew tagging and monitoring coho salmon behind the BDAs — a retired USFWS biologist, the Scott River Watershed Council director, a Karuk Fisheries biologist and two trainees, and a high school student from a ranching family. The Karuk crew pulled a seine through a deep, wide, and cool pool directly upstream of a beaver dam analogue, scooping hundreds of fish into buckets. Back on the bank, we helped the crew identify, weigh, measure, and tag the coho, steelhead, and Chinook salmon fry. Birds sang in the thick willow and maple forest that had grown up in the tailings, and when we waded out into the stream, the icy water came up to our chests, a shock in the blazing sun of the thirty-nine-degree day. This series of beaver dam analogues has been colonized, maintained, and expanded by beavers and has raised groundwater levels at least 300 m out into the floodplain, where the watershed council measures groundwater levels in small monitoring wells (Charnley 2018). Further downstream, the Karuk Tribe and the Mid-Klamath Watershed Council have begun studying and working with beavers and beaver dams to restore stream and off-channel habitat for salmonids in the Karuk Tribe's ancestral territory downstream from the Scott (Harling 2010, 2013). The authors are currently partnering with the Karuk Tribe Natural Resources Department's Wildlife Division and two UW Capstone students, Maddison Hicks and Hannah King, to codesign beaver population and habitat survey tools to study the impacts of dam removal on beavers and better enroll beavers in river, floodplain, and riparian restoration practices in Karuk Aboriginal Territory.

## Bodega Watershed

In the Bodega Valley and surroundings, a deepening drought from 2011 to 2015 sparked renewed interest among residential and agricultural water users in connections between local aquifers and Salmon Creek. This stream harbors two anadromous salmonids, steelhead trout and coho salmon, and dries to a series of intermittent pools (separated by dry streambed) during the summer. In years when rainfall is average or better (~1,150 mm/year), both species survive in these pools, because hyporheic and shallow groundwater flow into the pools sustains oxygen levels, but in very dry years, when flow between pools dries up in early summer, less than 5 percent of the fish survived through September (Woelfle-Erskine, Larsen, and Carlson 2017).

Leading up to the drought, settler intervention had transformed the watershed into a much drier and less-hospitable place for aquatic species. Logging, grazing, road-building, and exurban development all created a less pervious landscape, increasing winter runoff and reducing the amount of water stored in ridgetop aquifers, in soil and duff, and in the former floodplain. Well-drilling and pumping from streams further dehydrated the landscape. The Gold Ridge Resource Conservation District (RCD) had for a decade or so been working with landowners to heal some of these wounds, providing funds and technical expertise to residential and agricultural residents to regrade roads to infiltrate runoff, fence livestock out of riparian areas, and build engineered logjams in streams.[3] For decades before this, however, the RCDs, flood control agencies, and the California Department of Fish and Wildlife had been bulldozing all debris from the streams every year, destroying fish habitat and increasing the stream's erosive power. Just before the drought, a partnership among the RCD, the watershed council, and a local NGO had focused on reducing summer pumping from Salmon Creek, paying for tanks and large ponds to store rainwater as an alternative irrigation source.

At a 2012 workshop Woelfle-Hazard coorganized with collaborators for local residents, participants agreed on the general shape of this history. But they differed in their opinions about which settler transformations of the watershed had contributed most to drying out the stream and to salmonid decline. In breakout groups that we and UC Berkeley colleagues facilitated, longtime residents and farmers were more likely to blame past logging and the massive floods of 1982 for salmon disappearance. More recent residents blamed residential development and vineyard water use, though they did not necessarily think their own water use was significant enough to affect fish. Fish biologists tended to see decline as "death by a thousand cuts," or attributable to multiple cumulative effects, but highlighted the disconnection of rivers from floodplains as a negative feedback loop that decreased groundwater storage, increased storm flows, and therefore degraded both winter and summer habitat.

Many of the participants had attended a recent workshop on beavers, hosted by Kate Lundquist of the Occidental Arts and Ecology Center's beaver project. She and codirector Brock Dolman were (and remain) die-hard beaver believers working to change state wildlife codes to allow beaver relocations onto state and private lands. They had found historical evidence of beaver occupation nearby but were seeking archaeological evidence of beaver dams along Salmon Creek and nearby streams, and they distributed flyers asking people to tell them about beaver sightings and chewed sticks or other dam artifacts. At both Lundquist's workshop and ours, participants held different opinions of beavers. None had direct experiences of beavers, and compared to landowners in the Klamath, most found it hard to imagine the problems beavers might cause or how their neighbors might react to their presence. This was true of agriculturalists as well; because there are no irrigation ditches and few commercial orchards near the floodplain, beavers' tree felling and dam building seemed less threatening, perhaps. One resident thought that local knowledge of managing other wildlife could be extended to living with beavers and thought that their return could contribute to the recent resurgence in wildlife he had noticed: "We see now, there's coho in there, and otters, and turtles . . . there was a deficit of wildlife there from 2002 to 2008 or 2009, but it's coming back now. It's really good to see."

Some participants, mostly those already familiar with the harmful effects of low flows on salmon, seemed to see beavers as a missing piece that could solve all of the problems with disconnected floodplains simultaneously. They saw regulatory hurdles as the biggest barrier, and they suspected that since beavers traveled so far, they were likely to be shot or trapped by unsympathetic landowners. Their excitement at beavers' recolonization potential referenced an Edenic landscape, untrammeled by settlers and their capitalist greed and wanton wreckage. All the dry streambeds, all the old mistakes would be flooded behind busy beavers' dams and give way to blue pools teeming with salmon yet presumably still interspersed with houses and gardens and all the other accoutrements of settler inhabitation. In imagining this return of beavers, some participants spoke of a renewed connection to the groundwater and a renewed sense of belonging to a watershed of interconnected flows.

However, this imagined pre-European settler landscape was not inhabited and governed by Pomo or Miwok people, nor did anyone advocate for decolonizing moves (such as recognition of Graton Rancheria's treaty claims, land transfers, or comanagement efforts) as part of restoring water flow through the landscape. For example, one government scientist echoed residents' lament of the lack of presettlement ecological knowledge. He said, "We have no ecological memory any older than we are. None of the living landowners have ever seen a functioning floodplain. It's hard for them to support something [like beaver reintroduction] they can't imagine." However, when Woelfle-Hazard asked local residents and scientists whether Graton Rancheria Tribal members might have knowledge to fill in these gaps, respondents stated that local Tribal members had "lost" their culture and ecological knowledge. To us, this exchange (which repeated, with minor variations, dozens of times during Woelfle-Hazard's six years of fieldwork in the area) demonstrates that settler colonial modes of thought can operate through beaver-inflected hyporheic imaginaries as readily as they do through existing engineering imaginaries.

## CONCLUSION

Through relations to beavers, two California communities have been able to articulate a hyporheic imaginary that allows them to make sense of connections between land use and water quality, surface and groundwater, and human and nonhuman worlds. As emerging hyporheic imaginaries recruit beavers and their dams to rehydrate dewatered California streams, they reconfigure rural livelihoods, economies, and political cultures as well as patterns in the timing and spatiality of wet and dry in California watershed communities. Recent ecohydrosocial experiments with beavers open new ways of understanding and stewarding the hyporheic zone across species lines, across the channel/floodplain boundary, and across the groundwater/ surface water divide, for both agricultural and environmental values and for use both now and later. However, as we demonstrated, the articulations of human-beaver relations through the hyporheic imaginary also displayed a tendency toward instrumentalizing beavers and beaver dams as a means to sustain human livelihoods and maintain a settler-dominated landscape. Beavers and their dam-building practices can potentially serve as an entry point to discussions about impacts of resource extraction and agrarian settler colonialism on floodplain ecocultural systems but only if they include Indigenous representatives and take place alongside discussions about decolonization, land rematriation, and cultural revitalization to fully address the legacy impacts of colonial land and water management. Power imbalances resulting from the marginalization and dispossession of Indigenous communities must be addressed to account for different communities' abilities to produce knowledge deemed credible by resource management agencies and prioritize which assemblages of species and habitat conditions to manage and restore for in beaver-engaged floodplain rehabilitation projects.

Similarly, beavers, beaver dams, and beaver dam analogues should not be applied uncritically as a solution to floodplain management in the Scott or Salmon Creek watersheds. Against human-centric instrumentalizations of beavers, we conclude by emphasizing the importance of grounding the hyporheic imaginary and beaver collaborations in an amphibious and multispecies ethnographic practice. We are inspired by the transgression of binaries that beavers accomplish, and beavers are good companions for thinking about and theorizing an amphibious anthropology. By remixing spatial distributions and temporalities of wet and dry, blurring the boundaries between land/water, channel/floodplain, surface/groundwater, now/ later, human/nonhuman, beavers inspire new modes of water governance and new ways for humans to relate and belong to watershed communities. Beavers help humans reconceptualize stored and infiltrated groundwater as water that supports habitat for others now and emerges downstream as habitat for others later in the season. In articulating a hyporheic imaginary that makes sense of connections between land use and water quality, surface and groundwater, human and nonhuman worlds, beavers inspire new modes of multispecies amphibious livelihoods along California rivers. A beaver-inspired hyporheic imaginary provides fertile grounds for a dynamic interspecies mode of knowledge-making, water governance, and earth repair, provided it can remain attentive to the diverse ways that individuals and communities in the Scott and Salmon Creek watersheds understand, value, and form relationships with beavers and to the power dynamics that underscore the evaluation of risks and benefits in the context of floodplain rehabilitation.

As an alternative to Morgan's figure of the "channels of blood," we close with reference to a more entangled (Barad 2007) discourse within ecology that recognizes salmon carcasses as a crucial source of marine nitrogen to upland forests, granting salmon the status of keystone species, whose absence makes the whole arch collapse (Power et al. 1996). Although salmon, unlike beavers, cross over into the terrestrial realm only in death, to consider them amphibious in their afterlives and in this broader sense that we are elaborating in this volume transfigures and performs the material connectivities among living organisms and their constituent elements and relations across the perpetually shifting wet and dry spaces of floodplain ecosystems. The amphibious can bring to light a dynamic, relational ecology in which humans' and other species' bodies are, if briefly, containers for the elements that circulate endlessly via water through the landscape and waterscape. Attention to love of multispecies watershed communities and pain of wounds to those loved landscapes and particular plants and animals can, to use Thom van Dooren's (2010, 273) phrase, make a "generative opening, drawing us into the tangle of accountabilities that emerge inside multispecies communities of living and dying."

Such an approach to amphibious anthropology revisits Morgan's work on beaver dams as rich sites for multispecies ethnography, as transmuters of land and water and vital crossover points between "human, animal, vegetable, and mineral worlds," with an "astonishing capacity to spawn new life" (Feeley-Harnik 2001, 59–60). As Feeley-Harnik demonstrates, the beaver dams of Marquette created a matrix of watery earth, animate bodies, and everyday life that allowed Morgan to view the "human body as derived from and returning to dust" and therefore a "kind of land that could be drained, watered, cultivated, channeled, and fertilized" (2001, 78). However, against instrumentalist appropriations of beaver dams to engineer better rivers and/or society, we see in beaver dams and ponds rich multispecies cascades of living and dying that compose the hyporheic zone and the potential to guide collaborative watershed restoration for multiple species, habitats, and human communities, in and out of the river channel, above and below ground, in floodplain ecosystems and along riparian corridors.

Taking a cue from Haraway, Tsing, Weir, Ogden, and others, we see beaver-engaged floodplain rehabilitation as an opportunity to decenter narratives of control of nature that infuse watershed science and governance. An amphibious anthropology of watershed relations rejects the rigid demarcations of the channel and levee to account for the messy entanglements of beavers, salmon, cows, hay, humans, and flows of water and sediment that constitute floodplain ecosystems and watershed communities. Our account of a beaver-engaged hyporheic imaginary brings attention to the ways in which humans and nonhumans collectively remix spatial patterns and temporal rhythms of wet and dry along California streams. As we have shown, it is critical to remain attentive to the ways that power, culture, and the histories and legacies of settler colonialism and resource extraction shape and constrain river restoration opportunities. Foregrounding Tribal watershed stewardship, land rematriation, and cultural revitalization is critical in the process of healing rivers, reconnecting floodplains, and rehabilitating riparian areas to recover from colonial fur deserts. Supporting Tribal sovereignty over hyporheic flows can work toward repairing multispecies assemblages that also help heal relationships with Indigenous communities and build resilience to planetary ecological disaster and climate change. Working with Indigenous communities to decolonize the river, floodplain, and its supporting hyporheic flows can enable flourishing amphibious multispecies commons, with beavers leading the way, one stick at a time.

## NOTES

1  Among other ecologists, Naiman, Johnston, and Kelley write of beavers and other floodplain species like cottonwoods as "ecosystem engineers." We are interested in the discursive potentials of this term, while recognizing the dangers of co-opting other species into anthropomorphic roles. Woelfle-Erskine and Cole (2015) investigate this transgressive potential of ecosystem engineering further.

2  Coppicing is a practice used for willow, alder, poplar, and related species: the tree is cut down < 1 m above the ground, and the tree responds by sending out many branches of fresh growth. People typically practice coppicing to secure straight, flexible branches for basketry; beavers strip the leaves and bark off the succulent branches, then add them to their dams.

3  Resource Conservation Districts are local entities active primarily in rural areas to provide technical assistance and grants to landowners. They descend from the federal Soil Conservation Service, which was created during the Dust Bowl of the 1930s to promote erosion control.

## REFERENCES

Apple, L. L. 1985. "Riparian Habitat Restoration and Beavers." In *Riparian Ecosystems and Their Management: Reconciling Conflicting Uses*, edited by R. R. Johnson, C. D. Ziebell, D. R. Patten, P. F. Ffolliott, and P. F. Hamre, 489–90. General Technical Report RM120. Fort Collins, CO: USDA Forest Service, Rocky Mountain Forest and Range Experimental Station.

Barad, K. 2007. *Meeting the Universe Halfway: Quantum Physics and the Entanglement of Matter and Meaning*. Durham, NC: Duke University Press.

Beard, E. B. 1953. "The Importance of Beaver in Waterfowl Management at the Seney National Wildlife Refuge." *Journal of Wildlife Management* 17 (4): 398–436.

Benda, L., N. L. Poff, D. Miller, T. Dunne, G. Reeves, G. Pess, and M. Pollock. 2004. "The Network Dynamics Hypothesis: How Channel Networks Structure Riverine Habitats." *BioScience* 54 (5): 413–27.

Bowman, J. 2013. "Beaver Valley." *Siskiyou Daily News*. October 5, 2013.

Bresnihan, P. 2013. "John Clare and the Manifold Commons." *Environmental Humanities* 3 (1): 71–91.

Burchsted, D., M. Daniels, R. Thorson, and J. Vokoun. 2010. "The River Discontinuum:

Applying Beaver Modifications to Baseline Conditions for Restoration of Forested Headwaters." *BioScience* 60 (11): 908–22.

California Dept. of Fish and Wildlife. 2009. *Animals Taken by Component, Method Type and Fate by Wildlife Services in California.*

Castro, J., M. Pollock, C. Jordan, G. Lewallen, and K. Woodruff. 2017. *The Beaver Restoration Guidebook: Working with Beaver to Restore Streams, Wetlands, and Floodplains.* US Fish and Wildlife Service. https://www.fws.gov/oregonfwo /ToolsForLandowners/RiverScience/Documents/BRG%20v.1.0%20final%20 reduced.pdf.

Charnley, S. 2018. "Beavers, Landowners, and Watershed Restoration: Experimenting with Beaver Dam Analogues in the Scott River Basin, California." Res. Pap. PNW-RP-613, 38, 613. Portland, OR: US Department of Agriculture, Forest Service, Pacific Northwest Research Station.

Chen, M. Y. 2012. *Animacies: Biopolitics, Racial Mattering, and Queer Affect.* Durham, NC: Duke University Press.

Fals Borda, O. 1979. *Historia Doble de La Costa.* Vol. 1, *Mompox y Loba.* Bogotá: Carlos Valencia Editores.

Feeley-Harnik, G. 1999. "'Communities of Blood': The Natural History of Kinship in Nineteenth-Century America." *Comparative Studies in Society and History* 41 (2): 215–62.

———. 2001. "The Ethnography of Creation: Lewis Henry Morgan and the American Beaver." In *Relative Values: Reconfiguring Kinship Studies*, edited by Sarah Franklin and Susan McKinnon. Durham, NC: Duke University Press.

Foglia, L., A. McNally, C. Hall, L. Ledesma, R. J. Hines, and T. Harter. 2013. *Scott Valley Integrated Hydrologic Model: Data Collection, Analysis, and Water Budget.* Final Report. University of California, Davis. http://groundwater .ucdavis.edu.

Grantham, T., et al. 2018. *North Coast Summary Report: California's Fourth Climate Change Assessment.* Publication number: SUM-CCC4A-2018.

Haraway, D. J. 2008. *When Species Meet.* Minneapolis: University of Minnesota Press.

———. 2015. "Anthropocene, Capitalocene, Plantationocene, Chthulucene: Making Kin." *Environmental Humanities* 6 (1): 159–65.

Harling, W. 2010. "Restoring Coho Salmon in the Klamath River, One Beaver at a Time." Unpublished Manuscript. Mid-Klamath Watershed Council.

———. 2013. "Coho Rearing Habitat Projects in Seiad Valley Show Promising Results." *News from the Mid Klamath Watershed Council.* Spring.

Heter, E. W. 1950. "Transplanting Beavers by Airplane and Parachute." *Journal of Wildlife Management* 14 (2): 143–47.

Kirksey, E., and S. Helmreich. 2010. "The Emergence of Multispecies Ethnography." *Cultural Anthropology* 25 (4): 545–76.

Koenigsberg, Sarah. 2018. *The Beaver Believers*. Walla Walla, WA: Tensegrity Productions. https://www.thebeaverbelievers.com/.

Morgan, L. H. 1868 [1986]. *The American Beaver and His Works*. New York: Dover.

Naiman, R. J., C. A. Johnston, and J. C. Kelley. 1988. "Alteration of North American Streams by Beaver." *BioScience* 38 (11): 753–62.

Ogden, L. A. 2018. "The Beaver Diaspora: A Thought Experiment." *Environmental Humanities* 10 (1): 63–85.

Ott, Jennifer. 2003. "'Ruining' the Rivers in the Snake Country: The Hudson's Bay Company's Fur Desert Policy." *Oregon Historical Quarterly* 104 (2): 166–95.

Peet, R., and M. Watts. 2002. *Liberation Ecologies: Environment, Development and Social Movements*. London: Routledge.

Power, M., David Tilman, James A. Estes, Bruce A. Menge, William J. Bond, L. Scott Mills, Gretchen Daily, Juan Carlos Castilla, Jane Lubchenco, and Robert T. Paine. 1996. "Challenges in the Quest for Keystones Identifying Keystone Species Is Difficult—but Essential to Understanding How Loss of Species Will Affect Ecosystems." *BioScience* 46, no. 8(September 1): 609–20.

Ruedemann, R., and W. J. Schoonmaker. 1938. "Beaver-Dams as Geologic Agents." *Science* 88 (2292): 523–25.

Sarna-Wojcicki, D. R. 2015. "Scales of Sovereignty: The Search for Watershed Democracy in the Klamath Basin." EScholarship. January 1, 2015. http://escholarship.org/uc/item/3tk5r3w2.

Stanford, J., C. A. Frissell, and C. Coutant. 2005. "The Status of Freshwater Habitats." In *Return to the River: Restoring Salmon Back to the Columbia River*, edited by Richard N. Williams. Academic Press.

Star, S. L., and J. Griesemer 1989. "Institutional Ecology, 'Translations' and Boundary Objects: Amateurs and Professionals in Berkeley's Museum of Vertebrate Zoology, 1907–39." *Social Studies of Science* 19 (3): 387–420.

Tappe, D. T. 1942. *The Status of Beavers in California*. State of California Dept. of Natural Resources Division of Fish and Game Bulletin No 3.

Tsing, A. 2012a. "Contaminated Diversity in 'Slow Disturbance': Potential Collaborators for a Liveable Earth." In *Why Do We Value Diversity? Biocultural Diversity in a Global Context*, edited by G. Martin, D. Mincyte, and U. Münster. *RCC Perspectives*, no. 9, 95–7.

———. 2012b. "Unruly Edges: Mushrooms as Companion Species." *Environmental Humanities*, no. 1, 141–54.

———. 2014. "Blasted Landscapes (and the Gentle Arts of Mushroom Picking)." In *The Multispecies Salon*, edited by Eben Kirksey, 87–110. Durham, NC: Duke University Press.

van Dooren, T. 2010. "Vultures and Their People in India: Equity and Entanglement in a Time of Extinctions." *Manoa*, no. 22, 130–46.

Van Kirk, R. W., and W. S. Naman. 2008. "Relative Effects of Climate and Water Use on Base-Flow Trends in the Lower Klamath Basin." *Journal of the American Water Resources Association (JAWRA)* 44 (4): 1035–52.

Weir, J., and K. Murray. 2009. *River Country: An Ecological Dialogue with Traditional Owners*. Canberra: Aboriginal Studies Press.

Wells, H. 1881. *History of Siskiyou County, California*. Oakland, CA: D. J. Stewart.

Woelfle-Erskine, C. 2014. "Thinking with Salmon about Rain Tanks: Commons as Intra-actions." *Local Environment* 20 (5): 581–99.

Woelfle-Erskine, C., and J. O. Cole. 2015. "Transfiguring the Anthropocene: Stochastic Re-imaginings of Human Beaver Worlds." *Transgender Studies Quarterly* 2 (2): 297–316.

Woelfle-Erskine, C., L. G. Larsen, and S. M. Carlson. 2017. "Abiotic Habitat Thresholds for Salmonid Over-Summer Survival in Intermittent Streams." *Ecosphere* 8 (2) e01645: 1–23.

Wolf, E. R. 2010. *Europe and the People without History*. 3rd ed. Oakland: University of California Press.

Worster, D. 1985. *Rivers of Empire: Water, Aridity, and the Growth of the American West*. Oxford: Oxford University Press.

Wright, J. P., C. G. Jones, and A. S. Flecker. 2002. "An Ecosystem Engineer, the Beaver, Increases Species Richness at the Landscape Scale." *Oecologia* 132 (1): 96–101.

PART III

Through the Muck

CÉLINE GRANJOU / STÉPHANIE GAUCHERAND

# 7. Restoring Wetlands in Alpine Ski Resorts
## *The Biopolitics of Water, Land, and Snow*

Contrasting with the close rocky slopes interspersed with thorny bushes and scrub, a grassy flat area scattered with packs of strange wool-like white flowers swinging in the wind seems to be waiting for the lone hiker willing to plant her tent there for the night. Despite those seemingly welcoming charms, the soil of such a place may reveal itself to be unexpectedly loose and wet for those who try to walk across it in summer: this is indeed a typical Alpine wetland in which water circulates both in the close underground and aboveground, sustaining the life of water-loving frogs, dragonflies, reeds, cotton grass, and many other amphibious species.

Wetlands are often compared to big sponges storing water when it rains too much and releasing it when it is dry, simultaneously improving water quality and purity. As deltas, coastal ecosystems, and flooding rivers considered in this collective volume, wetlands compel us to reconsider conventional ideas about water and land as separate elements (Krause, Cortesi, and Camargo's introduction to this volume). They are amphibious ecosystems that mix and hybridize land and wetness in various, shifting proportions, depending on the seasons and rains. But while "many places are becoming wetter, forcing people to learn how to manage inconsistent and threatening waters" (Krause, Cortesi, and Camargo's introduction to this volume), marshes and wetlands have long been buried or drained and dried up, as they were viewed in terms of unhealthy and unproductive sites: the fragile mix of land and wetness that constitutes them has been deeply unsettled by trampling, water diversion, or damming. Yet today wetlands and peatlands are increasingly considered as fragile and endangered sites in need of attention and care. Though wetlands have already been protected by the international Ramsar Convention (Convention on Wetlands of International Importance) since 1971, their role in hydrological patterns (water circulation and filtering) and ecological functioning (habitat for amphibious biodiversity) was more recently emphasized in the Millennium Ecosystem Assessment (MA 2005) and is attracting a growing interest from mountain managers and researchers.

Far from being a fixed and given property, wetlands' amphibious character is thus a fragile, collective enactment of "keeping the land wet," as Paolo Gruppuso made clear in chapter 4 (see also chapter 9 on wetlands by Alejandro Camargo). Here we aim to address the practices, material objects, technologies, regulations, and worldviews contributing to enacting wetlands as fragile and functional places in need of attention and care, thus contributing to this volume's inspiring collective project of unpacking the "experiences and meanings of living in environments of ever shifting wetness" (Krause, Cortesi, and Camargo's introduction to this volume) in times of environmental and social changes.

How did wetlands come to be seen and dealt with, formerly as unproductive, unhealthy, and disgusting areas—their destruction considered as part of the "move toward civilization" (Fromageau 1998)—and now as fragile, beautiful, and highly functional ecosystems? Our contribution unpacks the material and discursive place-making processes that have been turning wetlands into functional wet lands in need of attention and care. Ecological functionality has become a powerful category justifying the development of a new politic of conservation with a strong emphasis on the functions and "services" rendered by ecosystems and biodiversity, yet little attention has been given to the types of material and affective encounters involved in (re)making nature as ecologically functional and productive in the field, and which sort of biopolitics is involved.

Drawing on a case study of wetland restoration in Val Thorens, a ski resort in the northern French Alps, we argue that this new status of wetlands is not reducible to the outcome of new constraining environmental legislation or to any sudden ethical conversion to environmentalism by local inhabitants and managers.[1] Instead, we would like to emphasize how people started to see wetlands differently through the progressive implementation of a range of material and discursive technologies that contributed to enacting wetlands as functional and productive sites. Our contribution is thus located within a growing body of "new-materialist" literature aiming to think about how materiality comes to matter in relation to situated practices and relationships (Bennett 2010), including by focusing on the livingness and agency of nonliving nonhumans such as water (Krause and Strang 2013). Our focus on environmental managers' work and how it "configures how and what environments are" is in line with recent literature on environmental management as situated practice (Lippert, Krause, and Hartmann 2015).

Our key point is that the transformation of those long feared and neglected areas into new places worthy of interest and conservation entails a hydrobiopolitics built on making "nature work" and rendering it productive and functional. The Foucauldian notion of biopolitics, first developed to account for technologies of governing the life of human populations, was recently discussed and extended to consider also nonhuman life (Lorimer 2015; Braverman 2016). Compared with the biopolitics of species conservation studied by Braverman, which consists in ordering species through a range of valuation and hierarchization operations, in our case local negotiations also entailed a range of decisions regarding which wetlands would be reanimated and restored, and which ones could not be saved. However, the case of wetland restoration and conservation highlights a biopolitics which is not only about letting die and making live but also about making a site ecologically productive; that is, identifying valued ecological functions and services like water filtration, water containment, water storage, and habitat for biodiversity, and making the place "work" as best as possible regarding the fulfillment of those functions and services.

Our contribution is grounded in a sociological investigation of wetland management and restoration in the Val Thorens ski resort, located in the northern French Alps in the county of Savoie. We draw on eighteen semistructured interviews with local managers, council representatives, inhabitants, and scientists, supported by observation during meetings and fieldwork.[2] The investigation results are also backed up with a reflexive approach to the personal experience of one of the authors, who is an ecologist and was personally involved in the wetland management program in Val Thorens: her involvement was part of a broader reorientation move of her research in land ecology toward a long-term program of research and restoration of wetlands and peatland.

## A SHORT ENVIRONMENTAL HISTORY OF VAL THORENS WETLANDS: FROM ERASURE TO RECOGNITION

The recent history of the Alpine ski resort of Val Thorens reflects the recent, broader requalification of wetlands as functional and biodiverse places. Val Thorens is part of a group of huge ski resorts built in the 1970s, when skiing was becoming increasingly popular. These new ski resorts, which are also called "third-generation ski resorts," were built in very high and isolated parts of the mountains in order to provide an increasing number of skiers with ultramodern and convenient facilities; that is, ski runs, ski lifts, and accommodation at the foot of the slopes (Marcelpoil and Langlois 2010).[3] Val Thorens ski resort is part of the mountain village called Saint Martin de Belleville, which is still today one of the wealthiest municipalities in France due to the international attractiveness and economic dynamism of its ski resorts (the two biggest ones being Val Thorens and Les Menuires). The village population has been increasing over the recent years (with one-quarter of the incoming people coming from abroad). It includes about 3,800 local residents, most of them being people working for tourism, senior executives (including working from home), and retired people, and only a very small number of farmers.

Because building high-altitude ski resorts entailed building new sites ex nihilo to accommodate tourists, leveling land for the longest possible ski runs, and using the most powerful ski lifts, those ski resorts had huge impacts on mountain landscapes, biodiversity, and ecosystems. In the case of Val Thorens, the environmental damages generated by the ski resort became a public matter of concern and contest at the end of the 1960s, when the expansion plans of the ski resort managers led to a national conflict between the ski resort and the Vanoise National Park, on the territory of which part of the ski resort is located (the episode is known as the Vanoise scandal).[4]

Since the building of Val Thorens ski resort, most local wetlands and peatlands have been considerably reduced, damaged, or even destroyed—as in most Alpine ski resorts. The ski resort itself was built on a big wetland that was totally destroyed in the process. In France, it is estimated that wetland area has decreased by more than 65 percent between 1950 and 2000, both in the lowlands and in mountain areas (Fromageau 1998). As early as the eleventh and twelfth centuries, wetlands were drained by monks in order to convey water to their mills and abbeys; in the sixteenth and seventeenth centuries, vast areas of wetlands were dried up because of fear of unhealthy fumes and contamination; once dried, they were cultivated (for more details on the historical requalification of wetlands, see Vileisis 1997 and Scaramelli 2021). In addition, in the northern Alps, wetlands tend to occupy flat areas, which are the most convenient sites for building roads, villages, or ski lifts.

As the ski resort was progressively expanded, wetlands were dried up in order to make available flat and convenient places to build ski lift stations and "easy" ski runs for beginners. Even where the wetlands were not dried up, their functioning was deeply disturbed and their biodiversity endangered by the diversion of water deep underground in order to build an increasing number of big water reservoirs. Because of the increasingly frequent lack of snow in winter due to climate change, those reservoirs have been used to produce artificial snow for the ski runs—reinforcing the links between Alpine wetlands and snow, which is and is not water at the same time, in their amphibious ability to blur the distinction between water and land. Wetlands were also often damaged by the use of snowcats for ski run maintenance: when flattening the snow, snowcats also compact the soil, and they can sometimes scratch deeply into the soil (Delgado et al. 2007). To make things worse, those ski runs that are located on wetlands need more preparation and flattening than others precisely because the presence of water fosters the formation of dangerous ice patches when it is cold and the formation of humid, treacherous snow when it gets warmer. The wetland called La Moutière, for instance, was one of the biggest and ecologically most sensitive wetlands in the ski resort and hosted hundreds of protected frogs. It had its functioning increasingly disturbed between the 1990s and the beginning of the 2000s by the construction of a ski run equipped with installations for producing artificial snow, ski lifts in the immediate surroundings, as well as a dirt road and a landing strip for mountain planes on the flat wetland (Gaucherand et al. 2010).

In 2006, Val Thorens ski lift company (i.e., the company that gets the financial benefits from skiing) was planning to build a new water reservoir for producing artificial snow in an area including a protected plant species (*Viscaria alpina*). In a context when the legal requirements related to the French application of the rule of mitigation were becoming stronger, the ski lift company had to carry out an environmental impact assessment that resulted in a requirement to compensate for the local destruction of the species.[5] Among other things, the ski lift company was required to complete a wetland inventory and finance a study to better understand the causes of wetland degradation within the ski area. The company was also legally required to better take wetlands into account in the further development of the ski infrastructures. In addition, the ski lift company voluntarily chose to restore the wetlands located in the ski resort when possible (i.e., insofar as it did not impact the ski activity). These efforts were in line with a broader requalification of wetlands since the 1970s, when they came to be seen as ecologically functional places fulfilling a number of crucial functions under the influence of environmentalists, particularly bird lovers. In France, the Ramsar Convention protecting big wetlands was signed in 1986, and two European directives for the protection of biodiversity and habitats (the Habitats Directive and the Birds Directive, published in 1991 and 1992) also fostered more attention to wetland biodiversity, as wetlands' role of hosting a number of particular and often sensitive and endangered species is also very often put forward.

Val Thorens ski lift company thus became involved in financing a range of local inventories and scientific studies of wetlands as an offsetting mechanism. Following the first county inventory, the local council of Val Thorens adopted a program to protect local wetlands with the help of the Conservatory of the Natural Heritage of Savoie, an organization in charge of monitoring and conserving nature in the Savoie County, with the help of the Vanoise National Park.[6]

The realization of increasingly refined inventories of the local wetlands made it clear that Val Thorens was located in one of the richest areas in terms of wetlands and peatlands in Savoie County (i.e., with the highest concentration of wetlands).[7] A local steering committee for managing wetlands was implemented, and the Val Thorens council developed a strategy to buy as much land as possible on which wetlands had been identified.

In order to help explore the possibilities for restoring wetlands' liquid functionalities and reanimating them as habitats for a range of living beings, the ski lift company contacted ecologists from the Research Institute for Environment and Agriculture (IRSTEA) in Grenoble, including one of the authors of the present contribution and her students. She had been trained in land ecology, and her previous research was dedicated to terrestrial vegetation—following the strong land/water division that still exists in ecological sciences between the research networks and journals devoted to studying land and those devoted to studying water. In the same way as they have been erased from local mountain landscapes and ecologies, wetlands have also tended to be forgotten in the research agendas of ecology, as the discipline has been organized along a long-lasting opposition between land and water, without paying attention to those in-between sites and beings located in the trading zone between land and water. Her growing interest in studying and helping restore Alpine wetlands in Val Thorens is telling of the shift of the status of those in-between places from a "non-place" (Augé 1995) to a "special" place worth of interest, efforts, and protection. Her initial involvement was linked to the feeling that it might be more efficient to try to protect the environment in places in which it is indeed degraded, rather than to focus on nature reserves only. Achieving small but critical results for nature conservation by identifying the ski infrastructures and practices causing the degradation and negotiating their modification with ski lift managers was part of her interest in getting involved. Her new research into wetlands also led her to acquire new knowledge and skills in hydrology, in order, for instance, to become able to use water probes.[8] Part of the challenge associated with this new research has been that of becoming able to document the functioning of the subterranean part of the wetland ecosystem and to "have some idea of what happens to this water underground."

The ecologists implemented a two-year study funded by the ski lift company in order to document the wetlands' status and the causes of their degradation and for the writing of a management plan, including the prioritization of restoration efforts and environmental guidelines for ski development,[9] with major consequences on shifting understandings and practices regarding local wetlands.

## HYDROLOGICAL TECHNOLOGIES: MAKING WETLANDS INTO BEAUTIFUL, FRAGILE, AND FUNCTIONAL PLACES

As suggested by a Vanoise National Park employee, wetlands have changed: "Wetlands were not part of . . . [our concerns]. We did not care about them particularly until two years ago. Today it's quite different." How, and to which extent, did wetlands come to matter in local inhabitants' and managers' everyday practices and activities? How did they become part of the world that "counts" not only for the scientists, the local conservationists, and the community council representatives but also for a number of local farmers, ski lift operators, snowcat conductors, and passing tourists? We argue that this shift may be conceived as the outcome of the implementation of a range of techniques and practices by which new aspects and meanings of the wetlands have come to be "activated" (Hawkins 2010, 120) — even though not with the same power for all of the people frequenting Val Thorens ski resort.

Here we take inspiration from Gay Hawkins's elaboration of how plastic bags have come to be seen as ethically "bad" through the actions of say-no environmental campaigns (Hawkins 2010). Hawkins argues that this new attitude to plastic bags should not be understood as a consequence of new environmental awareness. Instead, it is linked to a new situation in which matter itself (plastic) is enacted as bad and guilty: "say-no campaigns activate specific aspects of the materiality of the plastic bag" (Hawkins 2010, 123). Hawkins's key point is that "things have a capacity to assert themselves" (122), as specific aspects and meanings of their materiality are enacted through the different situations and associations in which they are embedded. Following her line of thinking, we argue that also wetlands are not a "passive object of reclassification with ontologically fixed properties"; instead, the shift in how they are considered comes from the fact that they "are materialized or dematerialized through different habits and associations," thus generating "a diversity of responses" (Hawkins 2010, 119). Say-no campaigns extended the ethical imagination of shoppers to the afterlife of plastic bags and established new connections with images of wildlife choking and beaches covered in waste. In a similar way, wetland restoration and conservation measures contributed to enmeshing wetlands within a range of meanings and images, for example, cotton grass, which has now become an iconic image representing the beauty of mountain wetlands. In the same way as plastic bags, wetlands have been historically enmeshed in various situated networks of associations by which they have come to matter in different ways.

The scientists from the Research Institute for Environment and Agriculture first introduced a range of material objects and infrastructures aiming to have ponds and surface water back in the wetland — let's call them hydrological technologies. The ski lift managers, who are used to realizing hydrological works in the resort, helped the scientists to design and implement works and infrastructures in order to modify the local flows of water and restore the wetlands. In the case of La Moutière wetland, the place had been partly dried up with drainage ditches and the water reoriented into the depth of the earth with shortcuts avoiding its stagnation at the surface of the soil. This resulted in splitting the wetland into two parts, one of which was completely isolated from water circulation and destined to die. Part of the wetland had also been buried by rocks and sediments conveyed by an upstream creek. Scientists decided to set up a pipe underground in order to bring the water back to the surface of the isolated part of the wetland, thus restoring and maintaining the flux of water needed for the ecological functioning of the wetland. The scientists also dug up a ditch at the entrance of the wetland in order to redistribute the surplus of upstream water. Instead of quickly running through the land within a single stream, the water is now diverted into smaller, slower creeks, as well as standing surface water and still, quiet ponds.

In a wetland located in Les Menuires, a ski resort very close to Val Thorens, on which a ski run for beginners was placed, removable locks were implemented by the scientists in order to stop the drainage and retain the water in the wetland during summer—and to continue to drain it in winter (figure 7.1). Underground pipes were also placed in different wetlands in order to have the water back from aboveground creeks that had been deepened and equipped with dikes.

Hydrological technologies are supported by biological technologies aiming to restore the vegetation in the wetland through planting and growing water-loving local species, using nets to protect the young plants very similar to those that are sometimes used in replanting sand dunes or eroded trails and paths. For the scientists involved in this work, these technologies clearly contribute to associating wetlands with imaginaries of life and plant growth.

In addition, discursive and communication technologies contributed to associating wetlands with new meanings and imaginaries also for local inhabitants and tourists. For instance, the scientists gave the names of the closest ski lifts (such as La Christine, Genepi, etc.) to Val Thorens wetlands, in order to be able to distinguish between them and to communicate easily with ski managers. A number of meetings and communication events were organized by local actors and groups involved in wetland restoration in order to explain the importance of local wetlands to local inhabitants, emphasizing particularly their role for water quality and water availability. The Val Thorens council explained the program of wetland restoration and conservation in its local news bulletin, *Belleville Infos*. Scientists communicated about the wetlands to the local mountain guides. A sign on the wetland site informs skiers and tourists of the existence of the ecosystem and its biodiversity, including in winter, when it is hidden under the snow. Nature trails were also implemented by the council in order to explain to tourists and local inhabitants what a wetland is, how it works, what its biodiversity looks like, and why it is worth conserving. Many of those communication initiatives use the now-popular vocabulary of ecosystem

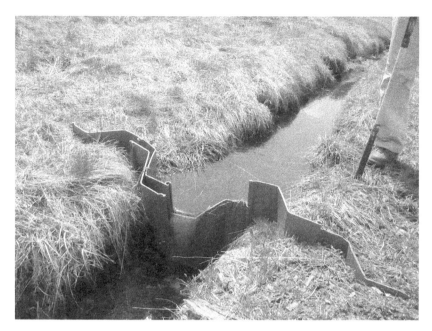

FIG. 7.1. Removable locks as placed by scientists on a wetland in Les Menuires ski resort. Photo by Stéphanie Gaucherand.

FIG. 7.2. Plantation of two herbaceous wetland species (*Trichophorum cespitosum* and *Eriophorum scheuchzeri*) to restore bare peat. The wooden planks limit peat erosion, and the straw protects the growth of young plants. Photo by Stéphanie Gaucherand.

services, defined by the Millennium Ecosystem Assessment as the services rendered by ecosystems to society, which insists that healthy ecosystems are vital to human well-being and social development (MA 2005).

Though some of the local inhabitants already knew of the localization of wetlands,[10] a number of new associations have been created in which wetlands are bound with trails, signs, names, and discourses on amphibious functionality—that is, the capacity of wetlands of slowing down and storing water in ponds and forming standing water, also allowing for the growth of specific biodiversity, and releasing water when it is dry. This communication aims to allow local actors and passing tourists to develop a feeling of how water gets filtrated through its slow journey through the vegetation of the wetland and of how the aspect of the place changes with the seasons and depending on the amount of water stored underground and aboveground. The scientists studying Val Thorens wetlands found that such aspects were of particular interest to the local people: "Speaking in terms of biodiversity is not sufficient because the people already know about it . . . issues of water quality, regulation of floods, and reduction of water's erosive strength are much more telling for the people," said a scientist involved in Val Thorens wetland restoration.[11]

Local actors got interested in the functionalities of wetlands for various reasons. The national firm in charge of the drinking water network (the Lyonnaise des Eaux company) has been especially sensitive to the question of water filtration because it had realized that works at high altitudes often make the water turbid in the rivers: consequently, the firm needs to pay to purify the water again. Ski lift managers have been more interested in the capacity of wetlands to reduce the local creeks' strength downstream: with storms, creeks can indeed cause floods, which can destroy ski runs, causing small landslides or even damaging inhabited areas. Local farmers are interested in wetlands in case of droughts, because they are then the only places that remain green and still have grass for the animals to graze. A member of the Conservatory of the Natural Heritage of Savoie emphasized the way recent droughts contributed to this interest: "In 2003, the drought made it very clear which areas remained green and were still interesting: those were the places which were still wet, and farmers are well aware that those wet areas are really of interest. . . . In 2003, the Conservatory was asked to open its wetlands for grazing because there was nothing left to eat for the herds because it was so dry. Yet the wetlands were still green; there was still grass: we implemented agreements with the farmers for their animals."

It remains difficult to measure the effects of wetland restoration. Yet there are a number of clues and anecdotes that suggest the role of restored wetlands in the reduction of landslides, the better quality of water, and the mitigation of drought episodes. Anecdotes include a case in which, as the scientists were explaining the benefits of wetland restoration to local actors (including the firm in charge of the drinking water network, ski lift managers, and local inhabitants) during a field trip in the ski resort, a restored wetland was found capable of cleaning the dirty water of an upstream creek containing a lot of sediments generated by ski run works. All the people present could see that, as part of that very cloudy creek was redirected into the wetland and made into slow and quiet surface water, the water coming out downstream of the wetland was perfectly clear and possibly clean enough to drink. In this occasion, the ski lift managers told the scientists of the flooding of the same place, which brought part of the soil of the ski run with it and required costly work to reconstruct it, and expressed the idea that such events and their consequences might be reduced by the restored wetlands.

The program of restoration and conservation thus contributed to transforming relations to wetlands and to constituting particular subjectivities as regards their value and their beauty. Since restoration measures were implemented, La Moutière wetland has been described as one of the most "spectacular" wetlands in the ski resort by a ski lift manager, who called it a "beautiful and big place in which one can see water running." Most local actors perceive degraded wetlands as ugly places that they associate with bare land, erosion marks, soil that tends to collapse, and dark water. In contrast, nondegraded or restored wetlands are recognized thanks to the dark green color of the vegetation, the flat surface, and the presence of cotton grass.

A number of interviews with ski lift managers, especially older ones close to retirement, suggest the awareness of wetlands' "fragility" and the decision to stop previous "damaging" practices. One of them, a lady in her sixties who was responsible for hygiene, safety, and environment-related issues in the ski lift company, explained, for instance: "Before, we drove through the wetlands with excavators . . . now we avoid them . . . and we are also careful not to block the watersheds." The associate director of the ski lift company, who was a man also in his sixties, explained that a number of former practices have been modified in order not to disturb the wetlands: "When we replace the ski lift poles, we are careful not to place the new poles in a wetland; anyway, the study forbids us to do to it. . . . The wetland is located between two ski runs and we were damaging this place with the snowcats, especially in spring, when we needed to shovel the ski runs up there, that was a handy place because it does not destroy the snowcats: that's why we drove on it, but now we try to drive somewhere else." The new attention paid to wetlands by ski developers is also partly due to a new socioeconomic context related to changing weather patterns: since the 1990s and 2000s, the lack of snow and the strategy of attracting more diverse categories of tourists have led most ski resorts to try to diversify tourism activities by developing, for instance, snowshoeing in winter and walking and biking in summer and by applying for environmental certifications of their practices as part of their reputation and marketing strategies. It is also probably partly related to the moment in their career when we met them: being closer to retirement, they may have felt less pressure related to the economic dimensions and more sensitivity to the aesthetic and environmental dimensions of their job.

Further, snowcat conductors are now supposed to slightly change their itineraries when preparing ski runs for skiing in order to avoid wetlands as much as possible—even though wetlands are very difficult to identify in winter because they are covered in snow. In order to help them spare the wetlands, snowcats mobilize the indications provided by GPS (Global Positioning Systems).[12] In Switzerland, georadar technologies, which measure the depth of snow under the machines, are also in use. A member of the council explained that the way of building new ski runs would be modified "in order to avoid building long drains along the roads, and to make instead channels so that the water is not diverted from the wetland and keeps feeding into it." The new practices and habits implemented by the scientists and the ski lift managers contributed to enacting a feeling that the wetlands are particularly "delicate" and "rich," justifying collective interest and care, said the council member.

The various technologies and material infrastructures of wetland conservation contribute to producing new practical habits that enact a new relationship with wetlands exposed as fragile places in need of attention and care — in the same way as our relations with birds threatened with extinction are transformed by the techniques and infrastructures of conservation and care that contribute to exposing their fragility (van Dooren 2014). They act as "techniques of conscience" constitutive of positive effects and ethical commitments toward wetlands as sites of water connectivity and ecological productivity. We use here Ian Hunter's term inspired by Foucauldian writings and used by Hawkins in her reflection on the aesthetics and ethics of plastic bags (Hunter 1993). While Hawkins wanted to understand how effects of environmental guilt are bound to the performativity of matter (i.e., plastic bags), here new relations have been generated by the scientists between the materiality of wetlands and new affects and ethics associated to the idea of amphibious functionality, emphasizing the wetlands' capacity of water storage and their resultant role in water filtration, decreasing water's erosive force, and the growth of a special biodiversity that flourishes in mixes of water and soil.

Water probes are another telling example of the embedding of wetlands within new practical habits and affects that make it possible to "see" the hidden water underground in the wetland and to develop a feeling of water circulation and connectivity between aboveground and underground. Routine checking of the wells and water probes participates in activating effects of amphibious functionality associated to the invisible presence of water underground. The associate director of the ski lift company told us that they also had to check that water was feeding properly into a wetland and sometimes fix a problem of blockage: "It's fragile, especially this one

## 210 Granjou and Gaucherand

... we have put back a small water stream that feeds into it, but sometimes it gets clogged, and we need to go and check and dig up a bit more in order to feed water into the wetland again."

Of course, not all of the local inhabitants and tourists buy into it, and the limits of the new sensitivity to wetlands should also be underlined. Some snowcat or quad drivers just do not care about wetlands or the environment: a ski lift manager told us that she needed to "be firm with the employees, or else they drive and drive again on the wetlands." Clearly those actors who were already committed to nature conservation, such as representatives and agents of the Vanoise National Park or the Conservatory of Natural Heritage of Savoie and ecologists, have been more sensitive to wetlands' new imaginaries and associations. The younger generation of ski lift managers seems to have been more open to caring for the wetlands, while older employees remained more insensitive.[13] More importantly, the efforts to preserve some wetlands are seen by some of the ski developers as a way to legitimize the ongoing pressure on the rest of the local landscape in a context in which snow is now massively artificially made to sustain ski tourism when "natural" snow comes to be lacking. Showcasing the preservation of a limited number of wetlands may, for instance, appear as a "greenwash" that justifies continuing to transform drastically the ecosystems and landscapes by installation of snow makers and building huge artificial reservoirs.

To what extent has wetland restoration actually modified the Alpine politics of snow and land dominated by the power of the skiing industry? What does the newly acquired status of wetlands mean for the broader Alpine biopolitics of water, land, and snow?

### BIOPOLITICS OF WATER, LAND, AND SNOW

The expansion of the skiing industry has heavily framed the society and the environment of the northern Alps for several decades—and is still often viewed as the major pathway toward mountain socioeconomic development, despite the heavy costs for local landscapes and ecosystems. Restored wetlands unsettle the dominating politics of snow because they store big amounts of water but not in the form of manageable and productive snow in terms of skiing activities: circulating as liquid fluxes or frozen in ice, wetland water is highly unproductive and even counterproductive from the point of view of ski managers, who need huge amounts of disposable snow to flatten and prepare ski runs. They have been extracting and utilizing wetlands' water in order to fill the water reservoirs, aiming to produce artificial snow, with highly detrimental consequences on the status and evolution of wetlands.

Even though a number of wetlands are listed as endangered and protected, most wetland species are not particularly charismatic or beautiful and are also quite elusive in the field precisely because they are visible only in summertime and may live underground. A number of them are listed in the European Birds and Habitats directives, and thereby protected as part of what is now often called "ordinary biodiversity," valuable because of its role in ecosystems rather than its iconic and remarkable "charisma" (Lorimer 2015). Wetland plants, for instance, play a crucial role in water filtration and storage. These reservoirs are now seen by the local actors, including at least some of the ski lift managers, as important to achieve clean and clear water and to reduce flooding and landslides. What is more, since ski resorts' developers in the northern Alps started to try to attract tourists not only in winter but also in summer, the restored amphibious biodiversity has been considered by Val Thorens managers as an extra economical asset for the ski resort. Wetlands are thus enmeshed in a biopolitics of water, snow, and land that seeks to make life and nature productive, both for themselves and for the humans whose activities depend on them. They are telling illustrations of the role of living beings in maintaining healthy and working ecosystems, including the services they render to human societies.

Wetland conservation is not indeed about enclosing iconic species in an uninhabited and rocky landscape but about maintaining a network of highly modified patches of ecologically functional nature. Braverman (2016) has unpacked the biopolitics of conservation enacted by the lists of endangered species, showing how the lists' categorization, prioritization, and hierarchization operations entail a certain ordering of nature through letting certain animals die while making others live: "Through their listing as threatened, certain species' lives are elevated to a political status, while the rest (initially, at least, the unlisted) remain biological, or mere, life" (Braverman 2016, 20). In the same way as these lists, wetland restoration and conservation were done through a range of negotiations and decisions between skiing promoters and conservationists regarding which sites were worth restoring and at what cost; that is, through a range of trials and hierarchizing judgments resulting in letting certain wetlands die and making other wetlands live. The local wetlands were diversely valued and hierarchized, certain wetlands being abandoned, often in exchange for the restoration and conservation of another one, considered more sensitive and important. Scientists and local managers sought for instance to distinguish between "the wetlands that are really exceptional and of major interest ... and the wetlands which are already quite degraded, do not have any protected species, and are not critical regarding hydrological functioning," a representative of the community council explained. In another ski resort (Les Menuires), ski lift managers' plans to build a new water reservoir entailing the destruction of a local wetland known for hosting an endangered plant species were accepted in exchange for their involvement in the conservation of another sensitive wetland in the ski resort. Some wetlands may simply not be restored and conserved because they do not host any protected species, or are too strategic for the ski resort, or too degraded and considered to be doomed—thus suggesting further extending the biopolitics concept to nonliving matter such as water.

For Braverman, "the power of threatened species lists emanates from their capacity to order life at the level of the biological species—what Foucault refers to as biopolitics" (Braverman 2016, 22). Wetland conservation is built less on the ordering of nature into species categories and regimes, but instead, it is about rendering a whole site productive, including plants, animals, water, and soil as components of the same amphibious ecosystem. Here the species is no longer the only "foundational ontological unit though which life can be calculated and known" (Braverman 2016, 23) and death can be understood and assessed. A different kind of death and life is defined and managed through techniques of wetland restoration and management, which tends to involve the whole ecological functioning in the valuing and ordering enterprise. Death is associated with the separation of running water from the land, while life is associated with the slowing of water flows and the (re)connection between water and land in an amphibious inhabited site. While species classifications work through the individualization of endangered entities and tend to separate them from their local context of growth by considering them as "endangered" in an abstract and general sense, the biopolitics of wetland conservation works through reestablishing wetlands' connectivity to the local landscape and ecosystem as well as local practices to maintain their connectivity over time. The reintegration of wetlands into local watersheds, creeks, and slopes is indeed actively performed by scientists, local conservationists, and ski lift managers through the routine work of maintaining and checking channels, pipes, trails, and signs and caring for not disturbing the fragile amphibious biodiversity.

In the wetlands deemed worth restoring and conserving, scientists and managers endeavored to recreate the amphibious functionality typical of healthy wetlands; that is, their capacity of storing and releasing water, including by slowing down running water into small ponds able to host plants. Importantly, wetland restoration and conservation opens up to a new awareness of how the amphibious "works" in Alpine wetlands by shifting water flows' temporality, slowing their quick pace downward, and allowing instead for the formation of fragile and ephemeral ponds that host standing water and foster the growth of amphibious biodiversity.

## CONCLUSION

Wetland restoration is less focused on nature's separation from society than on the valorization of wetlands' ecological functions and services as part of a search for compromises and conciliatory arrangements between conservationists, industry, and tourism developers. For a representative of the local council interviewed, the overall goal is "to manage to find systems in order for the water to circulate on ski runs and feed wetlands in summer, while it does not make ice in winter and does not create issues for skiing activities." Restored wetlands correspond to the emergence of a new socioecological "composition" in which wetlands are rebuilt and made productive in the terms of the current standards of ecological management closely inspired by the controversial notion of ecosystem services. As such, Val Thorens wetland restoration may thus be considered a telling example of the success and development of the conciliatory and management-based logic that is so vehemently criticized by Frédéric Neyrat (2016). Neyrat criticizes the pervasive development of a philosophy of conciliation and composition between society and nature that is strongly inspired by Latour's writings (Latour 1993) and culminates in the recent vocabulary of ecosystem services, paving the way for vast geoengineering initiatives. He calls for reestablishing an ethical distance and separation toward Nature defined as the part of the Earth on which any type of human intervention and management is (or should be) impossible.

As such, our case study contributes to demonstrating how "attention to the details of living in wet environments brings to the fore that oppositions like conservation and use . . . or natural and artificial often do not hold" (Krause, Cortesi, and Camargo's introduction to this volume). Clearly enough, wetland restoration is not about restoring wilderness defined as "a pristine exterior, the touchstone of an original nature" remote from any human presence and influence (Whatmore 2002; see also Cronon 1983).[14] Restoring wetlands is instead about multiplying human interventions in order to rebuild and manage small patches of closely monitored biodiversity within a densely frequented and exploited area. The restored wetlands no longer look the same as "natural" wetlands, because they are equipped with a range of objects, infrastructures, and instruments (pipes, locks, nets, ditches, signs, GPS, and georadars) that are proof and reminder of human intervention in order to rebuild nature. The new and somewhat fragile status of wetlands will not render those mountain areas destroyed by decades of skiing development back to their genuine beauty and virgin character.

Yet at the same time it is those particular objects, infrastructures, and technologies that participate in solidifying new practical habits, associations, and meanings by which wetlands come to matter as endangered and valuable places. Human technologies sustain the material but also help in the affective and ethical transformation of wetlands: it is precisely because of these technologies that local inhabitants as well as tourists came to care about wetlands as functional sites of amphibious ecology and trading zones between land and water, nature and artifact, nature conservation and skiing development.

Our case study thus suggests that ecological functionality is not only part of the language spoken by hard-nosed promoters of the financialization of nature through the valuation of ecosystem services: its success in fostering wetland conservation also provokes us to think more of the potential relevance of the ecosystem services argument for nature conservation. While restoring wetlands might be partly fostered by the economics of new tourism strategies, it also fosters new local sensitivities, practices, and care, reestablishing both the functioning and connection of wetlands to the local Alpine landscape and ecosystem. In this particular case at least, separating nature from human artifacts and objects may not make much sense: hybridity, fluidity, and connections are already inherently part of the amphibious biopolitics of wetlands.

## NOTES

We want to thank Isabelle Arpin for her very insightful comments on an earlier draft of this text. C. Granjou acknowledges Labex ITEM for funding her research on soil and the shifting soil/society relations (project ALpSols). She is grateful to the Institute of Culture and Society, University of Western Sydney, for inviting her to present this research and to Jeremy Walker for discussing its content and offering his generous and helpful comments.

1   Ecological restoration is the practice of renewing and restoring degraded, damaged, or destroyed ecosystems and habitats in the environment by active human intervention and action.

2   The interviews with ski managers, scientists, and local policymakers were realized by Berenice Commun in 2014, then a master student in social sciences supervised by Stéphanie Gaucherand, Emmanuelle Marcelpoil, and Isabelle Arpin at the Research Institute of Science and Technology for Environment and Agriculture (IRSTEA, University of Grenoble–Alps). Interviews were backed up with participant observation of the scientists' fieldwork.

3   While about eight thousand people stay in Val Thorens during summer holidays, forty thousand to forty-five thousand people are present in the ski resort during the peak skiing season.

216  *Granjou and Gaucherand*

4   Val Thorens ski resort is located in the buffer zone of the park (as opposed to the core zone), but some of the expansion was planned to take place in the core zone. The Vanoise National Park was created in 1963.

5   The rule of mitigation is part of the European Biodiversity Strategy and has been part of the French law since 1976 but was not really applied before the 2000s in France. It requires managers to avoid, reduce, or offset the detrimental impacts of new development projects. In the case of the project of the water reservoir in Val Thorens, ski lift managers could neither avoid nor reduce the impacts, so they were legally required to compensate for them by restoring and conserving wetlands.

6   The council is in fact that of the mountain village called Saint Martin de Belleville, of which Val Thorens ski resort is part.

7   While wetlands constitute 2.6 percent of the land in the county of Savoie, they constitute 3.7 percent of the land in Val Thorens (i.e., 401 wetlands occupying 601 hectares), on the basis of the official data available at the Observatoire des Territoires de la Savoie, accessed on March 19, 2018, http://www.observatoire .savoie.equipement-agriculture.gouv.fr/Atlas/4-environnement-inv.php.

8   Water probes are small electronic devices that emit a sound when water is detected, allowing for measuring the depth of groundwater surface.

9   The ski lift managers have paid €30,000 between 2007 and 2010 as a result of the offsetting measure and then decided to continue with €10,000 per year for the local wetlands.

10  The vernacular vocabulary is strikingly rich and diverse concerning those places: ponds, waterhole, marsh, swamp, wetland. Frogs and tadpoles are part of the fauna well-known among (rural) children. But local wetlands had seldom had names before the implementation of restoration and conservation measures.

11  In the same way, an employee of the ski resort explained that, as he was born in a rural area, he already knew what a wetland is, what wetland grass is, as well as reed, pond, frogs, and tadpoles, "but the hydrological of the wetlands, I did not know it."

12  GPS has been in use for a couple of years in order to update snowcat operators regarding dangerous places such as cliffs; it can also be used to alert them when getting close to a wetland.

13  This confirms previous research on the environmental sensitivities of national parks' employees, partly explained by the fact that former employees were often born in the same place in which they work, while younger ones

have gone through a national professional system devoted to environmental conservation (Mauz 2005).

14 The capacity of the notion of wilderness to provide a strong basis for conservation has become controversial also among the professionals working in protected areas themselves (Granjou 2013). Yet there is currently a renewed and very heated debate about wilderness among environmental social scientists (Monbiot 2014; Wuerthner, Crist, and Butler 2014).

### REFERENCES

Augé, M. 1995. *Non-places: Introduction to an Anthropology of Supermodernity.* London: Verso.

Bennett, J. 2010. *Vibrant Matter: A Political Ecology of Things.* Durham, NC: Duke University Press.

Braverman, I., ed. 2016. *Animals, Bio-politics, Law: Lively Legalities.* New York: Routledge.

Cronon, W. 1983. *Changes in the Land: Indians, Colonists, and the Ecology of New England.* New York: Macmillan.

Delgado, R., M. Sanchez-Maranon, J.-M. Martin-Garcia, V. Arnada, F. Serrano-Bernardo, and J. L. Rosua. 2007. "Impact of Ski Pistes on Soil Properties: A Case Study from a Mountainous Area in the Mediterranean Region." *Soil Use and Management,* no. 23, 269–77.

Fromageau, J. 1998. "Le droit de l'environnement: l'Exemple des zones humides." *Bibliothèque de l'École des Chartes* 156 (1): 173–85.

Gaucherand, S., F. Isselin-Nondedeu, and A. Bedecarrats. 2010. *Development of a Management Tool for the Conservation and Restoration of Wetlands within a Ski Area: The Case of the Ski Resort of Val-Thorens.* Communication to the Society for Ecological Restoration, Avignon, France, August 23–27, 2010.

Granjou, C. 2013. *Micropolitiques de la biodiversité: Experts et professionnels de la nature.* Bruxelles: Éditions Peter Lang.

Hawkins, G. 2010. "Plastic Materialities." In *Political Matter: Technoscience, Democracy and Public Life,* edited by B. Braun and S. J. Whatmore, 119–38. Minneapolis: University of Minnesota Press.

Hunter, I. 1993. "Subjectivity and Government." *Economy and Society* 22 (1): 123–34.

Krause, F., and V. Strang. 2013. "Introduction to SI 'Living Water.'" *Worldviews,* no. 17, 95–102.

Latour, B. 1993 [1991]. *We Have Never Been Modern*. Cambridge: Harvard University Press.

Lippert, I., F. Krause, and N. K. Hartmann. 2015. "Environmental Management as Situated Practice." *Geoforum*, no. 66, 107–14.

Lorimer, J. 2015. *Wildlife in the Anthropocene. Conservation after Nature*. Minneapolis: University of Minnesota Press.

Marcelpoil, E., and L. Langlois. 2010. "Protection de l'environnement et développement touristique en station: Du conflit à l'organisation des proximités." *Développement Durable et Territoires Dossier 7*: Proximité et Environnement.

Mauz, I. 2005. *Gens, Cornes et Crocs*. Versailles: Editions de l'Inra.

Millennium Ecosystem Assessment (MA). 2005. *Ecosystems and Human Well-Being: Synthesis*. Washington, DC: Island Press.

Monbiot, G. 2014. *Feral: Rewilding the Land, the Sea, and Human Life*. Chicago: University of Chicago Press.

Neyrat, F. 2016. *La part inconstructible de la Terre: Critique du géo-constructivisme*. Paris: Editions du Seuil.

Scaramelli, C. 2021. *How to Make a Wetland: Water and Moral Ecology in Turkey*. Redwood City, CA: Stanford University Press.

van Dooren, T. 2014. *Flight Ways: Life and Loss at the Edge of Extinction*. New York: Columbia University Press.

Vileisis, A. 1997. *Discovering the Unknown Landscape: A History of America's Wetlands*. Washington, DC: Island Press.

Whatmore, S. 2002. *Hybrid Geographies: Natures, Cultures, Spaces*. New Delhi: SAGE Publications.

Wuerthner, G., E. Crist, and T. Butler. 2014. *Keeping the Wild: Against the Domestication of the Earth*. Foundation for Deep Ecology.

SARAH WISE

# 8. Muddy Waters

## *Governing the Littoral in Andros Island, The Bahamas*

This chapter unfolds in the muddy tidal spaces of Andros Island, The Bahamas, to explore the ways people live, work, and govern the littoral. Andros Island is the largest landmass in the Bahamas archipelago, with a population of only 7,780, according to the 2022 census. Running one hundred miles long and fifty miles wide, the island is a mosaic of mud, mangroves, and aquatic caves. Human development sprinkles along the one road, running the length of the eastern shore. The west side of the island is a vast tidal flatland of thick and viscous sediment, leading to people calling the area "the mud." Although few live in the mud, the area has been actively used for commercial, recreational, and subsistence fishing as well as other resource use. In recent decades, Andros and its people have experienced dramatic social-ecological and climatic change. As the oceans warm, the island's thin freshwater lens has turned brackish in areas. Tidal creeks have shallowed, become more saline, or dried up altogether. The island gained notice within the conservation world as a space of opportunity, largely undeveloped with abundant wildlife. In 2002, as part of a larger national conservation campaign, the Bahamas government initiated a plan to create five protected areas (PAs) in Andros, covering over 1.5 million acres of land and sea. Much of the space slated for protection was undeveloped tidal wetlands, often described as empty and unused muddy expanses; however, Androsians actively engaged these areas to collect food, support their families and livelihoods, and live.

The people of Andros Island, The Bahamas, live and work in the broad, flat, muddy terrain of a tidal plain. The island sits barely a few feet above sea level, allowing the water to move across the landscape, washing out roads, lapping at houses, and punctuating island life. The island is strewn with tidal estuaries that connect as a labyrinth of waterways, sharing their names with nearby settlements—Fresh Creek, Cargill Creek, Stafford Creek, Staniard Creek—each one dividing the land, connecting the freshwater interior with the saline sea, ushering juveniles of marine species from mangrove nursery grounds to oceanic depths. Andros is only partially terrestrial, with its houses perched on stilts along the coastline or tucked tightly together on the gentle slopes that rise a few feet above water. Tides dictate access to space and resources, guide transport, and inform daily decisions. During low tide in Andros, waters retreat from the land to expose a vast and productive tidal-scape, the coastal littoral. Elders walk the shoals, fishing for conchs, sponges, and whelks. Women of all ages gather medicinal plants and small fish in the shallows. Children swim in the protected mangroves, pick dilly fruit (*Manilkara zapota*) and custard apple (*Annona reticulata*), and practice their spearing skills. They run to catch eels and boxfishes. Fishers pole their skiffs along the shallow coast, handlining for snapper (*Ocyurus chrysurus*) and grunts (*Haemulon plumierii*). US Naval cadets train along the edge of the deep water trench running the length of the coast and spear fish in the shallows while off duty. Scientists harvest the flora and fauna, the water, the air, the oral histories, and the dusty limestone for their research. When the tides rise, the creeks and bays fill, obscuring the muddy sea bottom, flooding the patches of mangroves, and redefining the stark line between land and sea, shoreline and deep water. As the tide fills the dry creeks, releasing the small fishing boats from their muddy moorage, the fishers head back out to sea.

Different sets of rules and social networks are observed during high tide. Children are forbidden to go out into the deeper waters, and elders move their work to land-based activities. Men in boats dominate the seascape, while the shoreline seems to empty of people once again. Like a rhythmic breath, human activity shifts with the tide: from nearshore to further out to sea, from harvesting littoral species to benthic, from a flurry of hard labor to rest. With each tidal breath, so changes the linkages among people and the animals and plants they depend on to survive.

This chapter addresses some of the unique relationships Andros residents have with their watery environment and how aquatic space works to fulfill multiple social ecological encounters to support valuable social networks, informational pathways, and meaning. Governing the littoral as an assemblage of encounters — under conditions of constant temporal, spatial, and social change — offers unique challenges. As an ecosystem centered on change, the littoral requires governance that addresses the material, social, and conceptual fluidity over time. When one reflects on enclosure conservation efforts in Andros Island as a case study, the need for a new resource governance system emerges, one that considers multiple meanings and addresses two central elements of the tidal littoral — that of time and fluidity — and that builds in the multiple facets of meaning making and intersection of use, perspective, and interaction. Given the fluid and changing conditions of a coastal littoral, what types of governance are appropriate to sustainably manage marine resources while improving food security and livelihood (Sherman et al. 2018)? What is the appropriate scale of management to protect mobile populations and a littoral environment that shifts across multiple scales (time, materiality, and human usage)? How do people encounter, imagine, or demarcate fluctuating boundaries, and in what ways does it differ from wet or dry spaces?

## MOSAIC OF MUD: THE LITTORAL

The littoral zone can be defined broadly as the area of shoreline experiencing tidal variance, measured from the highest to the lowest water marks. Physically, the tidal zone is defined by the presence of tidal waters and currents, marked by percentage of sunlight penetration and wave turbulence (Encyclopedia Britannica 2016). The Ramsar Convention defines wetlands as "areas of marsh, fen, peatland or water, whether natural or artificial, permanent or temporary, with water that is static or flowing, fresh, brackish or salt, including areas of marine water the depth of which at low tide does not exceed six metres" (Ramsar Convention Secretariat

2016, Article 1.1 and 2.2). Given these definitions, virtually all of Andros Island can be described as a wetland, and the people of Andros spend much of their life navigating what Anja Nygren (global development studies) and anthropologist Anu Lounela call "porous water-land fluctuations or, wet-lands" (Nygren and Lounela 2023, 296).

Ecologically, wetlands are considered some of the most productive and biodiverse ecosystems (Gopal 2009; Denny 1994; Barbier et al. 2011); however, globally, they have been underestimated and undervalued, as evidenced by the rapid decrease in wetlands by as much as 50 percent (Costanza et al. 2014; Davidson 2014; Fraser and Keddy 2005). Wetlands are considered extremely vulnerable to climate change, requiring careful management (Finlayson et al. 2017). The threats of climate change continue to reshape narratives surrounding wetlands: as protecting communities from storm surge and flooding and sequestering carbon (for examples, see Mitsch et al. 2013; Moomaw et al. 2018; Adhikari, Bajracharaya, and Sitaula 2009; Peimer et al. 2017; Villa and Bernal 2018). Recent research has emphasized the political ecology of wet-lands, showing how social and cultural perspectives about wet and dry spaces has changed over time, leading to shifts in definitions, bounds, and valuation (da Cunha 2018; Nygren and Lounela 2023) and place-making (Gearey 2022). What were once considered "wastelands" are now heralded as hot spots of biodiversity, habitats for important species, and hosts to electrical microbes (Denny 1994; Bobbink et al. 2006; Kingsford, Basset, and Jackson 2016; Pennisi 2020).

Anthropologists Richard Stoffle and Brent Stoffle (2007) examine the littoral as an important social and biological gateway for Caribbean islanders that provides important services to residents in Barbados and The Bahamas in terms of nutrition, environmental education, and cultural memory. The authors contextualize the littoral as a "social-ecological place" (Stoffle and Stoffle 2007, 547), and maintain that it allows for crucial adaptation and learning opportunities for residents. Pointing to the littoral's socioecological significance, the authors suggest that it is important to maintain people's access to the littoral rather than close it off to all human use through enclosure conservation.

Geographer Owain Jones's work builds on this notion, describing tidal areas as having a "distinctive cultural ecology of place" (Jones 2011, 2299), where community members have individual (and temporally specific) relationships with the sea-landscape or "hybrid timescapes" (Jones 2011, 2292). These cultural ecologies of place illuminate the role of interaction and relational linking of the social and the spatial. Jones terms the process of interaction between time and space as "rhythmpatterns" (Jones 2011, 1), the patterns in which time meets place to create spaces both recomposed and new.

Anchored by the rhythmic fluctuations of the tide, the littoral is neither dry land nor fluid sea. Tidal spaces have certain social and ecological properties that embody fluidity, interconnectivity, and a profound—often tactile—relationship with time-space patterns. The littoral is governed by its own hybrid rules: it hugs the coast, wedged between the material and regulatory structure of open sea and terrestrial shores. Land and the open seas have specific governance structures, but the stretch of littoral is liminal in that it occupies a transitional space: not solely subjected to the laws of the sea or land. The coastline moves, shifts with the seasons, dependent on lunar pull and tidal spread, and is highly dynamic. To be liminal is to occupy multiple states across a boundary, to reside in an ambiguous, transitory state. Geographers Philip Steinberg and Kimberley Peters write, "We understand the ocean not as a space of discrete points between which objects move but rather as a dynamic environment of flows and continual re-composition where, because there is no static background, 'place' can be understood only in the context of mobility" (Steinberg and Peters 2015, 11).

The area is a mobile space: the sea and wind currents churn, sand excavation and coastal development uproot, river mouths empty, and aquatic creatures hunt, forage, breed, and live. Steinberg and Peters refer to watery environments as "dynamic assemblages, in which mobile human and nonhuman (including molecular) elements and affects are not merely passively consumed but imagined, encountered, and produced" (Steinberg and Peters 2015, 10). The fluidity of the littoral shapes how people encounter space, lending meaning to wet-land spaces; these meanings shift to accommodate, facilitate, and resist encounters. The various and sometimes divergent discourses surrounding what human geographer

Ulrich Oslender calls "Aquatic Spaces" (Oslender 2001, 2004) work to inform management strategies for the littoral. Navigating these aquatic spaces requires social networks and governance strategies that account for the material and imagined realities of amphibious life. In turn, governing the littoral requires recognition of multiplicities in meaning and function.

## GOVERNANCE

Governance can be broadly defined as "the exercise of economic, political and administrative authority to manage a country's affairs at all levels" (UNDP 1997, 4), although it is well understood that the term is context dependent and can hold multiple meanings (Biermann and Pattberg 2008; Newaz and Rahman 2019). Scholars emphasize the importance of examining governance *processes* rather than *outcomes* (Rauschmayer et al. 2009; Armitage, De Loë, and Plummer 2012; Koebele 2015). Sustainability scholar David Manuel-Navarrete with coauthors writes, "Governance is a 'living' process through which social goals and objectives are achieved. It is not a given, but a changing set of procedures and processes" (Manuel-Navarrete, Pelling, and Redclift 2009, 15). Governance processes are reflexive and deeply entwined with the surrounding material and social conditions. Referring specifically to ocean governance, human geographer Lisa Campbell and coauthors suggest it is the sea's fluidity, as well as specific issues of actors, scale, and knowledge, that present challenges and a troubling move toward neoliberal policies in marine resource governance: "Contemporary governance often emphasizes market over regulatory mechanisms; for environmental issues, this often necessitates enclosure and privatization of the commons" (Campbell et al. 2016, 23). Other scholars have explored the simultaneous encroachment of neoliberal ideologies—what political economist Noel Castree (2008) called neoliberalizing nature—and the increase of enclosure in biodiversity conservation (for example, Büscher et al. 2012; Sullivan 2013; Arsel and Büscher 2012; Brockington, Duffy, and Igoe 2012). Building on Oslender's concept of "geographies of the 'pre-conditions'" (Oslender 2004, 958), governance can be understood as a spatially grounded social process, which does not develop in a vacuum but rather in a place of material, spiritual, and practical meaning. Governance structures reflect how people engage with and imagine space. Just as resources, practices, and social networks have evolved in communication with the everyday social interactions and daily rhythms of tidal life—leading to what Oslender calls an "aquatic logic" (Oslender 2004, 962)—so should the resource management frameworks that seek to govern use behavior reflect such a logic.

Research has shown the benefits of inclusive collaborative governance for complex social-ecological spaces such as wetlands (Cash et al. 2006; Heikkilä, Kopnin, and Volovik 2011; Norman, Bakker, and Cook 2012). The United Nations' Ramsar Convention guidelines highlight the value of participation and inclusion of stakeholders, declaring the need to "strengthen and support the full and effective participation and the collective actions of stakeholders, including indigenous peoples and local communities, for the existence of sustainable, comprehensive and wise use of wetlands" (COP14-15 2022). Collaborative governance promotes community organization and supports the legitimacy of sustainable management frameworks (Newaz and Rahman 2019; Turner et al. 2016). Effective governance requires a shared legitimacy among those affected by the organizational system.

Legitimacy can be defined as the shared belief in the right of one group to govern over another (Tyler 2006). Legitimacy is a social process central to social organization (Zelditch 2001) that links a particular object (such as a protected area) with a sense of rightful governing. As a social process, legitimacy shifts, given the social and ecological conditions in which the object is located. Encounters across human and nonhuman agents inform the process of legitimacy and governance through shared values and identities (Ruíz, Hes, and Schwartz 2011), as well as through meaning. Legitimate processes involved in governing aquatic resources can include both formal and informal management policies and decision-making pathways.

Given the mosaic of meaning and function within Andros's muddy spaces, flexibility and responsive governance would provide the fluidity and changeability necessary for resilience in the face of radical change. Amphibious governance builds on the core concepts of adaptive management, defined as "an intentional approach to making decisions and adjustments in response to new information and changes in context" (USAID 2018). While adaptive management incorporates uncertainty and transition within a management framework (Parlee and Wiber 2014), amphibious governance operates within the parameters of rhythmic and patterned change. The shifting conditions of tidelands are recurring and, in some ways, predictable to the people who have lived in the area for centuries (Raffles 2002, 2007). Amphibious governance can be responsive to the "rhythmpatterns" of the wet landscape to accommodate multiple uses and meanings across temporal and spatial scales.

Within the mud-scapes of Andros, the ways in which time and fluidity influence social-ecological practice and meaning in the littoral become visible, allowing the dynamic flows for the material and collective meanings of amphibious space. Drawing on eighteen months of ethnographic research in Andros, this work explores the interchange between space, place-making, and meaning-making, asking how the littoral shifts to reflect multiple meanings and make room for multifaceted marine governance, resource tenure, and perceptions of rightful ownership. Enclosure conservation disrupts the flow of the littoral, both socially and ecologically, and risks undermining the importance of human-nonhuman wetland encounters. Aquatic spaces allow for productive and malleable interactions to accommodate varied practices and meanings. These rhythmic encounters then shape and reshape the space and narratives embedded in wetlands.

Within Andros, the Crab Replenishment Reserve can act as a case study to illustrate the social and ecological complexities of governing aquatic spaces and ground this theoretical work in a watery mud-scape. A space once valued as a tidal commons, ideal for harvesting land crabs for subsistence and the cash economy, was recomposed as an exceptional and vulnerable space in need of protection. The model of enclosure conservation forces a rigid template for resource management and conservation: one that stands in stark contrast to the aquatic logic of between spaces in The Bahamas. An alternative possibility focusing on the multifaceted and dynamic conditions of the littoral over time, what may be called amphibious governance, allows for a collection of voices and a deep attention to temporal and spatial change. Complex social-ecological spaces require dynamic and interactive governance processes: amphibious governance embraces human-nonhuman relationships and the predictive qualities of change. As an important alternative to top-down enclosure approaches to resource management, amphibious governance can better address the plurality and fluid states of the littoral. Overly rigid management frameworks that ignore the heterogeneity of muddy, wet land risk ineffective and inequitable policies: protected areas that do not meet management objectives and do nothing to protect.

## DISRUPTING THE FLOW: THE SHIFTING LITTORAL AND THE MOVE TO ENCLOSE

In response to growing global concerns over declining fisheries and vulnerability of small island nations, the Bahamas government, in collaboration with the Bahamas National Trust (BNT), the nation's primary conservation organization, embraced enclosure as the solution for sustainable resource management by promoting a network of protected areas (PAs). Beginning in 2000, large tracts of land and sea were identified as ideal PAs throughout the archipelago nation. In 2002, the Bahamas National Park system doubled with ten new PAs, enclosing an additional 700,000 acres of land and sea (BNT 2008). In Andros Island alone, five PAs were created, enclosing over 1.5 million acres in total. By time of this print, there were thirty-two national parks in The Bahamas, protecting over two million acres (BNT 2008). Enclosure conservation delineates specific spaces for species uses (or non-uses): it cordons off space for certain goals, for example (to protect species, reduce habitat destruction, or mitigate the effects of climate change). The purpose of enclosure is to restrict access to a bounded space (which suggests manageability through monitoring and enforcement of that area). Within the area, there exist differentiated rules to modify human behavior according to desired outcomes (Wise 2014, 2015). Mangroves once used to collect medicinal plants or harvest fish may be transformed into a carbon bank or historical landmark. As a result, social-ecological relationships shift, further shaping identity and cultural meanings.

For centuries in The Bahamas, undeveloped land and sea were perceived as common pool resources, and thus available to all residents for use. Prior to enclosure, much of the islands was labeled as "Crown Land," government land held in public trust for Bahamians for resource use. Coastlines, beaches, and open waters could not be privately owned according to Bahamian law, allowing for the designation of marine PAs without concern for private property rights. The public trust doctrine, also known as the Law of the Commons, is difficult to pin down, even more so given the fluid materiality of the sea, or what anthropologist Bonnie McCay calls "patently slippery, muddy, and intangible subjects: waterways and the shores lapped by them, usually tidal and navigable" (McCay 1998, xx). Most Bahamians view common pool resources such as Crown Land and the marine environment as a form of social security, accessible areas to harvest food and other resources when money is scarce (Bethel 2000). Over centuries, families and individuals have made settlement claims to certain areas. These claims are based on conditions such as family lineage, age, gender, and race and depend on continued occupation (Wise 2014). Complex claims of ownership and access to marine resources are nested within a hierarchical framework of tenureship, including government regulations and customary laws. Changing the designation of space from a commons to a protected area transforms rightful access and use of that area to a select group—in a sense privatizing the space for a particular purpose (conservation) or entity (BNT). Through the process of enclosure, The Bahamas has been composed and recomposed as idyllic land- and seascapes for conservation to fulfill international conservation goals (see the Caribbean 30x30 Initiative 2023 and COP15 2022).

Most recently, The Bahamas' brackish wetlands have been promoted as valuable carbon sinks for global carbon emissions (Bastain 2023; The Bahamas Government 2022; Mandoske 2017). In Andros, international and regional conservation organizations made large territorial claims for the purpose of marine protection for biodiversity, protected species habitat, and flood protection. These claims were explained through the discourse of resource vulnerability, the duality of fragile and abundant ecosystems, and the wetland's unique abilities to protect from climate impacts. Andros's watery landscape was reimagined, creating the need for new governance mechanisms to accommodate pressing global needs.

## SHIFTING GOVERNANCE: ENCLOSING A COMMONS AND THE CALL FOR AMPHIBIOUS GOVERNANCE

In The Bahamas, claims to property emerged from a complex colonial legacy. Bahamian governance processes developed over centuries in close engagement with the physical environment. Access and ownership was managed though multilayered and multiplicitous customs and laws, including long-standing oral tenure institutions that shifted with respect to season and overlapped both temporally and spatially. The Bahamas archipelago comprises nearly seven hundred islands and cays, of which only thirty are currently inhabited (this includes private islands owned by wealthy foreigners). As early as 300 AD, seafaring Arawak peoples traveled from other regions of the Caribbean to live and fish in The Bahamas. Archaeological evidence shows Lucayan settlement from 900 AD onward. Upon arrival in 1492, Columbus documented about forty thousand Lucayans. Within twenty-five years of contact, the Lucayan people were wiped out through enslavement and disease. Piracy was rampant through the country, and the British struggled to maintain control over the thin spattering of islands spanning miles of shallow seas, contributing to a reputation of lawless and ungoverned space. In 1718, The Bahamas became a British crown colony, using land settlement structures to lay claim to vast island spaces and fueling British expansion through the slave trade.

Land claims in The Bahamas were always more than a parcel of dirt. In a nation with a painful colonial history with deep ties to slavery and racial oppression, access to land came to represent economic and social security, independence, and freedom. The institution of property in The Bahamas included both formal and informal rights: wealthy white land barons received titles, while "commonage land" was used by the poor, usually black, underclass that did not have the ability to formally claim title lands.[1] In a country divided along racial, ethnic, and class lines, access to and ownership of land provided opportunities for independence and even resistance among subjugated members of Bahamian society.

In Andros, the British made several attempts at large-scale commercial farming supported by slave labor, the lack of space and arable soil led to the frequent failure of plantations. Bankrupt landowners fled to Nassau, leaving their land and slaves behind (Craton 1962, 180). Those people who stayed behind relied on the land and sea to survive, building communities based on strong social networks and ties to the environment across generations. The geophysical environment of the islands—small, isolated patches of land that were difficult to govern, well suited for small-scale subsistence, but undesirable for commercial use—promoted flexible tenure claims to space based on physical occupancy and social networks.

Andros held historic importance as an island offering unclaimed and accessible land to black Bahamians. People escaping slavery in The Bahamas and the United States traveled to Andros, disappearing in the muddy swamps to evade capture and find freedom (Howard 2006). Andros developed an image as impenetrable, lawless, and wild, in some part due to its rugged and (often wet) shifting terrain. The lack of industrial and tourism infrastructure contributes to its characterization as a harsh place, sparsely populated with wild and lawless people. To quote one conservation official, "Androsians don't listen to anyone. They don't follow rules. They do what they want." Through multiple socioecological engagements, Andros became a place of independence and freedom for black Bahamians, and thus was associated with resistance to white colonial oppression. The vastness of Andros provided both the physical and psychological space for resistance. Through occupancy rights and commonage holdings, black Bahamians created and maintained independence.

Just as storm events and watery boundaries influence human behavior and physical space, laws and social norms shape patterns of resource extraction and use, as well as perceptions of natural resources. In his chapter on the material culture of tides, Jones focuses on the importance of rhythm and repetition of tidal spaces, drawing on assemblage theory to introduce the concept of "rhythmpattern consonance and dissonance" (Jones 2011, 19). Jones argues that consonance among social and tidal rhythms can maximize the use of ecosystem services and benefit both society and the environment. Alternately, conflict among social and ecological rhythms leads to dissonance, and it is this dissonance that can affect social networks and daily practice. In the case of the Crab Replenishment Reserve, the enclosure became a point of contestation and the area a place for resistance.

## AQUATIC NARRATIVES

As highly productive and malleable environments, tidal spaces have drawn human inhabitants for millennia. Daily necessities — such as food, work, water, building materials, protection, and play — are provided by these watery landscapes, driving continuous and evolving interaction. Specific governance strategies have emerged from these interactions and are molded by human–wet environment engagement. According to legal scholar Erika Torres-Fontánez, "The coast is construed in an array of meanings, forms and definitions, which evade, surpass and oftentimes ignore the legal and political definitions, which are not, and should not be the definitive ones" (Torres-Fontánez 2009, 40). The meanings of coastal waters differ depending on individual perspective and use of the area Carrier calls a "disputed landscape" (Carrier 2003, 226). How a person views and uses the landscape defines how he or she values the space. As neoliberal principles place monetary value on space, other forms of meaning — that is, historical, cultural, spiritual — may become obscured. Not only the littoral's unique physicality but socioeconomic and sociopolitical meanings shape perception of space and inform governance.

Tidal areas are a between space, interchangeably wet and dry, submerged and exposed. McCay describes coasts as both littoral and liminal spaces: "Their boundaries are often vague, shifting, and contested. If not feared or tabooed, they do pose cultural, political, and survival challenges and opportunities" (McCay 2009, 8). The littoral is a boundary, but, as McCay and others suggest, it can be indistinct in its delineation. These vague and shifting boundaries contribute to the perception of uncertainty: of ownership, durability, and security. Anthropologist Rob van Ginkel delves deeper in his exploration of ritual and taboo among fishers, particularly in relation to crossing between land and sea. The liminal is a "threshold," a point of crossing over from one state to the next, what van Ginkel calls a "space between spaces" (van Ginkel 2013, 47). Van Ginkel argues that it is not the wildness or unpredictability of nature that causes apprehension at the liminal, but the act of *crossing over*, the actualized state of transition. "Thus, it is not only the coast as such that is liminal: the human transition from one zone to the other also is" (van Ginkel 2013, 48). In this way, the action of transgression—moving *across* a boundary—is a significant aspect of how people experience the space. The daily movement of tides, storm surge, sea level rise, and coastal development underscore the point that the littoral is not static. Instead, it shifts, evolves, submerges, and reemerges as new entities—materially in their geographic composition, but also in our minds as "mental symbols" (Grove 1996, 9).

Within the conservation world, mental symbols are often configured through various visitor encounters—whether tourist, climate scientist, or developer. Amphibious spaces—long-standing symbols of transitional wasteland, empty, unused, difficult to access, and unsuitable for permanent development—have become ideal locations for enclosure conservation. Within the conservation world, wetlands are depicted as bountiful, yet with finite (and thus vulnerable) resources: "Vegetated wetlands, such as swamps and marshes, are some of the most wildlife-rich ecosystems on the planet, their shallow waters and abundant plant life supporting everything from insects to ducks to moose. But these wetlands, as well as lakes, rivers and other watery environments around the world, are in peril, with many polluted or degraded as a result of climate change and human development" (UNEP 2023). This juxtaposition—a space both empty and used, yet rich with opportunity for conservation—enables the reconfiguration of these spaces, from wasteland to abundance, from undesirable to valuable, from dangerous and vulnerable to protected.

## RHYTHMIC ENCOUNTERS AND CULTURAL ECOLOGIES

Every year the storm come and the sea come, every year. My children move
the TV and things up. I stay and wait for the water to go. The sea right
there, see? Right there. (Interview, female, Eleuthera, 2006)

The Bahamas is a signatory of the Ramsar Convention, which defines wetlands as "all lakes and rivers, underground aquifers, swamps and marshes,
wet grasslands, peatlands, oases, estuaries, deltas and tidal flats, mangroves
and other coastal areas, coral reefs, and all human-made sites such as fish
ponds, rice paddies, reservoirs and salt pans" (Ramsar Convention Secretariat 2016). By this definition, much of Andros Island could be considered
wetland, in that the terrain is submerged at least part of the year, although
the island is not officially registered as a Ramsar site.

Encounters with Andros have shaped and been shaped by images, metaphors, and ideas that constitute the discourses used by different groups
to represent their understandings of and interests in the place and its
people. Many Bahamians, even those living in Andros, describe Andros
as the least developed, most rural, and least appealing of all the Bahamian
islands—often calling it "the back-of-the-bush" or "the mud"—meaning
the remote, wild, and uncivilized, difficult to access, and dangerous. One
Androsian man explained, "The bush is dangerous. Those big trees can fall
on your house. Snakes live in them. Biting flies like that shade. You people
always keeping the trees, planting more trees! I put in a few things I like.
Keep 'em small. I don't need no big trees to remind me that the bush is
there, close. It's the garden of Eden, not the bush . . . where'd Eve find that
snake? In the tree!" (interview, male, Andros, 2009). Not just the trees, but
most features of the porous landscape held menace: "The ground changes
underneath you. You are always seeing something new. Something you
have never see before. Walking out, it's dry, dry, then thick mud! You get
stuck, you can't get out! Or you fall in a hole. Someone always dying that
way" (interview, female, Andros, 2009). In talking with people living in
Andros across generations, stories emerged of drownings in the blue holes,

234 *Wise*

losing relatives while out crabbing, sometimes just for days, and sometimes they were never found.

Each family had a cautionary tale of loss in the watery terrain. "Those sticks from the old bridge. We used to walk down to Stafford Creek that way before the road was built. It's all bay now. My uncle lived there all his life, but his house done gone now. Sea take it" (interview, male, Andros, 2009). Rarely has Andros Island been described as picturesque or tropical. Wild, desolate, and at times starkly beautiful, Andros defies the quaint colonial picturesque. For decades, the tourist industry avoided Andros. The land was too wet and the scrub too dense to build large resorts popular on the other islands. The beaches were rocky with sharp porous stone that could cut your foot. The entire island was prone to flooding much of the year, allowing the mosquitoes and biting flies to flourish but discouraging tourism.

Occasionally developers or the government's department of tourism attempt to draw tourists to Andros, turning away from the stereotype of sun-baked white-sand beaches and tropical foliage and instead rewriting the tourist experience as an adventure in untouched, uninhabited, and unfamiliar spaces: "Of the 700 islands in the Bahamas archipelago, only Andros offers such a wide range of truly untouched natural wonders. Its 2,300-square-mile limestone base is riddled with underwater caves that surface as blue holes. Sliced with endless waterways, the island's acres of mangrove-lined wetlands open onto bonefish flats and secluded beaches" (Kamalame Cay 2023). Frequently Andros is defined by its waterways rather than its land features, further illustrating the wetness of the land. It is the assemblage of shallow waters, tidal creeks, and muddy bays that compose and recompose Andros Island. A small ecotourism lodge described Andros as

> the eco-tourism capital of The Bahamas and the 5th largest island in the Caribbean . . . Perhaps the greatest attraction is the Andros Barrier reef, the 3rd largest in the world. The variety of shallow reef dives, ocean and inland blue holes and wall diving in the Tongue of the Ocean make Andros the best diving destination in the Bahamas. The Tongue of the Ocean is a vast underwater canyon more

than a mile deep offering deep sea fishing and deepocean diving within a mile or two offshore. Andros is otherwise surrounded by the shallow seas of The Great Bahama Bank. This combination of barrier reef and sand banks provides the island with significant protection from tropical storms, hurricanes and high seas. If you are looking for a quiet place with an abundance of eco-tourism and relaxation, South Andros Island is the place to explore. More than 80% of South Andros Island is preserved in the West Side National Park. (Andros Beach Club 2023)

Another perspective common among tourists and Bahamians alike—also building on Andros's social isolation and lack of development—was that Andros is the center of Bahamian music, dancing, language, and food, where people are connected to the sea, men really know how to fish, women cook, and the land crabs and fish are the largest found in the islands. Accordingly, tourist literature described Andros as "the heartland" or "the backbone" of The Bahamas, representing the true or authentic Bahamas islands. Androsians promoted this viewpoint, proud in their resistance to large megaresorts and other development projects: "Andros is where all the crab be! And crab is Bahamian. You feed your family, put a couple dollars in your pocket, buy your children uniforms and school things. Crab do that, and Androsians do it best!" (interview, male, Andros, 2009).

Similarities occurred in conservation writings. Conservationists referred to Andros as exceptional, fragile, undeveloped, and highly productive wetlands: "The Andros West Side National Park protects more than a million acres of coastal wetlands that are the most productive marine nurseries in The Bahamas. This park also provides habitat for bonefish and flamingos" (BNT n.d.). Among international conservation agencies, Andros Island had become valuable for its globally significant biodiversity but also because of its natural abundance. It was depicted as having the largest swath of wetlands in the region, and as the prime source of freshwater in The Bahamas (Hargreaves-Allen 2010).

The Crab Replenishment Reserve illustrates how aquatic spaces have been reshaped through multiple encounters over time. The broader efforts

236 *Wise*

to enclose 1.5 million acres of tidal wetlands in Andros attempted to use a rigid model of enclosure governance, erecting boundaries, mapping ownership, and restricting access. Enclosure of such dynamic and fluid space ignored the multiplicity of voices, meanings, and values help deep within the mud and disrupted the social-ecological flow of human-nonhuman engagement.

## Case Study

> The crabs come with the rain. Some morning you wake up
> and they walking cross your screens, on the walls, everywhere.
> (Interview, female, Andros, 2010)

The move to enclose 1.5 million acres in Andros's aquatic lands for the National Park system can be explored through a deeper analysis of the Crab Replenishment Reserve, one of the five national parks slated for enclosure. Originally enclosed to conserve "the best land crab habitat in Central Andros" (ANCAT 2010), the reserve was a heavily used seasonally flooded plane, known throughout the island as prime territory for white land crabs (*Cardisoma guanhumi*). Exploring the implementation process illustrates some of the complexities of littoral governance and demonstrates the variety of ways people made meaning in shared spaces.

The Crab Replenishment Reserve was located along the eastern road dubbed "the Hollow," an area known for its crab density. Craggy and dry most of the year, during each rainy season, the area flooded, linking the inner flat scrubland with the sea. When the rains hit, the call to breed drives thousands of crabs across the island to the muddy shore to breed and lay eggs. As they move, many Bahamian men, women, and children wake at dawn and walk through the bush to collect crocus sacks full of the arthropods. In the rainy season of 2010, cars lined the road along the reserve, throughout the day and night. Whole families organized crab parties. Young children barely able to walk held crocus sacks for their older siblings; grandmothers rode in the back of trucks and urged people to run faster, reach deeper into the black depths of a crab hole, gather more.

Packs of kids roamed through the night, gleeful in their freedom, each one determined to get more crabs than her cousin, his neighbor.

Throughout the summer, late into the night, voices could be heard laughing and shouting directions: "That there a big one! You see his biter? Watch for him! Use the stick. The stick!" Families traveled together, meeting up with members from other settlements. Crabbing was intensely social and worked to strengthen networks as well as build economic opportunities through cooperative sharing of tools, crabs, transport, supplies, food, childcare, and gas. Boasts were made about the biggest crabs and strongest holding pens. Plans were made for the next outing and for transporting the catch to Nassau for sale. The interisland ferry filled with sacks of live crabs to sell on other islands and to ship to family members. The Hollow was not simply a seasonally watery landscape but a social space, what Oslender describes as "a collective space of social relations that are based on co-operation and solidarity" (2004, 967). The Hollow supported and hosted strong social linkages, which in turn created and sustained the community.

Andros has the largest, and some say, the tastiest land crabs. During the summer, the streets of Nassau line with people selling crabs from Andros. The money provides a significant portion of an Androsian family's annual income. A good night of crabbing can bring in several dozen crabs. Once fattened and sold in Nassau, a dozen crabs can bring in as much as sixty dollars. Androsian children frequently crab before school to pay for new school uniforms and other clothes. In every family, there is a favorite crab recipe—crab soup, crab dumpling, crab 'n' dough, grill crab, stuffed crab—many of which are featured during Crab Fest, a festival celebrating the bounty of the season's land crabs.[2] People travel from around the world to sample Auntie Thelma's crab 'n' dough or crab soup. Crab is eaten fresh, never frozen. It is a highly valued food, in large part perhaps because it is only available for a limited time every year. During the season, the Andros littoral comes alive with crabs depositing eggs, as well as people scurrying after them to catch, sell, sauté, and eat.

During crab season, resource governance systems shift to accommodate the seasonal fluctuations. As people walk the island flats, individual property claims are rarely recognized: residents follow the crabs across the watery landscape—regardless of tenure—to harvest during their short season. Children run across the island, around fences, through yards to catch crabs. Once caught, the live crabs are placed in pens to cleanse and fatten. Pens are usually constructed from scrap materials and are often shared by families or whole communities. Pens are a collective structure, held in common by a self-identified group. Androsians can harvest any free-roaming crabs, but there exist strict penalties for anyone bold enough to "thief crab"—or pillage a neighbor's crab pen. Profitable crabbing requires intensive physical effort and strong social linkages. Labor is divided among the able bodied—those with time and ability to catch a fast-moving crab—while the social networks of older family members facilitate successful sales. Nearly everyone takes a break from normal routines to catch crabs when they are running, but it is someone known for their shrewd marketing skills who is sent to sell crabs off the island. Crab season reinforces family bonds and provides needed food and income for the rest of the year.

Soon after the Andros protected areas were approved by the Bahamas government, signs began to arrive along the eastern roads of Andros Island announcing the "Crab Replenishment Reserve." Most signs were small, green rectangles, declaring in white lettering that the space was a Bahamas National Park, managed by the Bahamas National Trust. Each sign, no matter how small, held the Bahamas National Trust's crest: blue sea in the foreground, a small island mound in the background, two flying pink flamingos, a pink conch nestled at the bottom, and, above it all, a crown. The signs signaled BNT's claim to the land under formal mandate of the national government, and ultimately the British crown. The signs also signaled change for these spaces that had been regarded and used for centuries as a commons by Androsians for crabbing, farming, hunting, and gathering straw (Albury 1975). With the appearance of these signs, BNT and the national government declared the space to have conservation value for the country and the wider world, offering a new hierarchy of meaning and making a governance claim that modified ownership, belonging, and access.

At first, the signs seemed to pass unnoticed—crabbing continued—and then the signs quietly disappeared, pilfered by nearby residents. BNT staff replaced the signs quickly, but they never lasted long. Some signs were damaged, uprooted, and knocked over. Conversations shifted from planning the night's hunt and boasts about previous hauls to talk about the reserve and new regulations. Many people wondered how the new regulations might affect the annual Crab Fest. A local man was awarded a position with BNT to assist in monitoring and enforcing PA regulations. The position came with social status, authority, and additional income, further complicating questions of equity and security surrounding protected areas (Kelly and Ybarra 2016; Kelly and Gupta 2016).

When discussing the signs, people were dismissive: "Yeah I see those little bitty signs. What they for? I crab here. My grammy crab here. No little sign gonna do nothing 'bout that." While the signage seemed a futile exercise in excluding crab harvesting, the subtle shifts in how people regarded the space were still likely to change. According to many Androsians, the attempt to claim the land as conservation space failed. The claims were deemed illegitimate and thus regarded by the people living in and using the space as insufficient. However, the arrival of the signs shifted, if only slightly, how people used and thought about the area and its meaning, as well as how they viewed local conservation efforts. People continued to crab, but "the Hollow" became a site of resistance and a symbol for elite intervention, as well as for the inefficacy of the national conservation organization. The move to enclose areas of land and sea that were long understood as a commons was viewed by many Androsians as a shift in governance scale and structure, from interactive and locally meaningful negotiations to internationally significant management agendas with material consequences.

This shift in governance imbued a new—globally significant—value to the aquatic space. Simultaneously, it threatened to disrupt existing governance processes and social linkages that considered specific realities and complexities of place, transposing instead a rigid model of environmental governance. By restricting access and activity in the area, the reserve threatened to disrupt the existing undersigns and relationships among community and space. Social networks shifted, lending status and social capital to new groups, such as the people involved with conservation efforts.

240 *Wise*

A resident explained his view of the conservation organization leading the move to enclose protected areas throughout The Bahamas: "It's a club, and if you ain't in it, that's it." The park project became an unrightful claim by conservation elites to an area that had once belonged to Androsians. The enclosure acted as an inflexible boundary line that threatened to disrupt the flows of aquatic space by restricting movement of people and resources as well as blocking existing governance processes. Conservation enclosure of the littoral disrupted the social flow. Once a well-used site of collective harvest and social networks, the area now also signals conflict, dispute, and dispossession.

When the Bahamas National Trust introduced the idea of protected areas in Andros, the responses among residents were mixed. Some people felt the island was large enough to enclose some areas, while allowing for people's continued livelihood. Others were suspicious of any interventions from "outsiders" (anyone not from Andros). From the perspective of the resource managers and conservationists, the discourse centered on rich, valuable biodiversity, "unpeopled" spaces, and the need to conserve "pristine wilderness," biodiversity, and "important fish and crab nurseries" of the coastal littoral (BNT 2008). Brochures and outreach materials described Andros as vast open and empty space: "The largest and least populated of the Bahamian islands, Andros Island is a place of vast, uninhabited expanses and mystery" (TNC 2016). In addition, they claimed it was in danger of losing abundant biodiversity.

The lands and seas of Andros have been shaped by human engagement for centuries. The shores of Andros were sites of industry, whether harvesting sponges, aragonite, or lobsters. Before roads, Androsians traveled by boat, sculling over the shallow bays to see family, celebrate deaths, obtain medical treatment, and transport goods. Boats and their drivers waited for specific hours and seasons for certain channels to clear and routes to open. For centuries, the shallow seas around Andros have hosted several commercial fisheries, including spiny lobsters (*Panulirus argus*), stone crabs (*Menippe mercenaria*), sponge species, queen conchs (*Strombus gigas*), and various scalefishes.

Environmental anthropologist Manuel Valdés-Pizzini argues that the tidal coast is a "sea-landscape" deeply embedded in a complex social-ecological history (Valdés-Pizzini 2009, 40). The shoreline has been depicted as a place of first landings, conquest, and trade. Specifically, Valdés-Pizzini describes the littoral as "indeed a liminal space that provides the means for important transitions, constructions and desires of identity" (Valdés-Pizzini 2009, 40). He goes further to hint at the space as an actively experienced place, writing that the coast is a "porous boundary of cultural and material exchange" (Valdés-Pizzini 2009, 41). This locates the littoral in the agentic realm, as a kinetic and dynamic space rather than a mere stage. Valdés-Pizzini emphasizes the role of colonial politics and capital labor in constructing—both literally and figuratively—the coastline as a refuge, as well as a boundary marker and access way to resources, identity, and belonging. For many, he writes, "the coast is hope" (Valdés-Pizzini 2009, 40). Historically, for many Bahamians, the shores of Andros did mean hope, in the form of freedom from slavery. Throughout the late 1700 and 1800s, British colonialists tried their hand at plantation-style agriculture with slave labor across Andros. The combination of inadequate wet and muddy soil and a difficult climate led to repeated failures. Eventually, the plantation owners moved on, abandoning their land and the enslaved as failed investments, adding to the narrative of Andros as a barren and difficult island. The formerly enslaved people continued to work and encounter the land, making homes and building communities (Albury 1975; Craton 1962; Craton and Saunders 2000). Later, having heard of the vast space of Androsian and free black Bahamian settlements, others fled slavery and oppression to resettle in Andros, contributing their stories, histories, and experience to the island (Goggin 1939, 1946; Howard 2006). In Andros, the littoral became a site of resilience, resistance, and survival for centuries. Access to resources is dictated by the tides and linked to notions of "rightful" access—often communicated through informal pathways loaded with meanings about gender, race, place, and belonging. Although much of the island spends a good deal of the year submerged, a wet land of mangroves and mudflats, Androsians continue to depend on the land- and seascapes to build their houses, crab, fish, sponge, hunt, and play across the island in ways that are meaningful and enduring.

## CONCLUSION

In the fluid, muddy littoral, amphibious governance offers an alternative to the rigid boundary-making of enclosure governance. PA management proves ineffective for tidal spaces, given their temporal and spatial dynamism, and perhaps more significantly, it is likely to disrupt vital social linkages that support community resilience. In an effort to manage rapidly declining resources, conservation managers may disregard valuable social-ecological linkages and the intricacies of those changing multifaceted relationships across humans and the littoral.

Enclosure management is a static form of governance: it does not account for the mobility and flow of the social and physical landscape. Rather, enclosure simply constructs barriers to fluidity. Terrestrial boundary markers are comparatively stable; however, tidelands are between spaces and, as such, require specific marking strategies that can withstand fluidity. Tracking mobile populations across temporal (i.e., seasonal or tidal shifts) and material (wet, dry, muddy) boundaries requires an understanding of ecosystem as well as social interactions. Even more importantly, the ways in which humans live within—and in relation to—dynamic tidal lands require a shift in the way space and behavior are governed. The two concepts of enclosure and connectivity are at odds, unable to capture the multiplicity of uses that have evolved with the fluid littoral for centuries. Enclosure conservation bounds space and potentially disrupts fluidity while the littoral flows across and recomposes boundaries in its fluidity. By restricting flows—of people, information, and social networks—enclosure conservation reshapes community organization, away from amphibious engagement and toward a static, and perhaps less responsive, governance.

Material and cultural conditions interact to create a space contingent on fluidity and repeated, rhythmic encounter. Through varied and specific interventions, mud-scapes can be shaped and reshaped to fulfill multiple applications. Andros's littoral spaces fluctuate—often dramatically—with time, season, and use. Where the ocean meets the land cannot be called firm ground or fluid sea; it is a transitory liminal space. The littoral, the point where ocean meets land, signifies a material and symbolic delineation, between marine and terrestrial worlds and all they can characterize. But as the tidal lands of Andros show, the littoral is also a lived place, populated with people surviving, working, and experiencing the rhythm-patterns of daily life.

The shoreline moves beyond a physical boundary and toward a moment of experienced transformation. Governance systems in Andros developed over centuries of colonial rule and deep-seated resistance to prejudicial authority. Andros Island held deeply rooted historical and culture meanings for Bahamians. For Androsians, the mud was closely tied to Bahamian culture and Androsian identity as self-sufficient and independent people living on the periphery of mainstream society. Creating effective protected areas in these spaces would require a new form of governance that derives legitimacy through the inclusion of multiple meanings and multifaceted uses of the fluid landscape. Amphibious governance would allow for responsive and legitimate management of these and dynamic spaces.

In a flowing dynamic space such as the littoral, amphibious governance—a type of management that incorporates temporal and multidimensional considerations—could better reflect the interconnectedness sustained by the social-ecological landscape, as well as the multiplicities of the people using the space. The term suggests a versatile form of governance that takes a processual approach to interconnectedness, both adaptable in the specificity of its practice and distinct in its response to the unique spatiotemporal processes shaping these spaces. Focusing on the processes of management, amphibious governance is multidimensional and adaptive to a range of uses and shifting material and temporal conditions.

The threat of climate change has only strengthened the drive for enclosure conservation to protect important resources and valuable habitat and most recently to act as a tool to mitigate climate change; however, enclosure strategies do other forms of work in the land- and seascapes. Enclosure governance disrupts flows by restricting access, mobility, and human-environment interactions. Littoral spaces center on movement, interaction, and change, requiring an amphibious governance that considers flow. When thinking about the effects of human activities on the marine environment, it is easy to imagine feats of mechanical engineering: structural barriers such as dams, levees, or breakwaters that modify the coastline and block and redirect watery flows; wetlands drained, "reclaimed," and formed into newly created land; sand dredged to build up islands or secure higher ground. These operations are manifestations of physical change of the land- and seascapes as well as the spaces in between. In a place such as Andros, where people are profoundly dependent on the land-sea interface, amphibious governance, framed in the rhythmic and spatial patterns of place, can reflect the fluidity and hybridity of the area as well as the dynamic social and ecological interactions. In practice, amphibious governance is fluid in its inclusion: it is a complex and hybrid governance process embracing customary laws, government regulations, environmental histories, and daily material experience of the littoral. The littoral requires a dynamic and interactive governance process specifically relevant to its temporal and special configurations and able to consider multiple and varied voices in the collective governing of a tidal space. The Andros case study can shed some light on the complexities of tidal coastal management by bringing into the conversation a multiplicity of voices, uses, perceptions, and claims to that space.

## NOTES

1    Common property is an institutional framework describing property held collectively by a group. That group is able to share some aspects of property rights and/or obligations, although not necessarily equally (McCay 2000; Ciriacy-Wantrup and Bishop 1975; Schlager and Ostrom 1992).

2    The annual Crab Fest is held in June after the first flush of crab harvest. According to the Bahamian Tourist Bureau, the purpose of the Crab Fest is to stimulate the local economies through domestic and international tourism and celebrate the traditional crab-catching ways of Andros Island. The Island of the Bahamas, "All Andros Crab Fest," accessed February 8, 2025, https://bahamasgeotourism.com/entries/all-andros-crab-fest/f654e9c5-f475-4598-9db8-b829a5051ce2.

## REFERENCES

Adhikari, S., R. M. Bajracharaya, and B. K. Sitaula. 2009. "A Review of Carbon Dynamics and Sequestration in Wetlands." *Journal of Wetlands Ecology* 2 (1): 42–46.

Albury, P. 1975. *The Story of the Bahamas*. London: Macmillan Educational.

ANCAT (Andros Conservancy and Trust). 2010. *Andros National Parks*. http://ancat.org/index.php?option=com_content&view=article&id=59&Itemid=57.

Andros Beach Club. 2023. "Andros Island." https://www.androsbeachclub.com/andros-island-bahamas-2/.

Armitage, D., R. De Loë, and R. Plummer. 2012. "Environmental Governance and Its Implications for Conservation Practice." *Conservation Letters* 5 (4): 245–55.

Arsel, M., and B. Büscher. 2012. "Nature™ Inc.: Changes and Continuities in Neoliberal Conservation and Market-Based Environmental Policy." *Development and Change* 43 (1): 53–78.

The Bahamas Government. 2022. "Climate Change and Carbon Market Initiatives Act." Climate Change Laws of the World. https://climate-laws.org/documents/climate-change-and-carbon-market-initiatives-act-2022_c676?id=climate-change-and-carbon-market-initiatives-act-2022_db37.

Bahamas National Trust (BNT). 2008. *Proposal for the Westside National Park*. Nassau, Bahamas: Bahamas National Trust.

———. n.d. "Observing World Wetlands Day." Accessed August 1, 2023. https://bnt.bs/news/observing-world-wetlands-day.

Barbier, E. B., S. D. Hacker, C. Kennedy, E. W. Koch, A. C. Stier, and B. R. Silliman. 2011. "The Value of Estuarine and Coastal Ecosystem Services." *Ecological Monographs* 81 (2): 169–93.

Bastain, A. 2023. "Beyond Natural Beauty: The Carbon Credits Market & The Bahamas." *International Investment*. https://www.internationalinvestment.net/feature/4118449/natural-beauty-carbon-credits-market-bahamas.

Bethel, N. R. M. 2000. "Navigations: The Fluidity of National Identity in the Postcolonial Bahamas." PhD diss., University of Cambridge.

Biermann, F., and P. Pattberg. 2008. "Global Environmental Governance: Taking Stock, Moving Forward." *Annual Review of Environment and Resources*, no. 33, 277–94.

Bobbink, R., D. F. Whigham, B. Beltman, and J. T. Verhoeven. 2006. "Wetland Functioning in Relation to Biodiversity Conservation and Restoration." In *Wetlands: Functioning, Biodiversity Conservation, and Restoration* (Ecological

Studies, vol. 191), edited by R. Bobbink, B. Beltman, J. T. A. Verhoeven, and D. F. Whigham, 1–12. Berlin: Springer.

Brockington, D., R. Duffy, and J. Igoe. 2012. *Nature Unbound: Conservation, Capitalism and the Future of Protected Areas.* Routledge.

Büscher, B., S. Sullivan, K. Neves, J. Igoe, and D. Brockington. 2012. "Towards a Synthesized Critique of Neoliberal Biodiversity Conservation." *Capitalism Nature Socialism* 23 (2): 4–30.

Campbell, L., N. J. Gray, L. Fairbanks, J. J. Silver, R. L. Gruby, B. A. Dubik, and X. Basurto. 2016. "Global Oceans Governance: New and Emerging Issues." *Annual Review of Environment and Resources*, no. 41, 2.1–2.27.

Caribbean 30x30 Initiative. 2023. https://caribbean30x30.org/.

Carrier, J. G. 2003. "Biography, Ecology, Political Economy: Seascape and Conflict in Jamaica." In *Landscape, Memory, and History*, edited by P. Stewart and A. Strathern, 210–28. London: Pluto Press.

Cash, D. W., W. N. Adger, F. Berkes, P. Garden, L. Lebel, P. Olsson, L. Pritchard, et al. 2006. "Scale and Cross-Scale Dynamics: Governance and Information in a Multilevel World." *Ecology and Society* 11 (2): 8.

Castree, N. 2008. "Neoliberalising Nature: The Logics of Deregulation and Reregulation." *Environment and Planning A* 40 (1): 131–52.

Ciriacy-Wantrup, S. V., and R. C. Bishop. 1975. "Common Property" as a Concept in Natural Resources Policy. *Natural Resources Journal* 15 (4): 713–27.

COP14–15. 2022. UN Biodiversity Conference. Resolution XIV.4: Review of the Fourth Strategic Plan of the Convention on Wetlands, Additions for the Period COP14-COP15 and Framework for the Fifth Strategic Plan. https://www.cbd .int/cop/.

Costanza, R., R. de Groot, P. Sutton, S. Van der Ploeg, S. J. Anderson, I. Kubiszewski, S. Farben, et al. 2014. "Changes in the Global Value of Ecosystem Services." *Global Environmental Change*, no. 26, 152–58.

Craton, M. 1962. *A History of the Bahamas.* London: Collins.

Craton, M., and G. Saunders. 2000. *Islanders in the Stream: A History of the Bahamian People: From the Ending of Slavery to the Twenty-First Century.* Vol. 2. University of Georgia Press.

da Cunha, D. 2018. *The Invention of Rivers: Alexander's Eye and Ganga's Descent.* Philadelphia: University of Pennsylvania Press.

Davidson, N. C. 2014. "How Much Wetland Has the World Lost? Long-Term and Recent Trends in Global Wetland Area." *Marine and Freshwater Research* 65 (10): 934–41.

Denny, P. 1994. "Biodiversity and Wetlands." *Wetlands Ecology and Management*, no. 3, 55–611.

Encyclopedia Britannica. 2016. *Littoral Zone, Marine Ecology*. https://www .britannica.com/science/littoral-zone.

Finlayson, C. M., S. J. Capon, D. Rissik, J. Pittock, G. Fisk, N. C. Davidson, K. A. Bodmin, et al. 2017. "Policy Considerations for Managing Wetlands under a Changing Climate." *Marine and Freshwater Research* 68 (10): 1803–15.

Fraser, L. H., and P. A. Keddy. 2005. "The Future of Large Wetlands: A Global Perspective." In *The World's Largest Wetlands: Ecology and Conservation*, edited by L. H. Fraser and P. A. Keddy, 446–68. Cambridge: Cambridge University Press.

Gearey, M. 2022. "Place-Making in Waterscapes: Wetlands as Palimpsest Spaces of Recreation." *Geographical Journal* 190 (2): 1–15.

Goggin, J. M. 1939. "An Anthropological Reconnaissance of Andros Island, Bahamas." *American Antiquity* 5 (1): 21–26.

———. 1946. "The Seminole Negroes of Andros Island, Bahamas." *Florida Historical Quarterly* 24 (3): 1–6.

Gopal, B. 2009. "Biodiversity in Wetlands." In *The Wetlands Handbook*, edited by E. Maltby and T. Barker, 65–95. Blackwell.

Grove, R. H. 1996. *Green Imperialism: Colonial Expansion, Tropical Island Edens and the Origins of Environmentalism, 1600–1860*. Cambridge University Press.

Hargreaves-Allen. 2010. "An Economic Valuation of the Natural Resources of Andros Islands, Bahamas." *Conservation Strategy Fund for The Nature Conservancy*. https://www.conservation-strategy.org/sites/default/files/field-file /Andros_Exec_summary_II.pdf.

Heikkilä, T. T., N. B, Kopnin, and G. E. Volovik. 2011. "Flat Bands in Topological Media." *JETP Letters*, no. 94, 233–39.

Howard, R. 2006. "The 'Wild Indians' of Andros Island: Black Seminole Legacy in the Bahamas." *Journal of Black Studies* 37 (2): 275–98.

Jones, O. 2011. "Lunar-Solar Rhythmpatterns: Toward the Material Cultures of Tides." *Environment and Planning A* 43 (10): 2285–303.

Kamalame Cay. 2023. "The All-Natural Beauty of Andros" https://www.kamalame .com/the-island.

Kelly, A. B., and A. C. Gupta. 2016. "Protected Areas: Offering Security to Whom, When and Where?" *Environmental Conservation* 43 (2): 172–80.

Kelly, A. B., and M. Ybarra. 2016. "Introduction to Themed Issue: 'Green Security in Protected Areas.'" *Geoforum*, no. 69, 171–75.

Kingsford, R. T., A. Basset, and L. Jackson. 2016. "Wetlands: Conservation's Poor

Cousins." *Aquatic Conservation: Marine and Freshwater Ecosystems* 26 (5): 892–916.

Koebele, E. A. 2015. "Assessing Outputs, Outcomes, and Barriers in Collaborative Water Governance: A Case Study." *Journal of Contemporary Water Research & Education* 155 (1): 63–72.

Mandoske, J. 2017. *Can Blue Carbon Further Conservation? Approaches to Conservation through a Portfolio of Blue Carbon Options: A Case Study in the Bahamas.* UC San Diego: Center for Marine Biodiversity and Conservation.

Manuel-Navarrete, D., M. Pelling, and M. Redclift. 2009. "Governance as Process: Powerspheres and Climate Change Response." *Environment, Politics and Development Working Paper Series* 9.

McCay, B. 2009. "The Littoral and the Liminal; or Why It Is Hard and Critical to Answer the Question 'Who Owns the Coast?'" *MAST* [Marine Anthropological Studies, University of Amsterdam] 17 (1): 7–30.

McCay, B. J. 1998. *Oyster Wars and the Public Trust: Property, Law, and Ecology in New Jersey History.* University of Arizona Press.

———. 2000. "Sea Changes in Fisheries Policy: Contributions from Anthropology." In *State and Community in Fisheries Management: Power, Policy, and Practice,* edited by E. Paul Durrenberger and Thomas King, 201–17. Bloomsbury.

Mitsch, W. J., B. Bernal, A. M. Nahlik, Ü. Mander, L. Zhang, C. J. Anderson, S. E. Jørgensen, et al. 2013. "Wetlands, Carbon, and Climate Change." *Landscape Ecology,* no. 28, 583–97.

Moomaw, W. R., G. L. Chmura, G. T. Davies, C. M. Finlayson, B. A. Middleton, S. M. Natali, J. E. Perry, et al. 2018. "Wetlands in a Changing Climate: Science, Policy and Management." *Wetlands* 38 (2): 183–205.

Newaz, M. W., and S. Rahman. 2019. "Wetland Resource Governance in Bangladesh: An Analysis of Community-Based Co-management Approach." *Environmental Development,* no. 32, 100446.

Norman, E. S., K. Bakker, and C. Cook. 2012. "Introduction to the Themed Section: Water Governance and the Politics of Scale." *Water Alternatives* 5 (1).

Nygren, A., and A. Lounela. 2023. "Remaking of Wetlands and Coping with Vulnerabilities in Mexico and Indonesia." *Water Alternatives* 16 (1): 295–320.

Oslender, U. 2001. "Black Communities on the Colombian Pacific Coast and the 'Aquatic Space': A Spatial Approach to Social Movement Theory." PhD diss., University of Glasgow.

———. 2004. "Fleshing Out the Geographies of Social Movements: Colombia's Pacific Coast Black Communities and the 'Aquatic Space.'" *Political Geography* 23 (8): 957–85.

Parlee, C., and M. Wiber. 2014. "Institutional Innovation in Fisheries Governance: Adaptive Co-management in Situations of Legal Pluralism." *Current Opinion in Environmental Sustainability*, no. 11, 48–54.

Peimer, A. W., A. E. Krzywicka, D. B. Cohen, K. Van den Bosch, V. L. Buxton, N. A. Stevenson, and J. W. Matthews. 2017. "National-Level Wetland Policy Specificity and Goals Vary According to Political and Economic Indicators." *Environmental Management*, no. 59, 141–53.

Pennisi, E. 2020. "The Mud Is Electric." *Science*, no. 369, 902–5.

Raffles, H. 2002. *In Amazonia: A Natural History*. Princeton University Press.

———. 2007. "Fluvial Intimacies." In *Waterscapes: The Cultural Politics of a Natural Resource*, edited by Amita Baviskar, 314–39. Permanent Black.

Ramsar Convention Secretariat, 2016. *An Introduction to the Convention on Wetlands* (previously *The Ramsar Convention Manual*). Ramsar Convention Secretariat, Gland, Switzerland.

Rauschmayer, F., A. Berghöfer, I. Omann, and D. Zikos. 2009. "Examining Processes or/and Outcomes? Evaluation Concepts in European Governance of Natural Resources." *Environmental Policy and Governance* 19 (3): 159–73.

Ruíz, A. G., E. Hes, and K. Schwartz. 2011. "Shifting Governance Modes in Wetland Management: A Case Study of Two Wetlands in Bogotá, Colombia." *Environment and Planning C: Government and Policy* 29 (6): 990–1003.

Schlager, E., and E. Ostrom. 1992. "Property-Rights Regimes and Natural Resources: A Conceptual Analysis." *Land Economics* 68 (3): 249–62.

Sherman, K. D., A. D. Shultz, C. P. Dahlgren, C. Thomas, E. Brooks, A. Brooks, D. R. Brumbaugh, et al. 2018. "Contemporary and Emerging Fisheries in The Bahamas—Conservation and Management Challenges, Achievements and Future Directions." *Fisheries Management and Ecology* 25 (5): 319–31.

Steinberg, P., and K. Peters. 2015. "Wet Ontologies, Fluid Spaces: Giving Depth to Volume through Oceanic Thinking." *Environment and Planning D: Society and Space* 33 (2): 247–64.

Stoffle, B. W., and R. W. Stoffle. 2007. "At the Sea's Edge: Elders and Children in the Littorals of Barbados and the Bahamas." *Human Ecology* 35 (5): 547–58.

Sullivan, S. 2013. "Banking Nature? The Spectacular Financialisation of Environmental Conservation." *Antipode* 45 (1): 198–217.

TNC (The Nature Conservancy). 2016. "The Bahamas, Andros Island." http://www.nature.org/ourinitiatives/regions/caribbean/bahamas/placesweprotect/bahamas-andros-island.xml.

Torres-Fontánez, E. 2009. "Law, Extralegality, and Space: Legal Pluralism and

Landscape from Colombia to Puerto Rico." *University of Miami Inter-American Law Review* 40 (2): 285–300.

Turner, R., J. Addison, A. Arias, B. J. Bergseth, N. A. Marshall, T. H. Morrison, and R. C. Tobin. 2016. "Trust, Confidence, and Equity Affect the Legitimacy of Natural Resource Governance." *Ecology and Society* 21 (3).

Tyler, T. R. 2006. "Psychological Perspectives on Legitimacy and Legitimation." *Annual Review of Psychology*, no. 57, 375–400.

UNDP (United Nations Development Programme). 1997. *Governance for Sustainable Human Development.* New York: UNDP Policy Document.

UNEP. 2023. "Drive to Protect World's Wetlands Gains Momentum." UNDP. https://www.unep.org/news-and-stories/story/drive-protect-worlds-wetlands -gains-momentum.

USAID. 2018. "Discussion Note: Adaptive Management." Bureau for Policy, Planning and Learning. https://usaidlearninglab.org/library/discussion-note -adaptive-management.

Valdés-Pizzini, M. 2009. "Comments on: 'The Littoral and the Liminal: Challenges to the Management of the Coastal and Marine Commons.'" *MAST* [Marine Anthropological Studies, University of Amsterdam] 17 (1): 39–43.

van Ginkel, R. 2013. *The Cultural Seascape, Cosmology and the Magic of Liminality.* Eastbourne: Leisure Studies Association.

Villa, J. A., and B. Bernal. 2018. "Carbon Sequestration in Wetlands, from Science to Practice: An Overview of the Biogeochemical Process, Measurement Methods, and Policy Framework." *Ecological Engineering*, no. 114, 115–28.

Wise, S. 2015. "Conflict and Collaboration in Marine Conservation Work." In *Human-Wildlife Conflict: Complexity in the Marine Environment*, edited by M. Draheim, F. Madden, J. B. McCarthy, and E. C. Parsons, 97–111. Oxford University Press.

Wise, S. P. 2014. "Learning through Experience: Non-implementation and the Challenges of Protected Area Conservation in the Bahamas." *Marine Policy*, no. 46, 111–18.

Zelditch, M. 2001. "Theories of Legitimacy." *Psychology of Legitimacy: Emerging Perspectives on Ideology, Justice, and Intergroup Relations*, no. 33.

ALEJANDRO CAMARGO

# 9. The Contours of the Amphibious
## *Wetlands, Knowledge, and Politics in Colombia*

On October 22, 2020, Sandra Vilardy, a wetland scientist; Alejandro Gaviria, the then president of Colombia's most prestigious private university; and Carlos Vives, a famous singer, met in a public online event entitled "Amphibious Colombia: A Pressing Country Dialogue." This event was linked to the launch of the official video of Vives's latest song, "Cumbiana." The video tells the story of Cumbiana, a girl who lives in Nueva Venecia, a town built on stilts in the Ciénaga Grande de Santa Marta marsh in northern Colombia. The story focuses on how she continuously misses, remembers, and dreams of her father—a fisherman who was kidnapped by illegal armed groups. These scenes evoke memories of the massacre of 2000, when paramilitary groups murdered thirty-seven people in this fishing community. In the video, Cumbiana's story unfolds as images of the marsh, its inhabitants, and biodiversity constitute a particular landscape. The Ciénaga Grande de Santa Marta marsh is a unique wetland where water from the ocean, the rivers from the Sierra Nevada de Santa Manta mountain, and the Magdalena River merge. This marsh is one of the few Ramsar sites in Colombia, and it is currently at risk. The expansion of commercial farming on its perimeter, the construction of a road that altered the saltwater/freshwater balance and impaired the life of fish and mangroves, and the intentional diversion of the mountain rivers that feed it with freshwater have rapidly deteriorated this wetland ecosystem. In addition, illegal armed groups have long made this place unsafe and haunted by violence. The video ends with the following text: "May the music of water reminds us that an amphibious world exists in Colombia.

252 *Camargo*

That world wants to flourish anew, keeping its way of life in equilibrium. And upon this, which seems to be so simple, our future depends."[1]

"How do music, education, and science relate to the marsh?" the moderator asked to start the discussion. The speakers emphasized that Colombia is a *país anfibio* (an amphibious country) because, according to a recent scientific study (to which I will refer later), wetlands cover about 30 percent of its territory. Water, Vilardy pointed out, is more than a resource, since it also forms territories, makes life possible, and shapes cultural identities. Yet, she continued, Colombians as a nation have been unable to understand and properly value this amphibiousness. Consequently, development programs have long been implemented at the expense of wetlands, and many of them have disappeared. This is so because the state, according to Gaviria, has ignored the geographical and hydrological realities of Colombia. The Ciénaga Grande de Santa Marta marsh is but an instance of the critical state of wetlands in a country also ravaged by violence and environmental degradation. For Vives, amphibious territories have also been the places that have given birth to prominent artists. The speakers agreed that Colombians faced a pressing need to "reconcile" themselves with water. The idea of Amphibious Colombia, as the aspiration of this event, holds the promise of ecological, national, political, and epistemic integration.

This chapter questions and examines the idea of the amphibious as a terrain of knowledge production and political deliberation. It analyzes the implications of deploying the concept of the amphibious to imagine territories and peoples at the intersection of science, politics, and society. The amphibious, as approached in this volume, primarily refers to a particular analytical approach to environments in which wetness intertwines with more-than-human experiences, socialities, and politics. Yet the Colombian case compels us to also consider it in its discursive, public, and performative forms. I propose to do so by way of a concrete question: How does the idea of the amphibious come into being in public imagination, and what do people do with it?

In Colombia, the idea of the amphibious has two important antecedents. The first of these antecedents is the work of sociologist Orlando Fals

Borda (1979), who formulated the concept of *cultura anfibia* (amphibious culture) in the late 1970s. Through this concept, Fals Borda explained the diverse ways of life found between land and water developed by the riverine people of the Mompos Depression in northern Colombia. The Mompos Depression is a dynamic floodplain where multiple marshes, rivers, and streams connect according to seasonal rain and floods. The ways of life that characterize this milieu not only refer to particular livelihoods and relations with the environment. They also allude to the everyday challenges and struggles involved in living in a place where unequal access to land and unbalanced agrarian power relations prevail. The second antecedent is the La Niña–related catastrophic floods of 2010. This disaster affected most of the Colombian territory in one way or another, but it wreaked particular havoc in regions such as the Mompos Depression. The problem of floods led the Colombian state to formulate a national policy of adaptation to climate change that included large amounts of resources for scientific research related to wetlands. These studies sought to provide a more accurate view of the spatial distribution of these ecosystems to better inform public policy. Inspired by Fals Borda's work, the idea of Colombia Anfibia (amphibious Colombia) came into being in this context as a discursive device to bring together science, politics, and society in support of an environmentally conscious approach to wetlands and an integrative notion of the national territory. However, while Colombia Anfibia exposes the hydrological nature of the national territory, it also obscures the land question. This is a critical issue because the unequal distribution of land is paramount in Fals Borda's formulation of *cultura anfibia*, as well as in the everyday life of the amphibious people of the Mompos Depression. Furthermore, scientists, artists, and development practitioners use the idea of the amphibious for political and environmental purposes, but the people from the Mompos Depression rarely use it. These dissonances expose the current limitations of this idea.

The idea of the amphibious, as materialized in wetlands, can be examined as a "boundary object" (Star and Griesemer 1989), where various forms of knowledge and political claims intersect.[2] It should be noted that the production of new cartographies and scientific studies about wetlands in the aftermath of the 2010 floods opened the way to this popularization of the idea of Colombia Anfibia. Environmentalists, NGOs, artists, scholars, and government institutions have coined this term to produce a particular idea of these territories and ecosystems in the context of climate change, peace building, and environmental deterioration. Different languages, intentions, imaginaries, and technologies delineate the contours of the amphibious and make it instrumental in mobilizing a particular national identity and amplifying the criticism of development, capital accumulation, conflict, and state action.

## CONTOURS

The amphibious as a lens through which to view particular landscapes, environments, and people is primarily an academic construct. The idea of *cultura anfibia* is not an exception, as it is inspired by the work of sociologist Orlando Fals Borda (1979; see also the introduction to this volume). The scholars who have coined this concept use it to approach not just a single thing but an entanglement of materials, processes, and relations. For Morita (2016), the amphibious is materialized in the sociospatial configuration of deltas. These environments are located between the ocean and the river (thus merging parts of these two worlds) and where particular lifestyles take place. From this viewpoint, deltas stand in sharp contrast with modernist biases that lean toward the terrestrial (see also Morita and Jensen 2017). Krause (2017) sees the amphibious as the place where land, water, and human lives converge. In this way, the amphibious has the potential to transcend the simplification and singularization of elements such as water. This is particularly explicit in the work of Richardson (2018), who pinpoints the need to move beyond the focus on water and flow in deltaic environments and to also consider processes of sedimentation and the formation of solid places. The term *amphibious* allows her to encapsulate those elements and relations in a single idea. The amphibious, therefore, helps to conceptually integrate, or transcend, what would otherwise need to be explained by resorting to the conventional separation of elements and objects such as land and water. Yet the amphibious is not merely the amalgamation of water and land. It is a different formation of wetness, as several chapters of this book elaborate. This concept has been an analytical category and an approach to the study of people–environment relationships in wet environments.

Although the idea of Colombia Anfibia as an approach to a particular territory is an analytical category, its scope is not confined to the academic realm. Rather, this idea is best understood as a "boundary object" that inhabits "several intersecting worlds" and is "plastic enough to adapt to local needs" and coherent and "robust enough to maintain a common identity across sites" (Star and Griesemer 1989, 393; for wetlands as boundary objects, see Scaramelli 2021). As a boundary object, the amphibious has a discursive force intended to transform practice. Linguists and philosophers have long reflected upon the question of "how to do things with words" (Austin 1975), or the performative power of language. Scientists, activists, and other actors deploying the concept of the amphibious seek to do things with this concept in order to counteract the socioecological deterioration of wetlands as well as the political fragmentation of the nation and territory. The amphibious, in this sense, also constitutes a form of "ecological nationalism" (Cederlöf and Sivaramakrishnan 2006). In order for Colombia Anfibia to become a boundary object, however, knowledge about wetlands had to be produced, put together, and translated in different ways. Science-and-technology studies have long examined the politics and rearticulations involved in translating scientific knowledge into tools for policy makers in order to make "complex socioecological realities legible and therewith governable" (Carton 2020, 1355; see also Scott 1998 for an earlier elaboration of this idea). Territory is precisely a category that emerges at the convergence of science and politics through techniques of calculation and cartographic representation, thus becoming an "epistemic object" (Mahony 2014, 125). In times of climate change, the future of territory is a concern to the state and other national and international political actors engaged with anticipative management (Mahony 2014, 126).

This type of concern has been part of long-standing discussions about the science–policy gap. But more broadly, it refers to the encounter of multiple forms of knowledge and the ways they are produced, circulated, and utilized (Kohl and Knox 2016). To some extent, the integration of these forms of knowledge is seen as desirable both in the literature and in the policy domain. For instance, the lack of "hybrid conceptual frameworks" for the integration of dissimilar epistemologies appears as a barrier for an interdisciplinary dialogue about climate change (López, Jung, and López 2017, 31). Yet "dissimilar" may also mean conflicting, oppositional, and contradictory (see Jensen and Morita 2020). Achieving consensus is not a simple endeavor. It often involves the "messy" politics of antagonism and irreconciliation (Klenk and Meehan 2015). In this sense, devising and implementing alternative epistemologies is also crucial to envisioning the possibilities of more democratic and just responses to climate change (Rice, Burke, and Heynen 2015).

As a boundary object, the idea of the amphibious in Colombia has the potential to integrate different forms of knowledge under a particular representation of the national territory. This representation has been built through a process of technical, political, social, and semantic delineation intended to discern the contours of the amphibious. These contours consist of the physical and cartographic boundaries of wetlands, their political and legal status, the subjects whose lifestyles are encompassed by the amphibious, and the meaning of such a term in academia and public imagination. Defining the contours of the amphibious, however, also involves disagreement and antagonism, as wetlands incorporate dissimilar meanings and conflicting uses. Yet at the center of the amphibious lies a particular configuration of landscapes and people existing in wet environments.

## WETNESS

The La Mojana region has been one of the most meaningful landscapes for sustaining the idea of Colombia Anfibia because of its wet environments. La Mojana is an inland delta located in the Mompos Depression. Here, the Magdalena, San Jorge, and Cauca Rivers meet to form a dynamic hydrological network. Everyday life in La Mojana transpires as water moves under the sway of either scarce or abundant rain. Marshes expand and contract, and rivers and streams rise, often overtopping their banks (sometimes in catastrophic ways), and then fall and dry up unevenly. Although the movement of water dictates the rhythms of agrarian livelihoods such as fishing, crop production, and cattle ranching, people also interrupt, repurpose, and divert water flows. People open small channels branching off the river or other streams to divert water, to drain wetlands, or to create a shortcut for aquatic transportation. These new streams, once created, are known locally as *chorros*. People tend to assign a name to each *chorro*, usually after the owner of the land through which the stream flows. On the riverbanks, people and even local authorities have built levees and embankments to protect settlements from overflowing water. These interventions, however, may inadvertently result in catastrophic events. It is common to hear that during rainy times some *chorros* actually make floods worse. In 2010, catastrophic floods in some parts of La Mojana, especially in the Cauca River area, were associated with the collapse of levees and embankments that were meant to control flooding. The technology of *chorros* and levees has also been instrumental in draining marshes during the dry season, after which they are blocked to prevent the river from filling them up again. This practice has been used to appropriate the land of former marshes and to expand cattle ranching and monocrop commercial agriculture.

The constant movement of water configures wet environments where multiple ecological processes occur and amphibious people and other beings live. *Zapales* are one of these environments whose vitality is contingent on the preservation of wetness. *Zapales* are freshwater swamp forests that retain wetness during the dry season. In an interview, a biologist working in La Mojana referred to them as examples of the amphibious environment par excellence since they are neither fully terrestrial nor aquatic. They are like green patches of high biodiversity. *Zapales* in La Mojana are understudied because, according to this biologist, ecologists and other scientists in Colombia usually specialize in either aquatic or terrestrial ecosystems, but not in in-between environments. For the people of La Mojana, *zapales* are places where life abounds. Fishes, reptiles, rodents, fowl, and specific plant species inhabit these swamp forests, as do humans who also hunt and fish. Over the last decade, however, a new species has gained commercial importance and has spread throughout La Mojana: water buffalo

(*Bubalus bubalis*). An inhabitant of the San Jorge River explained to me that unlike other species, buffalo destroy *zapales* and contaminate them with their urine. Furthermore, he added, this species is symbolic of the inequalities prevailing in the area, as buffalo are owned by wealthy farmers whose practices have long had an adverse impact on marshes in the area. But wetness also prevents *zapales* from being fully rooted, thereby making them unstable under some conditions. That was the case in 2010, when, according to the people near the San Jorge River, the floods were so powerful that they actually moved some *zapales* from one place to another. When dry times return, the wetness of *zapales* secures life and livelihoods, instead of destroying them. This makes these ecosystems rather significant to the people of La Mojana, and their disappearance therefore constitutes a threat to different forms of life.

In arid periods, wetness is also preserved in areas known as *playones*. *Playones* are transition zones between water and land on the edge of marshes that are temporarily exposed during dry times as marshes shrink. These areas retain wetness, which, together with sediment and its nutrients, form fertile terrains. People grow food and grass for cattle in *playones* before water returns. However, cattle ranching and crop production are mutually exclusive in some areas, and consequently, there are frequent conflicts over the ownership and use of *playones*. Others choose to enter into agreements that delineate the collective or individual use of *playones* through customary norms, as will be explained later. During rainy seasons, the river fills marshes with water, sediment, and organic matter, thereby replenishing the future *playones*. When rivers and streams overflow their banks, sediment, water, and nutrients also make adjacent areas wet and suitable for crop production. People living along the banks of the river use fluvial mud, known locally as *barro*, *fango*, or *lodo*, as soil for their home gardens and another type of river sand for home construction. These home gardens are spaces for the cultivation of food for domestic consumption by the family. Chickens, dogs, and pigs, among other animals, also benefit from home gardens when produce is included in their meals, or when they manage to sneak into them. People prefer *fango* for gardens because of its wetness and reject other materials as being too dry. Preserving wetness provides the possibility of expanding and maintaining the motion of life.

The wetness of *playones* and *zapales* is crucial for the delimitation of their ecological and spatial contours. Yet, it must be remembered that wetness is contingent on annual flooding, which is cyclical but does not always occur in the same fashion. For example, the floods of 2010 redrew the contours of various marshes, opened new channels, and made extensive areas waterlogged for almost four years. This turned into a catastrophe, as hundreds of people lost their livestock, crops, houses, and land. Since floods have increasingly become a powerful sign of the intensification of global climate change, the 2010 calamity triggered the implementation of adaptation to climate change projects in La Mojana. These projects added to a longer history of international interventions intended to tame floods and to delineate the contours of wetlands to make them legible to governmental powers. In other words, these interventions have ultimately created a new frontier for development and climate adaptation.

### FRONTIER

San Marcos is a town located where the savannahs meet La Mojana, and it's called the "Pearl of the San Jorge." This town has historically been an important economic center and port where goods such as fish and rice leave La Mojana, while others enter it to be distributed across the region. At the port of San Marcos, one sees a sculpture of el hombre hicotea (hicotea man), a half-human, half-turtle being who faces a magnificent marsh connected to the San Jorge River and the Caño Carate stream. The hicotea (*Trachemys callirostris*) is a turtle that inhabits the marshes and other wetlands in La Mojana and is also part of people's diet, especially during Holy Week. Fals Borda (1984, 27B; see also McRae 2015) observed that the "*dureza cultural*" (cultural hardship) of the "amphibious man," whereby "he" endures and copes with adverse circumstances, mimics the endurance of hicoteas during the harshness of the dry season. José Villegas, who built this sculpture in 1999, was inspired by Fals Borda's concept of amphibious culture. His mission was to find an object to represent the region. Since then, the hombre hicotea has been an icon of La Mojana (although one

260 *Camargo*

of his arms was broken for a long time). While the local government hesitated to make any money available to repair the arm of hombre hicotea, thousands of US dollars from international institutions have entered the region via San Marcos to improve the life of the people of the "amphibious culture," and to imagine wetlands anew in disparate ways.

The area between the urban center of San Marcos and the home of my friend José and his family on the bank of the San Jorge is but one of the places where those international funds mentioned above have materialized. I have traveled between these two spots countless times since I began my fieldwork in La Mojana in 2003. This experience has given me a sense of how things have changed over the years. In June 2019, for instance, I was on my way to José's house when I noticed that part of the road, which is unpaved, had been recently repaired, as it proceeded to a small community called El Torno. Beyond this point, the road was in bad condition as usual. I asked the motorbike taxi driver about this partial repair, to which he replied, "Ah, the mayor repaired this part of the road for the prince's visit to El Torno." "The prince, what prince?" I asked. "I don't know, a prince from Arabia or somewhere far away. A prince with lots of money." After browsing online, I found out that it was Prince Haakon of Norway, who visited El Torno in February 2019 as an ambassador of the United Nations Development Programme (UNDP). In his speech, the prince highlighted the work the UNDP has accomplished together with the Colombian government. These efforts have sought to adapt La Mojana to climate change, to make it more resilient, and to reduce its vulnerability (UNDP 2019). The first of these projects was funded by the Kyoto Protocol through the Adaptation Fund from 2015 to 2019, and the second project received funds from the Green Climate Fund to be implemented from 2019 to 2026. In the vicinity of El Torno, I saw billboards on the road advertising these projects and other specific interventions such as stream restoration. I finally arrived at José's house and was surprised to see on its walls the logo of the UNDP and the Adaptation Fund, as well as phrases like "crop diversification," "risk management in the face of flooding and drought," "efficient irrigation system," and "adaptation to climate change." José told me that his daughter had been working with the UNDP project as a local promoter and had taken training courses about adaptation to climate change and risk management. In recent years, La Mojana has become a new frontier of climate change governance in Colombia.

These are not the first international interventions in La Mojana. Aspirations to make La Mojana into a frontier have dated back at least to the 1950s. In 1955, Dutch engineer Hugo Vlugter recommended the Colombian government to reclaim 400,000 hectares located between the San Jorge and Cauca Rivers through a system of polders in order to make them suitable for agricultural development (Currie 1960). In the 1970s, the Dutch and the Colombian governments made an agreement to conduct a comprehensive study of the Cauca and Magdalena Rivers. This study also proposed the regulation of floods in La Mojana, but neither this nor Vlugter's suggestions actually materialized. The UN Food and Agriculture Organization (FAO) also visited La Mojana during this decade and pinpointed the underexploitation of fisheries due to inadequate fishing equipment. This organization called attention to the importance of increasing the productivity of fisheries through more-efficient technologies. The FAO returned in the early 2000s to initiate the "Program for the Sustainable Development of the La Mojana Region," in which, paradoxically, they expressed concern about the overexploitation of fishing (Camargo 2009). For some experts, the FAO sustainable development project is little different from the Colombia-Dutch project in its intention to drain marshes for economic and infrastructural development (Galvis and Mojica 2007). Labeled as climate change adaptation, current projects contribute to a growing history of interventions aimed at making La Mojana a terrain for the materialization of the goals of development.

The configuration of La Mojana as a new venue for climate change adaptation policies has involved financial resources, experts, programs, knowledge production, pedagogical activities, and the transformation of the landscape. The production of a discourse about the success of adaptation programs in this region has also been instrumental to legitimate these interventions and resources. The prince's visit and his laudatory words concerning the achievements of adaptation projects was but one legitimizing discourse, among others. In November 2020, the minister of the environment visited La Mojana and referred to it as "an example to the whole country" (El Meridiano 2020). The first adaptation project included the creation and implementation of a drought and flood early warning system, the production of new hydroclimatic data to support decision making, agroecological and silvopasture projects in communities, home gardens, community centers, water harvesting systems, training workshops, elevated houses, and wetland restoration programs. One of the most important newspapers of the country published an article entitled "La Mojana: How an Amphibious Community Adapted to Floods" (Casas 2020b), in which some of these interventions are depicted as being successful. This article also highlights the focus on water of the second and ongoing project as a continuation building upon the success of the previous one.

It is beyond the scope of this chapter to assess whether these interventions are actually successful or not. During my fieldwork, however, I have heard dissimilar opinions. Community projects, participation, and leadership have been useful to depict the success of these projects. In the several public events aimed at presenting the progress and outcomes of a particular intervention, project managers emphasized the central role of community involvement and the exchange of knowledge required for the success of the different activities. Wetland and stream rehabilitation, for instance, has been undertaken with the direct participation of local inhabitants. This is the case of Pasifueres, where a group of women led a rehabilitation project in coordination with scientists (Casas 2020a). The long tradition of critical development studies has repeatedly exposed the gaps between what is promised or expected and the actual outcomes in these types of projects. The literature has shown that not everyone benefits and that winners and losers do not come into being naturally: "They are selected" (Li 2007, 20). A person from a community who has participated in training workshops held by UNDP agents explained to me that sometimes attendance at these events is not as expected because "people are busy; they need to look after their livestock and crops, so it is not easy for them to take the time to come to meetings." A local leader also mentioned that "the UNDP team recruited people from the communities who became local promoters, but others who did not participate in the project felt excluded, so there is some resentment within some communities for that reason." Community gardens are symbolic of people's participation and empowerment, not only in the context of this particular project but in the world of development more broadly. But in a fishing community I visited in 2016, the garden was paradoxically flooded. In another community, home gardens were abandoned. I asked a fisherman about the deterioration of the garden, and he argued that he was more concerned about the recovery of fishing stocks (which have dramatically depleted over the last decades) than about gardens. For some people, current interventions in the area are in fact seen as a threat to fishing. Marshes are known locally as *ciénagas*, but recent projects have promoted the term *humedal* (wetland), a common word in the language of academics, development agents, and conservation practitioners. One fisherman argued that he mistrusts those who speak of *humedales* (the plural form of *humedal*) because, for him, *humedales* are human-free conservation areas where fishers won't be allowed to make a living (see Grupusso in this volume for a similar tension in Italy).

Nevertheless, while some people complained about current projects, others saw them as important initiatives. In a house near a *zapal*, certificates from training courses and workshops on adaptation and risk management hang on the wall. For the man who lives there with his family, these courses contributed greatly to his knowledge of what they face during droughts and floods. The language of adaptation, climate change, and risk management reshaped the epistemological contours of the amphibious people of La Mojana. Their adaptive skills and knowledge, initially seen as successful, have eventually being questioned by the UNDP project under the assumption that people need to learn about adaptation to climate change. The boundaries of wetlands were also reimagined, delimited, and materially reconfigured through the scientific knowledge of those promoting conservation and rehabilitation.

## BOUNDARIES

While dry land lends itself to the delineation of limits, the dynamic nature of water in floodplains, its unfixed shape, fluidity, and capacity to infiltrate, poses serious challenges to human efforts to determine its boundaries. Floods are particularly and dramatically illustrative of this indeterminacy. Floods can be understood in different manners and imply manifold biophysical processes (see Camargo and Cortesi 2019), but in La Mojana floods mean a constant reconfiguration of the spatial distribution of water and wetness. The use of *playones* is precisely contingent on the expansion and contraction of marshes' boundaries. Since water moves continuously, these boundaries fluctuate, thereby shaping how people inhabit and draw their own boundaries on these newly delineated wet places. The wetness of *playones*, which makes them rather fertile, is also reinforced as surface water recedes. *Playones* are communal areas, and small farmers are legally entitled to use them for subsistence purposes. Informal agreements among different actors with specific interests in *playones* have given rise to *derecho de ciénaga*, a customary right to use and work in those spaces (Camacho 2015). Yet the use of *playones* operates not only within a grid of adjacent plots. Interests overlap spatially, and therefore, exclusion and conflict emerge. For example, some wealthy and powerful cattle ranchers have historically appropriated *playones* for cattle grazing through violence and intimidation (Camargo 2022). Elusive property boundaries are at the center of these conflicts, as every rainy season may bring about different spatial patterns of flooding, and therefore the boundaries of *playones* may change.

Determining the boundaries of *playones*, private property, floodwaters, and marshes has become a matter of concern in light of these various instances of conflict and violence. In October 2020, a farmer who has long been a leader in the collective defense of *playones* against cattle ranchers' attempts to appropriate them was shot (Bustamante 2020a). He survived, but a few days later five other men were murdered. They were members of a community organization working for the defense of *playones* and communal savannas (Bustamante 2020b). These conflicts are only part of a broader history of agrarian struggles over land and property rights, which has historically permeated rural life in Colombia. Yet in La Mojana, the land question is also a hydrological one, as water shapes land in multiple ways. In 2018, the Ministry of the Environment and Sustainable Development enacted a legal regulation that provides guidelines to define the limits of the transition zones between aquatic and terrestrial spaces. These guidelines bring together geomorphological, hydrological, and ecosystemic components to determine the boundaries of such zones. La Mojana was one of the first regions in which these guidelines were applied as a method to discern the spatial limits of land and water in wetland areas. The Agencia Nacional de Tierras–ANT (National Land Agency) undertook this study as part of its institutional mandates to clarify property rights and resolve land conflicts. An expert in hydrodynamics who has worked in La Mojana explained to me that bringing together the aforementioned components is absolutely necessary. Nevertheless, in environments such as La Mojana, undertaking these studies is challenging. As water moves constantly and yearly floods reconfigure the landscape in myriad ways, determining the boundaries and limits of wetlands is difficult and contentious.

Since the La Mojana terrain is flat, any geomorphological change may alter water flows, level, and distribution. For instance, researchers identified two events of avulsion in the Cauca River that occurred during the 2010 floods.[3] These avulsions generated, among other biophysical changes, a connection between the river and a major wetland, thereby increasing the wetland area temporarily and altering the annual fluctuation of its level. These researchers believe that these avulsions may have disrupted the sedimentation patterns as well (Pérez-Consuegra et al. 2021). The UNDP project has also fostered these landscape transformations by rehabilitating silted up or vanished streams. In addition, a spatial delimitation of boundaries conducted in a specific moment must necessarily be revisited and revised one year after. This, however, demands additional resources, which cannot be guaranteed given the limited—and often shrinking—budget of state institutions such as the ANT. Determining the boundaries of wetlands is as much a technical project as it is a political and social endeavor.

Concerns about the boundaries of wetlands have not been restricted to La Mojana. The 2010 floods set the stage for a national debate about the spatial limits of these ecosystems. This catastrophe exposed the flaws of risk management policies, the lack of knowledge about the dynamics of wetlands, and the need for a more robust approach to adaptation to climate change. In particular, floods called attention to the importance of enhancing resilience through the maintenance of ecosystem integrity and water regulation (Arce 2016, viii). Alongside wetlands, *páramos* became crucial in this debate about the place of water in climate adaptation. *Páramos* are neotropical alpine ecosystems that are considered "the major water provider for the Andean highlands of Venezuela, Colombia and Ecuador, extensive parts of the adjacent lowlands, and the arid coastal plains of North Peru" (Buytaert et al. 2006, 54). The hydrological and ecological importance of wetlands and *páramos*, however, stands in stark contrast with their historical deterioration. Since the 1990s, Colombia and other Latin American countries have embarked on a series of legal reforms to attract international investments in the mining sector. Consequently, the scope of extractive industries in their territories has rapidly expanded (Saade Hazin 2013). *Páramos* have been one of those territories that are attractive to international mining companies in search of resources such as gold and coal. In a number of instances, these ecosystems have become contentious spaces in which the interests of communities, environmentalist NGOs, the state, and mining companies have collided (Osejo and Ungar 2017). Wetlands, on the other hand, have probably had a longer history of deterioration and disappearance as a consequence of the expansion of urban, agricultural, and industrial frontiers (e.g., Patiño and Estupiñán-Suárez 2016). In the aftermath of the 2010 floods, a large amount of public money went into scientific studies aimed at determining the spatial limits of *páramos* and wetlands. This endeavor was meant to offer technical and scientific data to support public policy in climate change adaptation, risk management, and economic development.

In this context, the recently created Adaptation Fund provided the financial resources for what is known today as "the most complete and extensive scientific work about Colombia's wetlands" (Ayazo Toscano et al. 2020, 321).[4] The Humboldt Institute, a public scientific institution, led this project with an interdisciplinary team of scientists, including biologists, ecologists, and engineers. The study was also conducted in collaboration with national and international institutions where geologists, climatologists, hydrologists, geographers, and social scientists all participated. Of particular significance was the use of radar imagery from the Japanese

Aerospace Exploration Agency. This imagery allowed for a more precise, detailed, and cloud-free visualization of bodies of water, and, together with geomorphological, hydrological, edaphological, and vegetation and land cover data, provided the input to produce a 1:100,000 scale map for the spatial identification of wetlands (Flórez et al. 2016). The production of this map set a baseline for a new conceptualization and classification of these ecosystems in Colombia. From the broad concept provided by the Ramsar Convention,[5] scientists moved toward the definition of wetlands as "a type of ecosystem that, due to geomorphological and hydrological conditions, allows the accumulation of water (temporarily and permanently) and gives rise to characteristic types of soil and organisms adapted to these conditions" (Ricaurte et al. 2019, 972; see also Vilardy et al. 2014).

The wetlands map also allowed scientists to formulate "the first system for wetland classification at the national level in Colombia," in which eighty-nine macrohabitats were identified (Ricaurte et al. 2019, 972). Yet, one of the most surprising findings was that wetlands currently cover 30,781,149 ha (about 27 percent) of the national territory. This is significant because before this study, official data varied considerably from 2,649,312 ha in 1992 to 26,422,367 ha in 1997 and 20,252,500 ha in 1998 (Andrade 2016, x). These outcomes were compiled in *Colombia Anfibia: Un país de humedales* (Amphibious Colombia: A country of wetlands), a two-volume open-access publication. This publication contains the map, the classification of wetlands, and a rich body of data regarding the socioecological dimensions of these environments. References to Fals Borda's work adequately support the conceptual component. Furthermore, it is written in a language accessible to nonexpert audiences and is presented in a design that is visually attractive. Shortly after the publication of the map, a CD called *Colombia Anfibia: The Music of Wetlands* was launched and freely distributed. The introduction and dissemination of these materials opened the way for the popularization of the idea of Colombia Anfibia and the widespread adoption of this term in government, academia, and civil society spaces, as well as the related public events, such as the one mentioned earlier.

Delineating the geographical boundaries and the technical and conceptual

268 *Camargo*

contours of wetlands had political consequences. Colombian legislation designates wetlands as public property. This designation excludes any form of private property and, therefore, it would allow for the protection of eco-systems by setting spatial limits to activities such as large-scale agriculture and mining (Rodríguez 2020). But if this were to be enforced throughout the country, a number of conflicts would inevitably emerge. For instance, many towns, villages, farms, and other human settlements are legally lo-cated in wetland areas. This means that it would be nearly impossible to treat these areas as public lands or areas for conservation. Furthermore, a specific plan for each of these areas would need to be formulated, and large amounts of resources would need to be secured in order to materialize these plans. To date, the wetland map has not been officially recognized and incorporated into the legal frameworks of the Colombian state, even though it was funded with state resources. According to two experts I interviewed, political interests forestall such incorporation. The map is currently a key reference for scholars, NGOs, and some local government officials, but its influence on national public policy is limited. Meanwhile, the idea of Colombia Anfibia gains currency, and the relevance of the map is regularly acknowledged in public events and academic settings. The amphibious came into being as a powerful boundary object to make the diverse spatial, social, and epistemological contours of wetlands visible. It has also become a controversial idea threatening political and private interests.

## CONCLUSION

While the amphibious is gaining currency as an analytical lens to under-stand wet environments, in Colombia, this term has also functioned as a tool to create a public notion of the national territory. The amphibious has been mobilized at the intersection of science, policy, and civil society in a moment of wetland degradation, social conflict, and abrupt climate change. For these reasons, the amphibious is endowed with optimism and the promise of a better future for wetlands, humans, and other beings. In a somewhat different context, Knox (2020, 23) reflects on how climate change challenges ways of thinking, creates "new kinds of discipline," and transforms conventional practices. A similar view can be taken of the amphibious. It is a novel academic lens through which to approach nature differently and, more specifically, as a discourse to reimagine Colombian wetlands and the inhabitants thereof. It is inspiring the work of water scientists and seeking to inform conservation, adaptation, risk management, and everyday practices.

The amphibious, when imagined as a territory, takes shape in a conjuncture of fragmentation. The idea of Colombia Anfibia helps to create the national identity of a country that has been described as fragmented and divided (Safford and Palacios 2002). Yet the political dissonances and contradictory interests around wetlands prevent this discourse from actually materializing or producing desirable practices. As Cantor suggests (in this volume), amphibious places have long been considered as wastelands, dangerous places, and areas suited mainly for drainage and exploitation. The discourse of the amphibious seeks to defy that worldview by exposing the relevance of these ecosystems not only for the preservation of life but also for the common future of a nation torn by conflict. In this sense, the amphibious has nurtured a form of ecological nationalism that places nature at the center of a process of national identity and territory building (Cederlöf and Sivaramakrishnan 2006; Yeh 2009).

The discourse of the amphibious helps delineate the contours of particular ecosystems in order to make them legible to different forms of governance (in Scott's [1998] terms) and also incite their defense. However, a crucial cause of national fragmentation has not yet been sufficiently addressed: the problem of land concentration and inequality in amphibious territories. Fals Borda coined the term *cultura anfibia* to think of the land-based historical inequality and struggles of La Mojana. Yet, the current use of the amphibious term is mainly circumscribed to its hydrological dimension. The amphibious occurs between land and water, but it all too easily slips into water, thereby obscuring land. This is clear in the case of climate adaptation projects in La Mojana, as they focus on the rehabilitation of bodies of water but without considering the distribution of land. Attending the land question does not mean to return to the binary that the amphibious defies but to acknowledge that the dynamics of land and water may profoundly affect the amphibious.

It seems that the promise of integration embedded in the amphibious as a boundary object is not readily attainable in practice. Scientists, environmentalists, and development practitioners deploy the word *amphibious* in different scenarios in order "to do" something with it and effect social change. Nevertheless, the question of how the amphibious people of La Mojana use this concept is yet to be answered. Although the amphibious, both as a scholarly concept and as a discourse about the national territory, has transcended the academic realm, it has not yet become an actual tool for action in people's everyday lives. I do not mean to say that it should necessarily incite action in communities. But the question of why this word has not achieved popularity in the very region that gave it birth deserves more attention. This is crucial because the amphibious in the Colombian case is not merely a socially constructed idea but also a boundary object with ontological implications. More broadly, we must ask, What do scholars deploying the idea of the amphibious want to do with this word when it comes to imagining possible futures? The futures of whom?

We must keep before us the problem of knowledge integration. The amphibious as a boundary object constitutes a terrain in which different epistemologies converge. The amphibious is a lens, an analytical category, an approach, and a lived experience. It is through the integration of these epistemologies that the contours of the amphibious take shape. Science plays a central role, as it provides mapping technologies that make the contours of wetlands visible. Furthermore, scholars in Colombia have begun to consider the amphibious in their analysis of topics such as dispossession in wetland areas (e.g., Campo and Escobar Jiménez 2021). The appropriation of this knowledge has also involved the use of other languages such as music, radio, and video. Yet, in places such as La Mojana, the role of its inhabitants in defining the contours of the amphibious is far from obvious. One of the most influential contributions in the work of Fals Borda was his elaboration on the participatory action research approach. This approach is not only about community participation but also about community's active role as researchers and intellectuals in projects aimed at producing social change. Participatory action research refers to research committed to support grassroots social mobilization (Rappaport 2020). By sidestepping the land question, the idea of the amphibious bypasses an important realm of social mobilization. Some of the amphibious people of La Mojana who have struggled to protect wetlands have been killed and attacked, as mentioned earlier. It is a struggle against the disappearance and dispossession of wet environments that also has an epistemic dimension. While researchers determine the contours of wetlands on a map or through discourse, the dwellers of amphibious territories draw and redraw these contours through the elaboration of particular forms of knowledge and in their everyday practices of wetland use and occupation. The difficulties in making these contours overlap expose the elusiveness and changeability of the amphibious.

## NOTES

1 "Que la música del agua nos recuerde que en Colombia existe un mundo anfibio. Ese mundo quiere florecer de nuevo, conservando su forma de vida en equilibrio. Y de eso, que parece tan sencillo, depende el futuro de todos." Carlos Vives, "Cumbiana (Official Video)," YouTube, posted October 15, 2020, https://youtu.be/baUk9YcCxBQ?si=mA5zkUJ_MXGuqjjg.

2 I am grateful to Lina Pinto for pointing out the relevance of the concept of the boundary object in science-and-technology studies to the way I elaborate on the amphibious in this chapter. I also thank Úrsula Jaramillo and Jerónimo Rodríguez for helping me understand the politics of wetlands in Colombia.

3 The *Oxford Dictionary of Geology and Earth Sciences* defines *avulsion* as the "lateral displacement of a stream from its main channel into a new course across its floodplain" (Allaby 2020).

4 The Adaptation Fund (Fondo de Adaptación) in Colombia was created in 2011 to administer the funds for the reconstruction of the areas affected by the La Niña phenomenon. It has nothing to do with the international Adaptation Fund.

5 The Ramsar Convention on Wetlands of International Importance Especially as Waterfowl Habitat defines wetlands as "areas of marsh, fen, peatland or water, whether natural or artificial, permanent or temporary, with water that is static or flowing, fresh, brackish or salt, including areas of marine water the depth of which at low tide does not exceed six metres" (Ramsar 2016, 9).

## REFERENCES

Allaby, M. ed. 2020. *A Dictionary of Geology and Earth Sciences*. 5th ed. Oxford: Oxford University Press.

Andrade, G. 2016. "Introducción." In *Colombia Anfibia: Un país de humedales*. Vol. 2, edited by Ú. Jaramillo, J. Cortés-Duque, and C. Flórez-Ayala, x–xi. Bogotá: Instituto de Investigaciones Biológicas Alexander von Humboldt.

Arce, G. 2016. "Adaptándonos a un país de agua." In *Colombia Anfibia: Un país de humedales*. Vol. 2, edited by Ú. Jaramillo, J. Cortés-Duque, and C. Flórez-Ayala, viii–ix. Bogotá: Instituto de Investigaciones Biológicas Alexander von Humboldt.

Austin, J. L. 1975. *How to Do Things with Words*. Oxford: Oxford University Press.

Ayazo Toscano, R., W. Ramírez, A. C. Santos, O. L. Hernández-Manrique, A. Batista, and M. Roa. 2020. "Amphibious Colombia: A Country of Wetlands." *Wetlands Science & Practice* 37 (4): 321–22.

Bustamante, M. V. 2020a. "Atentan contra líder campesino en San Benito, Sucre." *El Heraldo*. October 20, 2020. https://www.elheraldo.co/sucre/atentan-contra-lider-campesino-en-san-benito-sucre-767122.

———. 2020b. "'El que reclama tierras, recibe plomo': Lucha campesina en Sucre." *El Heraldo*. November 22, 2020. https://www.elheraldo.co/sucre/el-que-reclama-tierras-recibe-plomo-lucha-campesina-en-sucre-775094.

Buytaert, W., R. Célleri, B. De Bièvre, F. Cisneros, G. Wyseure, J. Deckers, and R. Hofstede. 2006. "Human Impact on the Hydrology of the Andean Páramos." *Earth-Science Reviews* 79 (1–2): 53–72.

Camacho, J. 2015. "Paisaje y patrimonio en La Mojana, Caribe colombiano." *Geografia Ensino & Pesquisa*, no. 19, 90–100.

Camargo, A. 2009. "Una tierra bondadosa: Progreso y recursos naturales en la región del río San Jorge, Siglo XX." *Historia Crítica*, no. 37, 170–91.

———. 2022. "Land Born of Water: Property, Stasis, and Motion in the Floodplains of Northern Colombia." *Geoforum*, no. 131, 223–31.

Camargo, A., and L. Cortesi. 2019. "Flooding Water and Society." *Wiley Interdisciplinary Reviews: Water* 6 (5): e1374.

Campo, R. G., and K. Escobar Jiménez. 2021. "Territorio anfibio y despojo en una zona de humedales protegida del Caribe colombiano." *Revista de Estudios Sociales*, no. 76, 75–92.

Carton, W. 2020. "Rendering Local: The Politics of Differential Knowledge in Carbon Offset Governance." *Annals of the American Association of Geographers* 110 (5): 1–16.

Casas, P. A. 2020a. "Las mujeres mojaneras, lideresas en la adaptación al cambio climático." *El Espectador*. November 19, 2020. https://www.elespectador.com/noticias/medio-ambiente/las-mujeres-mojaneras-lideresas-en-la-adaptacion-al-cambio-climatico/.

———. 2020b. "La Mojana: Así se adaptó la comunidad anfibia a las inundaciones." *El Espectador*. November 25, 2020. https://www.elespectador.com/ambiente/la-mojana-asi-se-adapto-la-comunidad-anfibia-a-las-inundaciones-article/.

Cederlöf, G., and K. Sivaramakrishnan, eds. 2006. *Ecological Nationalisms: Nature, Livelihoods, and Identities in South Asia*. Seattle: University of Washington Press.

Currie, L. 1960. "Program of Economic Development of the Magdalena Valley and North of Colombia: Report of a Mission." Manuscript.

El Meridiano. 2020. *La Mojana, ejemplo para el país: Ministro Correa*. El Meridiano. November 15, 2020. https://m.elmeridiano.co/noticia/la-mojana-ejemplo-para-el-pais-ministro-correa.

Fals Borda, O. 1979. *Historia doble de La Costa*. Vol. 1, *Mompox y Loba*. Bogotá: Carlos Valencia Editores.

———. 1984. *Historia doble de La Costa*. Vol. 3, *Resistencia en el San Jorge*. Bogotá: Carlos Valencia Editores.

Flórez, C., L. M. Estupiñán-Suárez, S. Rojas, C. Aponte, M. Quiñones, Ó. Acevedo, S. Vilardy, and Ú. Jaramillo. 2016. "Identificación espacial de los sistemas de humedales continentales de Colombia." *Biota Colombiana* 17 (1): 44–62.

Galvis, G., and J. Mojica. 2007. "The Magdalena River Freshwater Fishes and Fisheries." *Aquatic Ecosystem Health & Management* 10 (2): 127–39.

Jensen, C. B., and A. Morita. 2020. "Deltas in Crisis: From Systems to Sophisticated Conjunctions." *Sustainability* 12 (4): 1322.

Klenk, N., and K. Meehan. 2015. "Climate Change and Transdisciplinary Science: Problematizing the Integration Imperative." *Environmental Science & Policy*, no. 54, 160–67.

Knox, H. 2020. *Thinking Like a Climate: Governing a City in Times of Environmental Change*. Durham, NC: Duke University Press.

Kohl, E., and J. A. Knox. 2016. "My Drought Is Different from Your Drought: A Case Study of the Policy Implications of Multiple Ways of Knowing Drought." *Weather, Climate, and Society* 8 (4): 373–88.

Krause, F. 2017. "Towards an Amphibious Anthropology of Delta Life." *Human Ecology* 45 (3): 403–8.

Li, T. M. 2007. *The Will to Improve: Governmentality, Development, and the Practice of Politics*. Durham, NC: Duke University Press.

López, S., J. K. Jung, and M. F. López. 2017. "A Hybrid-Epistemological Approach to Climate Change Research: Linking Scientific and Smallholder Knowledge Systems in the Ecuadorian Andes." *Anthropocene*, no. 17, 30–45.

Mahony, M. 2014. "The Predictive State: Science, Territory and the Future of the Indian Climate." *Social Studies of Science* 44 (1): 109–33.

McRae, D. 2015. "El hombre hicotea y la ecología de los paisajes acuáticos en Resistencia en el San Jorge." *Tabula Rasa*, no. 23, 79–103.

Morita, A. 2016. "Infrastructuring Amphibious Space: The Interplay of Aquatic and Terrestrial Infrastructures in the Chao Phraya Delta in Thailand." *Science as Culture* 25 (1): 117–40.

Morita, A., and C. B. Jensen. 2017. "Delta Ontologies: Infrastructural Transformations in the Chao Phraya Delta, Thailand." *Social Analysis* 61 (2): 118–33.

Osejo, A., and P. Ungar. 2017. "¿Agua sí, oro no? Anclajes del extractivismo y el ambientalismo en el páramo de Santurbán." *Universitas Humanística* 84 (84): 143–66.

Patiño, J. E., and L. M. Estupiñán-Suárez. 2016. "Hotspots of Wetland Area Loss in Colombia." *Wetlands* 36 (5): 935–43.

Pérez-Consuegra, N., N. Hoyos, J. C. Restrepo, J. Escobar, and G. D. Hoke. 2021. "Contrasting Climate Controls on the Hydrology of the Mountainous Cauca River and Its Associated Sedimentary Basin: Implications for Interpreting the Sedimentary Record." *Geomorphology*, no. 377, 107590.

Ramsar. 2016. *An Introduction to the Ramsar Convention on Wetlands*. Gland: Ramsar Convention Secretariat.

Rappaport, J. 2020. *Cowards Don't Make History: Orlando Fals Borda and the Origins of Participatory Action Research*. Durham, NC: Duke University Press.

Ricaurte, L. F., J. E. Patiño, D. F. Restrepo Zambrano, J. C. Arias-G, O. Acevedo, C. Aponte, R. Medina, et al. 2019. "A Classification System for Colombian Wetlands: An Essential Step Forward in Open Environmental Policy-Making." *Wetlands* 39 (5): 971–90.

Rice, J. L., B. J. Burke, and N. Heynen. 2015. "Knowing Climate Change, Embodying Climate Praxis: Experiential Knowledge in Southern Appalachia." *Annals of the Association of American Geographers* 105 (2): 253–62.

Richardson, T. 2018. "The Terrestrialization of Amphibious Life in a Danube Delta

'Town on Water.'" *Suomen Antropologi: Journal of the Finnish Anthropological Society* 43 (2): 3–29.

Rodríguez, J. 2020. *Retos jurídicos y científicos de la delimitación y gestión integral de humedales continentales en Colombia*. Bogotá.

Saade Hazin, M. 2013. *Desarrollo minero y conflictos socioambientales: Los casos de Colombia, México y el Perú*. Santiago de Chile: Organización de las Naciones Unidas, Cepal.

Safford, F., and M. Palacios. 2002. *Colombia: Fragmented Land, Divided Society*. Oxford: Oxford University Press.

Scaramelli, C. 2021. *How to Make a Wetland: Water and Moral Ecology in Turkey*. Redwood City, CA: Stanford University Press.

Scott, J. C. 1998. *Seeing Like a State: How Certain Schemes to Improve the Human Condition Have Failed*. New Haven, CT: Yale University Press.

Star, S. L., and J. R. Griesemer. 1989. "Institutional Ecology, 'Translations' and Boundary Objects: Amateurs and Professionals in Berkeley's Museum of Vertebrate Zoology, 1907–39." *Social Studies of Science* 19 (3): 387–420.

UNDP (United Nations Development Programme). 2019. "Discurso del príncipe heredero Haakon de Noruega, embajador de buena voluntad del PNUD, en La Mojana: Clima y vida." February 3, 2019. https://www.co.undp.org/content /colombia/es/home/presscenter/pressreleases/2019/02/discurso-Mojana.html.

Vilardy, S., Ú. Jaramillo, C. Flórez, J. Cortés-Duque, L. M. Estupiñán-Suárez, J. Rodríguez, Ó. Acevedo, et al. 2014. *Principios y criterios para la delimitación de humedales continentales: Una herramienta para fortalecer la resiliencia y la adaptación al cambio climático en Colombia*. Bogotá: Instituto de Investigaciones Biológicas Alexander von Humboldt.

Yeh, E. T. 2009. "From Wasteland to Wetland? Nature and Nation in China's Tibet." *Environmental History* 14 (1): 103–37.

STUART MCLEAN

# Amphibious Epilogue

The summer of 2021, when I began writing this epilogue, is already being described as a season of extremes—of violent contrasts, jarring juxtapositions, and wild oscillations. Despite the rollout of vaccines and the accompanying lifting of lockdown restrictions (in some parts of the world at least), the spread of the new and highly contagious delta variant demonstrated forcibly that the coronavirus pandemic was far from over. The summer's most remarked-upon extremes, however, were those of the weather. In the Chinese city of Zhengzhou, dams and flood defenses were breached, and passengers on commuter trains drowned in flooded underground railway tunnels. In London, during the second-wettest July on record, a typical month's worth of rain fell in a single twenty-four-hour period, flooding homes, roads, and public transport stations. In the Rhineland-Palatinate region of Germany, rivers burst their banks, and floods rendered roads impassable, cutting off power to tens of thousands of households and claiming more than a hundred human casualties. At the same time, a record-breaking heat wave cooked mussels, clams, and other sea creatures alive in their shells off the coast of Vancouver, and wildfires raged across the West Coast of North America, southern Europe, and the taiga forests of Siberia and Russia's Far East. August 2021 also saw the publication of the first installment of the sixth and latest report of the Intergovernmental Panel on Climate Change, which reiterated the urgent need to reduce greenhouse gas emissions and warned that as global temperatures continued to rise, extreme weather events like those of summer 2021 were likely to become more frequent—and more extreme.

As forests burn and wayward waters inundate the seeming solidity of humanly constructed residential spaces and urban infrastructure, it seems that the wet and the dry are indeed out of control. One might ask, of course, whether they have ever been fully in control. Over the course of Earth's long-term geological history—a history extending back far beyond the first appearance of humans—sea levels have risen and fallen, glaciers have advanced and retreated, islands have risen from and sunk into the ocean depths, shorelines have been resculpted by the action of winds and tides, and shifting tectonic plates, gliding upon their bed of subterranean magma, have disassembled and reassembled continents, time and again—and again, and again. Considered thus, the story of the wet and the dry is one not of dichotomous poles but of a continuous, metamorphic interplay, of which humans (and other living beings) are not only the sometime agents but also the long-term products. Perhaps, to adapt a phrase from an eminent science studies scholar, we (that is, humans as a species) have never not been amphibious (Latour 1993). Perhaps, too, the aspiration to definitively separate watery indeterminacy from humanly inscribed terra firma is itself part of a Euro-American, modernist project of ordering and differentiation (not least of "culture" from "nature"), one moreover of relatively recent historical provenance, albeit forcibly internationalized on the back of imperial expansion and capitalist globalization.

If so, it is surely amphibious spaces and lifeworlds, fluctuating ambivalently between wet and dry, or partaking simultaneously of both, that have given the lie most emphatically to such compartmentalizing and dichotomizing efforts. These amphibious zones and the practices, lifeways, and imaginings they have called forth have often been ignored or cast as anomalous (and therefore undeserving of sustained consideration) by virtue of their recalcitrance to binary classification, but the contributors to this volume remind us that they are in fact numerous and widely distributed: the Lazio region of central Italy; southwestern Estonia; the suddenly appearing sinkholes of Israel-Palestine's Dead Sea coast; the Salton Sea of Southern California (alternating sometimes centuries-long periods of wetness and dryness); the ski slopes of the French Alps; the fluctuating tidal landscapes of The Bahamas; the human-beaver collaborations being enlisted to protect Northern California's streams; the fluvial landscapes of North Bihar, India; and the often divergent claims to amphibiousness staked by scientists, environmentalists, development professionals, and

278 *McLean*

local residents in Colombia's La Mojana region. Amphibiousness, it seems, is everywhere and has been for a considerable time. Yet it also appears urgently and distinctively of the present, affording a timely description of the predicament in which increasing numbers of humans (and others) find themselves as temperatures and sea levels rise, not to mention a future in which many land-based habitats may find themselves subject to ever more frequent — or permanent — inundation, a future that already appears perilously close at hand in, for example, Bangladesh, or the low-lying Pacific island nation of Tuvalu.

Today, the sense that the wet and the dry have indeed loosed themselves from their long-standing definitional enchainment to sharply etched dichotomies speaks not least to an all-too-contemporary anxiety about changing climates and environments and the unevenly distributed responsibilities and vulnerabilities of different communities in relation to them. If the aspiration to separate definitively the wet and the dry has always been untenable, it has surely become spectacularly and undeniably so under present circumstances.

Accordingly, amphibious anthropologies are obliged to combine a recognition that wetness and dryness are always and everywhere uncertainly demarcated with an attentiveness to many and varied ways in which such categorizations and their undoings are played out in different settings and in relation to different (human and other) populations. The marshlands of Estonia's Soomaa region appear very differently to local farmers engaged in a protracted struggle against flooding and waterlogging and to the owners of a tourism company offering "wilderness experiences." The sinkholes that appear on the shores of the Dead Sea, in the border regions between Jordanian, Palestinian, and Israeli territories, swallow factories and permanently shut down tourist beaches but provide employment for a Bedouin caretaker, who thus acquires the paperwork to cross legally into Israel for the first time in his life. In North Bihar, India, the "ecology of absences" informing managerial and infrastructural projects aimed at regulating the riverine landscape through zoning, river linking, and the construction of embankments and dams contrasts with the situated and embodied ecological knowledges of local populations.

Amphibious anthropologies demand a commitment both to the specificity of ethnographic cases and to a comparative vision capable of recognizing that, as the scope of the present volume attests, amphibiousness is a multiple phenomenon, demanding as such a multiplicity of modes of engagement. The latter might encompass not only a plurality of research methods but also a willingness on the part of researchers to question familiar terms of analysis, insofar as these have often betrayed amphibiousness in their very attempt to name and designate it. Such is arguably the case with the increasingly ubiquitous term *wetland* (or *protected wetland* in the case of Lazio, Italy). As the conspicuously less habituated looking *wet land* attests, however, sometimes a touch of the space bar is enough to make the familiar appear newly strange! Such concerns are far more than aesthetic quibbles. Conceptual and lexical displacements can manifest new possibilities of ecological engagement. In Val Thorens, in the northern French Alps, idioms of amphibiousness suggest new approaches to conservation premised on the valuing of existing landscapes rather than the restoration of a disturbed ecological status quo.

A sensitivity to verbal nuance and connotation can also foreground the dangers and pitfalls attendant upon attempts to formulate new approaches to conservation and governance, including new alliances between constituencies of humans and other-than-humans. In Southern California, conservationists' attempts to enlist beavers as allies take shape within colonial histories of land expropriation and present-day power relations. On Andros Island in The Bahamas, the tidal flatland known as "the mud" emerges as a site of contestation, as government conservation initiatives, involving the enclosure of designated protected areas, collide with local practices of engagement dating back to the era of plantation slavery and its aftermath. In Colombia, the term *amphibious* itself (more specifically *Colombia Anfibia* or "Amphibious Colombia"), initially given currency by the sociologist Orlando Fals Borda, becomes a "boundary object" that is laid claim to in a variety of ways by (among others) environmentalists, NGOs, artists, scholars, and government institutions, all of which have, arguably, served to divert attention from the question of land distribution that remains no less pressing for many of the people of the La Mojana region. If the amphibious is constantly eluding categorization (including the modernist classificatory binaries that have structured much academic research up to the present) then perhaps not the least of the challenges it poses is that of continuously renewing or reinventing scholarly (and other) idioms and vocabularies, and of maintaining an openness to alternatives to canonical academic prose, in the forms of (for example) narrative, poetry, or mixed media. To attend to the amphibious is not only a political act but also, inescapably, a creative one.

In this regard, it is worth noting too that for many artists and writers, amphibiousness, far from being an ontological embarrassment, has often provided a powerful source of inspiration. Take, for example, the Hong Kong performance artist Frog King (a.k.a. Kwok Mang-ho), who has stated that he was drawn to the animal from which he borrows his name for a number of reasons: its metamorphic life cycle; its capacity to move freely between land and water; and its bulging eyes (a recurrent feature in many of his artworks), suggesting at once watchfulness, a bridge between Chinese and Western artistic influences, and a boat for traveling to new and uncharted spaces. Part of Frog King's practice involves the creation of extemporized exhibition and performance spaces (known as Frogtopia) incorporating a variety of found objects, photographs, and fragments or photocopies of past works. Visitors are invited to participate in the creative process by drawing, painting, paper folding, or dressing up in improvised costumes, the aim being to establish, at least temporarily, an amphibious zone of indistinction between artist and audience, art and life (Ming 2011).

A writer drawn to indeterminate zones of interchange between wet and dry is the Mexican American novelist Chloe Aridjis, who has spoken of her attraction to "unstable topographies." In Aridjis's first novel, *Book of Clouds* (2009), set in Berlin, the city's own unstable history finds an embodiment and counterpart in condensation of water vapor into clouds hanging over the urban landscape and thickening to impenetrable fog at the story's end (Aridjis 2009). In her most recent novel, *Sea Monsters* (2019), a teenage girl runs away from her middle-class home in Mexico City to Oaxaca on the Pacific Coast, where she wanders in the elusive, interstitial zone of the beach, encountering beachcombers, drifters, storytellers, and a character described as a "merman" (Aridjis 2019). Yet the fluctuating states of matter of the tidal zone, like the clouds floating over Berlin in the earlier novel, suggest also that the city she has left behind may, in its own way, be no less amphibious a space than the one where she has taken refuge. Of both books, Aridjis states in a recent interview, "The beach and the city are often seen as opposing topographies, but they're both unstable landscapes, constantly shifting" (Baum and Appignanesi 2021, 23). Certainly, the residents of many cities around the world learned such a lesson forcibly during the summer of 2021! It can be learned too, however, by less destructive means. Is the capacity to discern the shifting, mutable character of that which appears solid and permanent one that amphibious anthropologies share with art and literature?

All of this, of course, attests to the (thoroughly amphibious) polyvalence of the concept of amphibiousness itself—at once a symptom of rapidly accelerating anthropogenic climate change (with the lion's share of historical responsibility falling, needless to say, upon the capitalist West); an existential human and planetary condition instantiated in the *longue durée* of geological time; and a source of new possibilities and imaginings, even in the face of seemingly impending ecological catastrophe; and perhaps more besides. A word should be said too about that most amphibious of writerly devices, the epilogue. As Jacques Derrida noted many years ago with reference to that other textual outlier, the preface, such instances of "Outwork" are notable not least for complicating and confounding notions of beginning (or ending), of what can be said to lie inside or outside a text (Derrida 2016). Neither a chapter in its own right nor straightforwardly a commentary on or summary of the assembled contributions (of the kind that, say, an editors' introduction might provide), an epilogue seems an amphibiously undecidable, in-between thing—neither integrally a part of nor unambiguously distinct from the text with which it is associated. Perhaps an epilogue is best thought of as an amphibious intermediary between the body of the text—already a thoroughly porous, leaky, uncertainly bounded body—and the world into which it is sent forth to be read, commented on, and responded to. As such it is perhaps no less an emissary too between past, present, and future—between a titularly past scene of research and writing that is never fully and decisively past, a readerly present that can never be said to coincide exactly with itself, and a nondetermined future in which the effects of these will reverberate. It seems only fitting, therefore, that the author of the present epilogue should sign off by commending this volume, exploring the possibilities of amphibious anthropologies, to the future, a future that is still unscripted but that will assuredly—in at least one of many possible senses—be amphibious.

### REFERENCES

Aridjis, Chloe. 2009. *Book of Clouds*. New York: Vintage.

———. 2019. *Sea Monsters*. New York: Random House.

Baum, Devorah, and Josh Appignanesi. 2021. "Fluidity, Indeterminacy, Interdependence: A Conversation with Chloe Aridjis." *Wasafiri* 36 (2): 23–28.

Derrida, Jacques. 2016 [1972]. *Dissemination*. Translated by Barbara Johnson. London: Bloomsbury Academic.

Latour, Bruno. 1993. *We Have Never Been Modern*. Translated by Catherine Porter. Cambridge: Harvard University Press.

Ming, Fay. 2011. "Tadpole to Frog King." In *Frogtopia Hongkornucopia: Kwok Mang-ho (a.k.a. Frog King). La Biennale di Venezia 54th International Art Exhibition*, edited by Benny Chia, 30–33. Hong Kong: Hong Kong Arts Development Council.

# Contributors

ALEJANDRO CAMARGO is an assistant professor at the Department of History and Social Sciences at Universidad del Norte, Colombia. He is interested in water-related disasters, fluvial environments, the environmental history of development, climate change adaptation, and the political ecology and economy of agrarian change. He currently works on two projects. The first project examines the impacts of green urbanization and industrial development on fishing livelihoods in two Colombian port cities. The second project is a study on the social life of fluvial sediment on a climate frontier in northern Colombia.

ALIDA CANTOR is an associate professor of geography at Portland State University. She is a political ecologist who studies water governance and environmental justice. She is interested in the intersections of water with communities, food, energy, and environmental justice and is currently researching the hydrosocial impacts and imaginaries of renewable energy development in the US West.

LUISA CORTESI is tenured assistant professor of water, disasters, and environmental justice at the International Institute of Social Studies, Erasmus University, the Netherlands. She works on floods and water contamination, resilience and adaptation, technologies and environmental knowledge, from the perspective of Bihar, India, and other parts of the globe. She has edited *Split Waters* (with K. J. Joy). Her current projects include the Water Justice and Adaptation Lab and From Flood-Prone to Flood-Ready.

STÉPHANIE GAUCHERAND is an ecologist at INRAE, the National Institute for Food, Agriculture and Environment, Grenoble, France. She studies restoration ecology in wetland and high-altitude ecosystems. She is generally interested in the ecological impacts humans have on the natural environment and how to improve the mitigation of these impacts on biodiversity. Her publications include "Transplanting Success of Two Alpine Plant Species in Combination with Mulching during Restoration of a High-Elevation Peatland," *Wetlands Ecology and Management* (2019), with F. Isselin.

CÉLINE GRANJOU is a professor at INRAE, the National Institute for Food, Agriculture and Environment, Grenoble, France. With a background in science studies and environmental sociology, she works on the production of ecological knowledge, human/soil relations, and the politics of anticipation. Her recent publications include "Bringing Soils to Life in the Human and Social Sciences," *Soil Security* (2023), with G. Meulemans, and "Researching Cities, Transforming Ecology: An Investigation into Urban Ecology Agendas," *Nature and Culture* (2023), with J. Salomon Cavin et al.

PAOLO GRUPPUSO is an anthropologist working as a research fellow within the Horizon Europe research project "BioTraCes: Biodiversity and Transformative Change for Plural and Nature Positive Societies" at the University of Catania, Italy. His research focuses on societal relations with wetlands and rivers in Europe. He has published articles in journals such as *Conservation & Society*, *Social Anthropology/Anthropologie Sociale*, and *Theory, Culture & Society*. From November 2024 he will conduct a research project on European wetlands funded by the German Research Council and based at the Rachel Carson Center for Environment and Society, at LMU, Munich, Germany.

FRANZ KRAUSE is professor of environmental anthropology at the University of Cologne. His research and teaching revolve around water, social and ecological transformation, and climate change in the Circumpolar North and elsewhere. Franz is codirector of Multidisciplinary Environmental Studies in the Humanities (MESH). He is the author of *Thinking Like a River: An Anthropology of Water and Its Uses along the Kemi River, Northern Finland* (Transcript, 2023) and coauthor of *Environmental Anthropology: Current Issues and Fields of Engagement* (Haupt/UTB, 2023).

STUART MCLEAN is professor of anthropology at the University of Minnesota. His regional focus is North Atlantic Europe, and his interests include anthropology of art, ecological anthropology, and experimental writing and poetics. He is the author of *The Event and Its Terrors: Ireland, Famine, Modernity* and *Fictionalizing Anthropology: Encounters and Fabulations beyond the Human*, and he is the editor (with Anand Pandian) of *Crumpled Paper Boat: Experiments in Ethnographic Writing*. He is currently completing a manuscript provisionally titled "Surviving Europe."

SIMONE POPPERL is editor for broadcast at KFF Health News, an independent national newsroom that produces in-depth journalism about health issues. She edits audio reporting that airs on NPR, Marketplace, and CBS radio, as well as KFF Health News' award-winning long-form podcasts. Her academic work has been published in the *International Journal of Middle East Studies, Middle East Report*, and *American Anthropologist*.

DANIEL SARNA-WOJCICKI currently works with the Karuk Tribe Department of Natural Resources Wildlife Program on research, policy, and planning. His research uses interdisciplinary and community-engaged participatory approaches to support policy advocacy for ecosystem rehabilitation and social and environmental justice. He has been working with the Karuk Tribe since 2009 on supporting ecocultural revitalization efforts through research and advocacy related to climate resilience, food sovereignty, watershed restoration, and wildlife ecology.

SARAH WISE is an anthropologist at the National Marine Fisheries Service who focuses on the intersection between science, policy, and human experience in marine and coastal ecosystems. Sarah's work explores the ways people engage with marine governance and decision-making under conditions of rapid social and environmental change.

CLEO WOELFLE-HAZARD is a fire adviser with UC Cooperative Extension, where he is partnering with Native basket weavers and cultural practitioners on cultural fire and fire-water interactions on California's North Coast. His most recent book is *Underflows: Queer Trans Ecologies and River Justice*.

# Index

Page numbers in *italics* refer to illustrations

agriculture. *See* farming

Agro Pontino, 114, 116–21, 127

Alps, 195–215

amphibious, 7, 8, 11, 19, 120, 122–23, 132; as boundary object, 253, 256, 268, 270; as discourse, 255; epistemology, 100, 102; as a lens, 254; and nationalism, 255, 269; and wetness, 49–50, 140, 149, 153, 195, 255

amphibious anthropologies, 8, 10, 141, 144, 158, 170, 186

amphibious biodiversity, 196, 209, 211–13, 257

amphibious culture, 7, 178, 253, 259–60

amphibious ecology, 187, 215

amphibious functionality, 206, 209, 213

amphibious governance, 16–17, 226–27, 229, 242–44

amphibious knowledge, 99–100, 102

amphibious landscapes, 8, 11, 18, 50, 59–60, 166–68

amphibious life, 4, 17, 100

amphibious materiality, 59

amphibious multispecies worlds, 164–65, 168–69, 188

amphibiousness, x, xi, 72, 76, 99–100, 140, 277–81

amphibious territory, 269

Anthropocene, ix, 3, 42, 46–50, 59

Aridjis, Chloe (Mexican American novelist), 280

art and amphibiousness, 150–51, 184, 252, 279–81

Bahamas, 219–44

beavers, 15, 151, 154, 163; dams built by, 176, 179, 181, 186; ecology of, 177; as engineers, 178; in multispecies assemblages, 169–70; and restoration, 164, 18; trapping of, 173

binaries. *See* dichotomy

biopolitics, 196, 210–13, 215; hydrobiopolitics, 197

birds, 118, 128–30, 138, 146, 179, 182; bird lovers, 200; bones, 29, 40, 42; extinction, 209; habitat, 40–41; migrating, 30, 37, 39

Bonifica Integrale, 114, 116, 119

boundary object. *See* amphibious

California, 29–30, 34, 39–40, 47; Bodega Valley, 175; Department of Fish and Wildlife, 176, 183; Scott Valley, 172; water management, 165–66

288  *Index*

care, 171, 196, 209

categories, 3, 16–17, 157–58, 208, 212

climate change, 163, 166, 168, 227, 254,

climate change (*continued*)
256, 276, 281; adaptation to, 259–61,
263, 265–66; conservation and, 232;
floods as a result of, 259; and the
future of territory, 255; governance,
261; Indigenous communities and,
188; and lack of snow, 199; policy, 253;
scientists, 232; and wetland vulnerability, 222, 229, 232

Colombia, 251–54; Anfibia, 255–56, 267,
269; La Mojana, 256, 261, 265; legislation, 266, 268; páramos, 266; playones, 264; rivers, 261; San Marcos,
259; wetlands, 266

colonialism, 171–73, 186, 188; and colonial violence, 55. *See also* settler
colonialism

Colorado River, 29–30, 32, 40–41

commons, 16, 165, 226, 238; common
property, 244n1; communal areas,
264; communal resources, 142, 148;
law, 228; multispecies, 167, 170–71,
188; privatization of, 224

Cons, Jason, 13

conservation, 14, 17, 34, 155, 175, 219, 239,
279; of beavers, 154, 170; biopolitics
and, 197, 211, 213; enclosures, 221–22,
224, 226–27, 232, 240, 242; landscape,
145–46; NGOs and, 163; politics, 196;
postnatural, 47; wetland, 154, 197,
203, 207, 209, 211–13, 215, 263, 268

cycles, 36, 280; of wet and dry, 165, 178

Da Cunha, Dilip, ix, 13, 85, 112

dams, 85–88, 93, 166, 177, 244, 276; and
beavers, 154–55, 165, 167, 169–73, 176,
179–82, 184–88

Dead Sea, 55–73; mineral extraction of,
61–65; salinity, 60; tourism, 65–68

desert, 147, 166

dichotomy, ix, 3, 11, 33, 37, 177–78

drainage, 145, 148, 151, 157, 166, 195, 199,
244, 257, 261, 269; beavers and, 172,
188; bogs, 154–55; and restoration,
203–4. *See also* wetlands

drought, 206–7; irrigation, 176, 182–83;
risk management, 260, 262–63

ecohydrosocial, 167, 186. *See also* hydrosociality

ecology, 16, 187; of absences, 88–89;
land, 198, 201; reconciliation, 47

ecosystem services, 214–15, 231

embankment, 81–85, 91–92, 257; road,
149, 151

engineers, 44, 179, 188, 266; beavers as
ecosystems, 168, 171, 176, 178, 189n1;
civil, 101; hydraulic, 165–66; reclamation, 121, 261. *See also* US Army
Corps of Engineers

environmental management, 16, 32–33,
46–47, 124–25, 197

epistemology, 256, 263, 268, 270

Estonia: economy of, 146; environmental administration of, 154–55;
Mardu, 149–51; Soomaa, 139, 144,
156; Soviet Union, 147–48; tourism,
153, 156

ethics, 16, 209

extraction, 186, 188, 230; of land, 228; of
resources, 171, 173–75, 266; of water, 211

Fals Borda, Orlando, 7, 17, 178, 252–54, 259, 267
farming, 32, 119–21, 126, 145, 147–48, 173, 230, 238
fishing, 45
flood, 2, 30, 79–80, 264; control, 2, 81, 84–85, 91–92, 100
floodplain, 167, 188
France, 196, 198; Les Menuires, 204; Val Thorens, 198–200, 204; Vanoise National Park, 198, 201
Frog King (Kwok Mang-ho, Hong Kong performance artist), 280
functionality, 40; ecological, 196. See also amphibious: functionality
fur desert, 173–74, 176, 188

geomorphoanthropology, 89, 97–99
geomorphology, 158, 265, 267
governance, 142, 166, 221, 223–25, 229, 231, 237, 239–40, 269, 279; collaborative, 225; enclosure, 236, 242–43; groundwater, 180; littoral, 236; marine, 226; water, 165, 186- 87; watershed, 164, 188
grid, 81, 82, 264

hybrid, 37, 195, 215, 244; "conceptual frameworks," 256; timescapes, 223
hydrosociality, 5, 141. See also ecohydrosocial
hyporheic zone/hyporheic flow, 15, 164, 167–68, 170–72, 176, 179, 183, 186; imaginary, 163–65, 179, 185, 187–88

in-between, 11, 122, 123, 201, 257, 281
indeterminacy, 44, 45, 46, 168, 262, 277

India, 79, 83, 85, 89, 101; Ganga, 80, 91; nadiya, 90–91; North Bihar, 79–80, 85–86
infrastructures. See dams; embankment
Ingold, Tim, 12, 98, 99, 123, 130, 132
insects, 151–52, 157, 174, 232
instability, 42, 72
irrigation, 5, 181, 183–84, 260; for agriculture and pasturage, 172, 174, 178; and canals, 176; for drinking water, 142; privatization, 6; rural-to-urban transfer, 29–30; Salton Sea, 32; settler, 165
island, 141, 165, 219–22, 228–30, 233–44, 277–78; small, nations, 227
Israel, 55, 61, 67, 69; Ein Gedi, 69–70
Italy, 111; Agro Pontino, 114, 120, 131; Circeo National Park, 111, 114, 117–18; Fogliano, 116–17

Jensen, Casper Bruun, 8
Jordan, 55–56, 58, 70
Jordan River, 61, 63–64

knowledge, 76, 79, 201, 261–63, 270–71; conflicts of, 101, 180; ecological, 98, 185; ecology of absences, 88; and governance, 224; and Indigenous communities, 186; local, 184; production of, 17, 113, 130, 181, 187, 252, 255–56

Lahiri-Dutt, Kuntala, 84, 143
land question, 253, 264
landscape, 5, 76, 79, 89, 143, 157, 251, 256, 265; altered, 47, 49; degradation of, 183; Dust Bowl, 178; economy of, 231;

landscape (*continued*)

governance, 41, 229, 243; hydroge-ology, 86, 94; knowledge of, 113, 129; Memory Landscape project, 149; mountain, 198, 215; restoration, 3, 177–78; riparian, 176; sea-, 223, 231, 241; settler, 185–86; stochastic, 180; tidal, 277; wet/watery, 9, 13, 15–16, 18, 19, 121, 226, 237–38; wetland, 112, 115, 119, 124. *See also* amphibious: landscapes; conservation

lines, 12, 13

Linton, Jamie, 141

littoral, 219–24, 226, 231–32, 240–43

materiality, 140, 159, 197, 202, 203, 209, 228; relational, 31

Mathur, Anuradha, 13

McLean, Stuart, 13

modus vivendi, 122, 132

more-than-human, xi, 121–22, 126; entities, 14, 164–65; relations, 9, 16, 18, 170, 252

Morita, Atsuro, 8, 254

morphologics. *See* geomorphology

mud, 219, 220, 225–26, 233, 236, 241–43; fluvial, 258; -scape, 226, 242

multispecies commons, 167, 170–71, 188. *See also* commons

Native Americans, 35, 163–64, 175–76, 178, 185, 188

nature, 40, 111, 131, 196–97, 253, 269; conservation, 155, 201, 210, 215; control of, 166, 188; ecology, 211; financialization of, 215; and nationalism,

269; neoliberal, 224; pristine, 214; and society, 214–15, 277; trails, 204; and wetland restoration, 213

opposition, ix, 3, 11, 33, 37, 177–78

Pacific Flyway, 39, 41

Palestine, 55; British Mandate, 62–63, 65; West Bank, 67

performativity, 38, 43, 209; posthumanist, 38

political ecology, 222

Plumwood, Val, 33

queer ecologies, 33, 43, 171, 180

Ramsar Convention, 115, 196, 200, 221, 225, 233, 251, 267

reclamation, ix, 114, 155, 165

refuge, 147, 241, 281

replacement habitat, 41

resistance, 230, 235, 243; by farmers, 6, 119; material, 49, 92; in wetlands, x, 231, 239, 241

restoration, 30, 46, 49, 202, 207, 212; bog, 144–55; riparian, 183, 188; river, 90, 93, 94, 98; stream, 181, 260; watershed, 164, 188; wetland, 196–98, 202, 204, 206–7, 210, 212–14, 262. *See also* beavers

rhythm, 9, 166, 220, 223, 225–26, 230–31, 242, 257; rhythmicity, 158; "rhythm-patterns," 223, 226, 231, 243–44

riverine ecosystems, 166; habitat, 101, 169; people, 99, 101, 102, 253; spaces, 84; species, 179 sacrifice zone, 30, 50

separation, 16, 92, 143, 164, 213, 214, 254

settler colonialism, 55, 56, 72, 173, 186, 188. *See also* irrigation; landscape

shapes, 76, *82*, 97–98, 263; of dams and embankments, 85, 87; landscape, 89, 122; river, 94, *95*, *96*, 100

ski resorts, 195, 198–200, 203, 207, 211

smell, 42, 43, 139

subjectivity, 5, 139

surface, 12, 146, 164–65, 167, 179, 185–87, 203–4, 207; sub-, 56, 58, 60, 67, 72, 73n2, 173, 179, 202

taskscape, 120, 122

temporality, 3, 8, 15, 34, 92, 213

terra nullius, 60, 72–73

territory, 236, 255; aboriginal, 172, 182; colonial, 174; and nation, 252–53, 255–56, 267, 269–70

third space, 3, 168

tidal spaces, 16, 219, 223, 230, 231, 242, 244. *See also* landscape

tourism, 65–71, 117; companies, 153, 156, 234; destination, 156, 157, 234; as economic activity, 139, 144, 149, 153, 156, 157, 198, 208, 210, 214–15, 235

uncertainty, 1, 17, 44, 45, 156, 226, 231, 278

United States of America, 35, 41, 163, 167–68; Bodega Valley, 175, 176–77, 182; California, 29–30, 165–66; Imperial Valley, 29–30, 35; Pacific Northwest, 163, 173; Scott River, 172–74, 181

US Army Corps of Engineers, 174

volatility, 13, 143

waterland, 8, 79, 80, 95

watershed, 171, 173, 175–76, 181, 185–86, 208, 213; coastal, 176; communities, 187, 188; councils, 181, 182, 183; inhabitants, 168; relations, 171, 179; repair, 170; science, 188. *See also* governance; restoration

West Bank, 67

wetland, 7, 111–13, 115, 118, 123–24, 126–32, 141, 143, 154, 158, 195, 199, 222, 232–33, 256, 263, 267; anthropogenic, 41–42; classification, 14, 48, 112–13, 119, 127, 267; drainage, 195, 199, 244, 257; fragility of, 208–9, 211; loss, 2, 39, 132; mutable, 124; property, 268; restoration, 196–98, 202, 204, 206–7, 210, 212–14, 262. *See also* conservation; Ramsar Convention

wetness, 3–4, 13–14, 140–44, 149–50, 152–53, 156–59, 252, 257, 264, 278; and land, 195, 234. *See also* wetland

*zona umida*, 111, 118

CULTURE, PLACE, AND NATURE

*Studies in Anthropology and Environment*

*Amphibious Anthropologies: Living in Wet Environments*, edited by
    Alejandro Camargo, Luisa Cortesi, and Franz Krause
*Viable Ecologies: Conservation and Coexistence on the Galápagos Islands*,
    by Paolo Bocci
*Crafting a Tibetan Terroir: Winemaking in Shangri-La*, by Brendan A. Galipeau
*China's Camel Country: Livestock and Nation-Building at a Pastoral Frontier*,
    by Thomas White
*Sustaining Natures: An Environmental Anthropology Reader*, edited by
    Sarah R. Osterhoudt and K. Sivaramakrishnan
*Fukushima Futures: Survival Stories in a Repeatedly Ruined Seascape*, by
    Satsuki Takahashi
*The Camphor Tree and the Elephant: Religion and Ecological Change in Maritime
    Southeast Asia*, by Faizah Zakaria
*Turning Land into Capital: Development and Dispossession in the Mekong Region*,
    edited by Philip Hirsch, Kevin Woods, Natalia Scurrah, and Michael B. Dwyer
*Spawning Modern Fish: Transnational Comparison in the Making of Japanese
    Salmon*, by Heather Anne Swanson
*Upland Geopolitics: Postwar Laos and the Global Land Rush*, by Michael B. Dwyer
*Misreading the Bengal Delta: Climate Change, Development, and Livelihoods
    in Coastal Bangladesh*, by Camelia Dewan
*Ordering the Myriad Things: From Traditional Knowledge to Scientific Botany
    in China*, by Nicholas K. Menzies
*Timber and Forestry in Qing China: Sustaining the Market*, by Meng Zhang
*Consuming Ivory: Mercantile Legacies of East Africa and New England*, by
    Alexandra Celia Kelly
*Mapping Water in Dominica: Enslavement and Environment under Colonialism*,
    by Mark W. Hauser
*Mountains of Blame: Climate and Culpability in the Philippine Uplands*, by Will Smith

*Sacred Cows and Chicken Manchurian: The Everyday Politics of Eating Meat in India*, by James Staples

*Gardens of Gold: Place-Making in Papua New Guinea*, by Jamon Alex Halvaksz

*Shifting Livelihoods: Gold Mining and Subsistence in the Chocó, Colombia*, by Daniel Tubb

*Disturbed Forests, Fragmented Memories: Jarai and Other Lives in the Cambodian Highlands*, by Jonathan Padwe

*The Snow Leopard and the Goat: Politics of Conservation in the Western Himalayas*, by Shafqat Hussain

*Roses from Kenya: Labor, Environment, and the Global Trade in Cut Flowers*, by Megan A. Styles

*Working with the Ancestors: Mana and Place in the Marquesas Islands*, by Emily C. Donaldson

*Living with Oil and Coal: Resource Politics and Militarization in Northeast India*, by Dolly Kikon

*Caring for Glaciers: Land, Animals, and Humanity in the Himalayas*, by Karine Gagné

*Organic Sovereignties: Struggles over Farming in an Age of Free Trade*, by Guntra A. Aistara

*The Nature of Whiteness: Race, Animals, and Nation in Zimbabwe*, by Yuka Suzuki

*Forests Are Gold: Trees, People, and Environmental Rule in Vietnam*, by Pamela D. McElwee

*Conjuring Property: Speculation and Environmental Futures in the Brazilian Amazon*, by Jeremy M. Campbell

*Andean Waterways: Resource Politics in Highland Peru*, by Mattias Borg Rasmussen

*Puer Tea: Ancient Caravans and Urban Chic*, by Jinghong Zhang

*Enclosed: Conservation, Cattle, and Commerce among the Q'eqchi' Maya Lowlanders*, by Liza Grandia

*Forests of Belonging: Identities, Ethnicities, and Stereotypes in the Congo River Basin*, by Stephanie Rupp

*Tahiti beyond the Postcard: Power, Place, and Everyday Life*, by Miriam Kahn

*Wild Sardinia: Indigeneity and the Global Dreamtimes of Environmentalism*, by Tracey Heatherington

*Nature Protests: The End of Ecology in Slovakia*, by Edward Snajdr

*Forest Guardians, Forest Destroyers: The Politics of Environmental Knowledge in Northern Thailand*, by Tim Forsyth and Andrew Walker

*Being and Place among the Tlingit*, by Thomas F. Thornton

*The Tropics and the Traveling Gaze: India, Landscape, and Science, 1800–1856*, by David Arnold

*Ecological Nationalisms: Nature, Livelihoods, and Identities in South Asia*, edited by Gunnel Cederlöf and K. Sivaramakrishnan

*From Enslavement to Environmentalism: Politics on a Southern African Frontier*, by David McDermott Hughes

*Border Landscapes: The Politics of Akha Land Use in China and Thailand*, by Janet C. Sturgeon

*Property and Politics in Sabah, Malaysia: Native Struggles over Land Rights*, by Amity A. Doolittle

*The Earth's Blanket: Traditional Teachings for Sustainable Living*, by Nancy J. Turner

*The Kuhls of Kangra: Community-Managed Irrigation in the Western Himalaya*, by J. Mark Baker

www.ingramcontent.com/pod-product-compliance
Lightning Source LLC
Chambersburg PA
CBHW020557300725
30256CB00002B/5